The Reparative in Narratives
Works of Mourning in Progress

Contemporary French and Francophone Studies 13

MIREILLE ROSELLO

The Reparative in Narratives

Works of Mourning in Progress

LIVERPOOL UNIVERSITY PRESS

First published 2010 by
Liverpool University Press
4 Cambridge Street
Liverpool
L69 7ZU

British Library Cataloguing-in-Publication data
A British Library CIP record is available

ISBN 978–184631–220–5 cased
978–184631–221–2 limp

Typeset by Carnegie Book Production, Lancaster
Printed and bound by CPI Group (UK) Ltd, Croydon, CR0 4YY

A Juliette et à Edith,
Belles comme la colère

Contents

Acknowledgements

am grateful to the organizers of conferences or events where the preliminary versions of the following chapters found generous and interested audiences. For their kind invitation and for making me feel at home away from home, I wish to thank Hakim Abderrezak, Alec Hargreaves and Bill Cloonan, Hafid Gafaiti and Patricia Lorcin, Karl Britto, Debarati Sanval, Soraya Tlatli and Suzanne Guerlac, Elizabeth Boyi, and Max Silverman. Thank you to the colleagues and students who took time out of their busy schedules to come and listen to talks delivered the University of California Berkeley, Stanford University, Florida State University, Texas Tech, Leeds University and the University of Minnesota.

I am also indebted to all the colleagues and friends who have invited me to contribute to collected volumes, providing me with the incentive to revise and rewrite the original conference papers. Their perceptive remarks and suggestions were welcome at a time when I was still trying to come to grips with the 'reparative'. I am grateful to Isaac Bazié, Sylvie Durmelat, Nacira Guénif, Chris Floyd, Joe Golsan, Alec Hargreaves, Peter Klaus, Murray Pratt and Vinay Swamy.

Thank you to the students enrolled in the Cultural Analysis MA programme and the PhD students at the Amsterdam School of Cultural Analysis. They remind me every day that research and teaching go hand in hand and that I have good reasons to love my job.

also wish to thank the colleagues I have met and worked with here in the Netherlands. Without Ieme van der Poel and Patricia Pisters, I may not have discovered the University of Amsterdam. Without the faculty members who teach the programme in comparative literature, life would be less complicated and less fun: thank you to Joost deBloois, Jan Hein Hoogstad, Esther Peeren and Murat Aydemir for their intellectual energy. A special note of gratitude goes to Sudeep Dasgupta who does not find it strange to talk about theory, cinema or literature at one o'clock in the morning.

Mike Katzberg's editorial help was invaluable: his patience and enthusiasm for the project kept me going when I was tempted to give up.

I am grateful to the friends who, sometimes without knowing it, helped me build a bridge of words between the theories developed in this book and the life we lead outside of academe. I wish to thank Jean-Xavier Ridon, Yves Clemmen, Carine Mardorossian, Lonny Morse, Catherine and Malcolm Pritchard, Philippe, Jacques and Alain Lombard for sharing their ideas, raising questions, questioning my academic language and forcing me to articulate my points in a much more coherent way,

Emilie and Dipti: thank you. You know why.

INTRODUCTION

From the Debate on 'Repentance' to the Reparative in Memorial Narratives

'Narratives' and 'reparative': these two words will be used throughout this book, and the nature of their relationship will remain unstable. Originally, I was looking for a working definition of what a 'reparative narrative' would be, might be. And positing that reparative narratives could be found was of the order of a theoretical hypothesis. I was not sure that they existed but it was clear that if they did, I needed them, and needed them badly. I wanted to learn at the same time how to identify them and to understand how they worked in order to recognize them and remember them, to let them nurture me and impart to me their wisdom, so as to be able eventually to share them and teach them.

The original search for pre-existing 'reparative narratives', however, was rather frustrating because they were a premature theoretical dream. This study, then, is not about reparative narratives but about *the* reparative *in* narratives. The objective is to analyse the relationship between the reparative and narratives, and to examine the conditions that enable these two words to coexist in productive tension. Depending on how you read the stories that constitute the building blocks of the chapters, each word, 'reparative' and 'narrative' will, at a given moment, qualify the other.

Global Reparability: Context and Theorization

The quest for something that would cross the narrative with the reparative was triggered by a specific historical and discursive moment that is important to elucidate, not so much to limit the scope of this research to a given time and space as to precisely ascertain the possibilities of extrapolation. It will be more meaningful to translate the answers that a specific issue has generated and to make them travel to other situations. Just as critics familiar with the cultural and narrative turn in the humanities and the social sciences recognize that it is prudent for authors to identify their subject position to avoid masquerading as universal authorities (even and especially if they wish to preserve a space of dis-identification between what they state and who they say they are), it is important not to immediately generalize or theorize what we discover when we scrutinize one specific historical node. The contours of the case study do not have to limit the validity of our conclusions but they do organize the shape of our research, which has already influenced the way in which we define our object of study.

My immediate historical and geographical context is both local and global. The following chapters focus on France, but France's spatial identity is questioned by narratives that struggle with the past. France becomes one node in a global network of pasts and presents because the redefining of boundaries is one of the effects of narratives that struggle with the reparative. France is therefore more than the sum of all that is French within or even outside its borders. The identitarian dislocation or relocation affects temporality as well. All the works studied here (films, novels, drama or non-fiction prose) have appeared since the very end of the twentieth century and since the beginning of the new millennium. Yet they make no cultural sense if we forget that they constitute contemporary ways of giving an account or accounts of the first tragic decades of the twentieth century, accounts that may clash with earlier ways of narrating the (supposedly same) past. From that point of view, contemporary France can be studied as a paradigmatic case: it is one of the self-identified modern democratic nations that has to deal with the current impact of two wars waged on its perceived core territories as well as conflicts of decolonization fought on lands that France claimed were differently French. In 1998, Henry Rousso wrote:

> the recent past is presented to us today with unequalled intensity. It is receiving unprecedented attention because of our difficulties in facing up to the tragedies of the twentieth century. Only now are we coming to realize the true proportions of these tragedies. We are living in the 'age of memory,' that is in a sensitive, affective and even painful relationship with the past. (Rousso, 2002, 1)

His 'we' refers to the French as well as to a community of rememberers and mourners whose identity is not clearly circumscribed. Memory discourses, in general, may have been a global obsession since the 1980s.[1] Yet the specific ways in which such issues are addressed in France or elsewhere, in French or in other languages,[2] enable us to refine the analysis of this highly contested memorial terrain.

Truth, the State and the 'Colonial Fracture'

n the Hexagon, a cacophonous ensemble of voices is currently struggling with and against a desire to give an account of their/our individual and collective past, and this study of the reparative in narratives aims to contribute to a conversation about the appropriateness of various narrativizations of national and individual memories. These memories are excruciatingly painful for individuals and quasi mind-boggling from an ethical, philosophical and political point of view. The legacy that the beginning of the twenty-first century narrativizes includes the Shoah and the violent dismantling of the colonial empire (Felman and Laub, 1992; Kritzman, 1995; Golsan, 1996; LaCapra, 1998; Wood, 1999; Hirsch, 2008).

Memory, here, means the memory of genocides and torture. Even for those subjects who cling to a nostalgic vision of their past experience,[3] the dominant mood is sombre. The memories that are evoked in these narratives are not only poignant because any story about the past points to what is irretrievably lost. The reparative, in this book, is not a response to some sort of disciplinary melancholy.[4] What narrators have to deal with is the kind of torment that has been analysed by trauma theory. At the same time, this book is not about trauma and while I owe a theoretical debt to trauma studies and to their contribution to textual analysis, I would suggest that the search for the reparative can begin only once a certain amount of working through trauma has already taken place. In the following chapters, when narratives struggle, they are not faced precisely with the forms of 'unsharability' that Elaine Scarry describes in the *Body in Pain*. In that book, she points out that the impossibility of sharing is sometimes due to the fact that 'physical pain does not simply resist language but actively destroys it' (Scarry, 1985, 4). As far as the reparative is concerned, the difficulty of producing and offering a tale that can reach or rather create a new audience is more accurately explained by the complex system of address and subjectivization that Judith Butler analyses in *Giving an Account of Oneself* (Butler, 2005). Even the least traumatized narratives are not full or even self-contained accounts. Even the heroes of the following chapters who seem to have come to terms with the necessity of telling the tale are not capable of formulating what limits their story. They have made conscious compromises before publishing a novel, staging a spectacle or preparing a trial, but even when their 'I' asserts his or her willingness to take responsibility and to account for the past, it is structured by the system of address that enables but also binds the narrative. The storyteller, always opaque to him or herself, speaking from that very opacity, produces an account that is both the only way of taking responsibility and the reiterated mark of his or her potential failure.

Still, I would argue that none of the stories analysed in the following chapters is to be confused with the manifestation of trauma. I do not wish to imply that once a narrative emerges, we are not or no longer in the presence of trauma. Yet I would like to keep alive the reparative potential of the distinction between the traumatized tale (or expression) of a traumatic event and the narrative produced from a position that has worked through the trauma. For what is perhaps even more remarkable than the overall anxiety over the past is the multiplicity of different threads of memorial discourses. And it is worth comparing them to each other while keeping in mind that they are surrounded by other national commemorative discourses. One of the issues at hand is to ask which values or agendas are promoted either by each narrative or sometimes by the hidden similarities between them.

On the one hand, French culture is affected by the supposedly global memory fever. So many discursive spheres are concerned that it is possible to talk about a culture of memorialization. The state, the legislator, professional educators are just as actively involved as academics (historians or social scientists in general). Cultural agents participate at all levels, be they artists (writers, filmmakers or comedians) or members of the culture industry (curators or festival organizers). Even what we think of as the general public is not left out: those who we might imagine as the target audience of such discourses are not reduced to the role of consumers. So-called ordinary people testify, associations make claims and groups launch manifestos. An interdisciplinary proliferation of voices is collectively trying to regulate and revise, to propose some narratives as legitimate, correct old ones and choose new ones to replace them.

What seems unavoidable, under such circumstances, is that each of the new narratives proposed, as well as all the old narratives questioned by the apparently unstoppable process, should be the object of furious battles. The multiplication of interventions exponentially accentuates the possibility of contradictions between competing narratives. It is not so much a question of state propaganda vs. what dissidents would wish to see recognized as a marginalized truth. The current debate highlights the limits of the 'counter-discursive' memorial paradigms.[5] The Republic is not the dominant pole. It is both one of the competing voices and, at the same time, the paradigmatic site within which conflicting tendencies are fought out. No simple binary opposition can be made between the former colonies and the former colonizer or between the state and specific individual or communitarian memories, given the imbrications of geographical spaces and historical layers.

Repentance

n this highly volatile context, one word has emerged and imposed an undesirable for-and-against logic. A few years ago, 'repentance' would not have meant much to the French public. Nowadays, it is unusual to start a discussion about memory without hearing this recently naturalized word whose '-ance' suffix is curiously reminiscent of a Derridean coinage.[6] Repentance obviously belongs to the semantic field of remorse, contrition and atonement but does not refer to the subject who repents and is not the word that the French usually use to express 'repentance'. 'Repentir' would be expected, not 'repentance' which connotes a process and suggests that something will never end, and that it is likely to be some sort of undesirable obsession with guilt, with the past constructed as a reason to feel guilty.

This book, in many ways, is an attempt to provide an alternative framework and to give readers a chance to sidestep the 'for or against repentance' false dilemma. The reparative is a response offered to those who use the word 'repentance' (usually to dismiss certain memorial practices) and to those who find it downright unhelpful and wish to redefine the parameters of the memory debate.

The reparative is not the opposite of repentance. It is, instead, what enables me to suggest that 'repentance' is not a concept but a rhetorical trap. Like an insult, 'repentance' overdetermines the rest of the conversation, it functions as a performative tautology: repentance is the name that I give to the kind of memory that I do not value. And the type of memorialization I do not value, I call repentance. Those suspected of repentance can therefore exhaust themselves in an impossible self-contradictory attempt to prove that they are not engaged in 'repentance' and/or that repentance may not be so undesirable after that.

The titles of books published by those who implicitly define themselves as 'anti-repentants' clearly suggest a political memorial agenda. We may wish to believe that both 'anti-repentants' and their targets are in good faith when they claim that they refuse to instrumentalize history. Yet, taken together, the essays, pamphlets or volumes that are visibly meant as a critique of 'repentance' orient the reader towards a very specific use of historical narratives. France, Frenchness, the nation and the Western world are implicitly defended against unfair accusations. In 2006, Max Gallo published *Fier d'être français* [Proud to be French], a manifesto whose more elaborate version *L'Ame de la France. Une histoire de la Nation* [France's Soul: A History of the Nation] appeared one year later (Gallo, 2006; 2007).[7] Pascal Bruckner severely condemned *La Tyrannie de la pénitence* (Bruckner, 2006) in what Nathan Bracher calls a 'vehement indictment of France's alleged penchant for sententious, anachronistic moralization of history that leads to political pusillanimity and intellectual auto-flagellation' (Bracher, 2007, 54–55). Nicolas Bancel and Pascal Blanchard, authors of *La Fracture coloniale*, point out that the subtitle of Bruckner's book (*Essai sur le masochisme occidental* [Essay on Western Masochism]) suggests that '... ce n'est pas seulement la France qui s'effondre sous le coup de butoir des "repentants", mais tout l'Occident' [It is not only France but the whole Western world that collapses under the 'repentants' relentless blows] (Bancel and Blanchard, 2007, 45). Even more explicitly, Daniel Lefeuvre proposed his ideal agenda and specifically linked 'repentance' to the colonial: *Pour en finir avec la repentance coloniale* [To Put an End to Colonial Repentance] (Lefeuvre, 2006).

The reparative in narratives, when it works, is a deliberate attempt to practise what 'repentants' (those who practise repentance) are accused of doing. Studying the colonial past and documenting the crimes committed in the name of the Republic would be an obvious example. Yet the deliberate embracing of what is systematically criticized as an undesirable stance is not meant as a defence of 'repentance'.[8] Like Catherine Coquery-Vidrovitch, who wrote an elaborate and very critical review of Lefeuvre's book, we can 'recuse' the word 'repentance' (2007) and object to the implicit definition of memory and history that the 'anti-repentants' defend.

The controversy over memory is directly connected to the definition of French national identity and to the way in which the French conceptualize the notion of minorities and ethnic communities. For 'anti-repentants', 'communautarism' looms large and the complex relationship between the national and a myriad of other identity markers continues to be simplified. Communitarism is what puts the Republic in danger. Those who wish to confront the legacy of the colonial past and to recognize the traces left by centuries of a slavery-based economy or colonization are accused of overemphasizing the 'colonial fracture'.[9] They are suspected of a self-complacent bad consciousness, and accused of perpetuating divisions and conflicts within France. A certain type of memorialization is held responsible for the fragmentation of the nation and especially France's social ills. The French are threatened, not by some external enemy, but by internal divisions. The national fabric is 'fractured' and 'repentants' are accused of contributing to or worsening the 'war of memory'.[10]

When, in 2005, young people rioted in French banlieues, the spectacular and highly mediatized few weeks of violence were examined in the context of repentance. While many other standard and often stereotypical explanations have been put forward to account for the 'fracture' between disenfranchised neighbourhoods and a supposedly homogeneous France as a whole, this time it did not seem absurd to blame memorial practices. 'In the wake of the fall 2005 suburban riots, some went so far as to decry a "France stricken with its colonial past" that it allegedly continued to deny, while others deplored the futile hand-wringing of a proverbial "imaginary invalid" paralysed by historical hypochondria' (Bracher, 2007, 55). Bracher points out that memorialization is treated as a 'disease' that generates more social ills.[11]

If certain types of memorial practices are accused of worsening France's social climate, repentants are also blamed for their methodology and their discursive or theoretical choices. From a theoretical point of view, repentance is linked with certain disciplines or fields of inquiry. Postcolonial theories, for example, are under suspicion and the few French academics who choose to make use of them are likely to be seen as 'repentants'. The idea that France can be studied through a postcolonial lens is rejected as a reactionary move that forces the observer to look back, to lose track of the present and to become obsessed with the past.[12] Such a position deliberately but implicitly rejects one common working definition of postcolonial studies which is the ability and the desire to assume that the present and the past are part and parcel of a narrative: from a postcolonial perspective, no simple chronological line goes from the colonial to the postcolonial period. Anti-repentants speak as though there was a colonial and then a postcolonial France, rather than a postcolonial way of analysing colonialism in the nineteenth century as well as the history of the post-independence era (which includes the memory of past conflicts of decolonization). The exaggerated picture that one gathers from the more virulent critiques of 'repentance' is that whoever studies the colonial past must be a melancholic scholar whose fascination for dusty archives goes hand in hand with a morbid obsession with horrible deeds that it would be much healthier to collectively forget, given that it is impossible to forgive let alone explain.[13]

One issue, however, should have reconciled public speakers who are caught up in the debate organized around the word repentance: no matter which 'side' one is perceived to agree with, everyone recognizes that it is undesirable and wrong to 'instrumentalize' memory or to subordinate history to morality. Like 'repentance', instrumentalization is the word that one is likely to use when the way in which others deploy historical narratives is deemed offensive, inappropriate or illegitimate. 'Instrumentalizing' has the power to do much cultural work in the absence of clear definitions of how memory should or should not be used, by whom, when and why. But the issue of who instrumentalizes and why is complicated rather than simplified by the consensus about the undesirability of 'instrumentalization' in general. In the case of the 2005 riots, it is hard to decide whether instrumentalization would have been acceptable had social harmony resulted from different memorial practices.

The ambiguity is rhetorically powerful and I am not sure that I want to spend much time arguing about whether or not 'instrumentalization' has occurred. Even after we all agree on what constitutes the politics of truth, we will continue to have heated arguments about the most appropriate, the most ethical or politically useful way in which history and memory might be mobilized by the nation and by individuals, and by different communities (including schools and the media as well as groups defined by age, gender, ethnicity or class). Historians who object to the way in which the state intervenes also oppose forms of instrumentalization. But they may themselves turn to the colonial past and suggest that they find some forms of memorial practices better than others. Different questions might then become more relevant: how exactly are memories differently instrumentalized in various contexts and by several cultural agents? s it possible to ascertain to what extent some instrumentalizations recognize the desirability or even the possibility of acting reparatively? If it is the case, which narrative, theoretical and political positions do they adopt?

Historians, Presidential Speeches and the Law

When historians intervene as writers and public intellectuals, they may choose to treat collective memory and memorial practices as one of their objects of study. They might argue in favour of some forms of commemoration and against others. Historians, too, grapple with the meaning of memory, even if their professionalism make us construct them, at times, as experts who speak from above the fray. In the case of the Algerian war, one of the theses defended by historians such as Benjamin Stora is that memory is a mosaic of self-contained narratives that remain compartmentalized and cannot be fused (Stora and Leclere, 2007; Stora 2001). Moreover, he argues that the relationship between them is hostile. One interpretation of his thesis is that he, too, is concerned by memorial tales that do not add up to one harmonious national narrative. Depending on the role they played during the war of Algeria, individuals acquired a collective identity that is now solidifying, precisely because it has become less relevant to the political and cultural present. The persistence of such potentially obsolete identity markers explains the development of certain types of memorial discourses that each community recognizes as its own. 'Pieds noirs' (European settlers) write their own memorial thread, which is different from that of 'harkis' (Algerians who fought on the French side), conscripts (young men sent to do their military service in Algeria), and 'porteurs de valise' (Europeans who militated in favour of an independent Algeria).

It would be hard to deny that Stora has an opinion about this type of memorial development and that he is implicitly or explicitly recommending what he sees as the best practices. He is clearly not thrilled with recent developments. If, in the 1990s, his priority was to make the colonial past and the Algerian war in particular visible to the French public, his more recent interventions have to do with the form that this memorial fabric has taken. And his voice participates in a debate that consciously or unconsciously emphasizes the status and uses of memorial discourse at least as much as its existence or the content of the stories that are finally revealed.

When Mohamed Harbi and Stora (an Algerian and a French historian) worked together on a book, they called their collection of articles *La guerre d'Algérie: de la mémoire à l'histoire* [The Algerian war: from memory to history]. They stated that they wished to offer 'une réflexion sur les *rapports* entre groupes porteurs de "la mémoire algérienne", des pieds-noirs aux harkis, des immigrés algériens aux soldats français, des militants algériens nationalistes aux partisans de l'Algérie française' [a reflection on the *relationship* between communities who are the guardians of 'Algerian memory', from pieds-noirs to harkis, Algerian immigrants to French soldiers, from nationalist Algerian militants to the advocates of Algérie Française] (Harbi and Stora, 2004, 13, my emphasis). But the challenge of this type of memorial project is to solve the problem that it contributes to creating by identifying it: Harbi and Stora suggest, when they critique the memorial practices of various 'communities', that each group has 'their' memory and that depending on which vision of the past is presented, one may deduce the community to which the narrating subject belongs. Each group, it is assumed, is relatively coherent, attached to their own melancholic version of their own past, and bent on defending their own sense of victimization. It is unclear what type of reconciliatory memory would emerge if all the memories emanating from different historically formed sub-groups were to be merged. One of the questions this book asks is whether it is possible to produce a reparative vision of the past without necessarily moving towards a common narrative which, sometimes, in other contexts (though certainly not in Stora's work) starts resembling old national myths.

When Nicolas Sarkozy was elected president, it became clear that he was interested in adding his voice to the memorial chorus. He has regularly taken advantage of public appearances to make proposals that blurred the distinction between the state and education (or more exactly the teaching of history understood as the preservation of a certain national memory and not as the self-reflexive analysis of how that story imposes itself). In February 2008, during a dinner with the 'Conseil représentatif des institutions juives de France (Crif)' [Representative Council of French Jewish Institutions], he suggested that pupils in elementary schools should adopt the memory of a deported Jewish child.[14] One year earlier, what had started the controversy was his suggestion that, every year, high-school students should be read the letter that Guy Mocket, a seventeen-year old resistant, wrote to his parents before being put to death in October 1941.

Yet even his most virulent detractors never accuse him of 'repentance'. Regardless of the position he adopts, Sarkozy views himself as one of the 'anti-repentants'. Even before the presidential election, he had repeatedly made it clear that he 'did not accept' repentance. In a speech delivered in Caen on 9 March 2007, he declared:

> ... la mode de la repentance est une mode exécrable. Je n'accepte pas que l'on demande aux fils d'expier les fautes des pères, surtout quand ils ne les ont pas commises. Je n'accepte pas que l'on juge toujours le passé avec les préjugés du présent. Je n'accepte pas cette bonne conscience moralisatrice qui réécrit l'histoire dans le seul but de mettre la nation en accusation. Je n'accepte pas ce changement systématique de la nation qui est la forme ultime de la détestation de soi. Car pour un Français, haïr la France c'est se haïr lui-même ... (Sarkozy, 2007)

> [... 'repentance' is a detestable fashion. I do not accept that we should ask sons to expiate their fathers' crimes, especially if they are not guilty. I do not accept that the past should be judged through the present's prejudices. I do not accept that a moralizing good consciousness should rewrite history only to accuse the nation. I do not accept the systematic changing of the nation, which is the ultimate form of self-hatred. For a French person, to hate France is to hate oneself ...]

The repeated 'je n'accepte pas' [I do not accept] singularizes the future president's declaration (this is, after all, his own opinion). But this 'I' obviously speaks from a position of such authority that it is legitimate to ask whether 'I do not accept' is going to have concrete consequences on what the French in general are allowed to accept or reject. Sarkozy obviously does not recuse the word repentance. Instead, he condemns repentance in the strongest possible terms. A 'detestable fashion' is tasteless and probably ephemeral. Repentants are fickle, they adopt the latest trend, and their position has extreme affective consequences: self-hatred. Interestingly, self-hatred and hatred for the nation are one and the same thing in this paragraph. And both are caused by what Sarkozy calls (and the formulation is so vague that one wonders if the speech was hastily written or if the delivery modified the original sentence) 'ce changement systématique de la nation'. By the 'systematic change of the nation' does Sarkozy mean the rewriting of history, the use of certain memories? Is it the systematicity or the change that he objects to, and why would 'the nation' (rather than history) be the object of such modifications? When new memorial threads appear, is the national fabric modified? The closer one reads, the fuzzier the message becomes. And yet something very clear emerges out of such speeches: the refusal of 'repentance' and a blanket condemnation of whoever is put in the position of the 'repentant'.

Sarkozy's speeches are not the only theoretically ambiguous texts on the matter. The Republic as a whole, when it is represented by the Parliament, does not seem interested in re-thinking the role of national history (does changing history change 'the nation'?) but does not hesitate to intervene and to propose a historical canon, changing the narrative rather than the role of the narrative. At the National Assembly, the past is sometimes turned into legal texts and the goal of the exercise is to prescribe not a mosaic of diverse narratives but one unique, hegemonic story that is to be understood and reiterated as the truth. This is a different type of instrumentalization, and it produces different effects. A few highly publicized laws have transformed a number of past events into narratives that are officially recognized as the only version that the Republic wishes to endorse. The Holocaust, slavery, the war between France and Algeria and the Armenian genocide have a legislative existence, and the law has something to say about how we should preserve that memory. What the French say or do, with or in the presence of such narratives, is carefully (if not unambiguously) codified. The series of memorial laws reach into spheres usually entrusted to the authority of historians, educators or cultural agents. Parliament has the power to forbid and impose, but perhaps more remarkably, Parliament cares, Parliament has an opinion.

The specific ways in which legal texts seek to authorize, promote or delegitimize memories vary.[15] Sometimes the objective is to replace one expression with another. The phrase 'opérations effectuées en Afrique du Nord' [operations carried out in North Africa] is officially and systematically replaced, wherever it appears, with 'guerre d'Algérie ou combats en Tunisie et au Maroc' [Algerian war or armed conflicts in Tunisie and Morocco].[16] The Loi Taubira, passed in May 2001, does not replace a phrase with another but introduces a narrative that makes us perceive earlier versions of the code as texts with gaps. The law recognizes that slavery 'constitutes a crime against humanity'. One of the articles also states that slavery be taught (although no specific content is indicated here), that archiving must be encouraged and that a date must be found for commemoration purposes. Perhaps more remarkably, a few words are added to the article of law about the freedom of the press: to article 48–1 of the law adopted on 29 July 1881 was added a recommendation to 'défendre la mémoire des esclaves et l'honneur de leurs descendants' [defend slaves' memory and the honour of their descendants]. Like most memorial laws, the Loi Taubira thus codifies not only what collective memories should be but also what the French should do with them. Naming slavery a 'crime against humanity' is already a way of admitting that it existed or exists. Moreover, some memorial practices are presented as legitimate (archiving, commemorating and teaching).

Legislative interventions are relatively rare but they never fail to launch theoretical debates about matters of principle (who is using or abusing history, what are the ethics and politics of historical truth?). So far, there have been relatively few similar laws but they all address particularly traumatic events or the aftermath of last century's conflicts. The opponents of such laws are often professional historians who are appalled by the transformation of their discipline into legislative texts even when they agree with what the new law says or implies. A recent petition thus states:

… L'histoire n'est pas un objet juridique. Dans un État libre, il n'appartient ni au Parlement ni à l'autorité judiciaire de définir la vérité historique. La politique de l'État, même animée des meilleures intentions, n'est pas la politique de l'histoire. C'est en violation de ces principes que des articles de lois successives – notamment les lois du 13 juillet 1990, du 29 janvier 2001, du 21 mai 2001, du 23 février

2005 – ont restreint la liberté de l'historien, lui ont dit, sous peine de sanctions, ce qu'il doit chercher et ce qu'il doit trouver, lui ont prescrit des méthodes et posé des limites. Nous demandons l'abrogation de ces dispositions législatives indignes d'un régime démocratique.

[History is not a juridical object. In a free state, neither Parliament nor the judiciary should define historical truth. State politics, even with the best of intentions, is not a politics of history. A series of laws (namely the laws of 13 July 1990, of 29 January 2001, of 21 May 2001, of 23 February 2005) have recently violated this principle, restricted the historian's freedom, and, under pain of legal sanctions, told him [sic] what he must find, imposed methods and set limits. We ask that such legislative dispositions, unworthy of a democratic regime, be abolished.][17]

By referring to the whole series of memorial laws, historians avoid being seen as biased in favour of any given type of instrumentalization. When the rejection of state intervention is a matter of principle, it is impossible to suggest that those who signed the petition are defending a specific ideological agenda. They would agree, for example, that slavery has to be taught and commemorated but find it unacceptable to insist on the positive aspects of colonization, as the controversial law of February 2005 originally suggested.

The beginning of the fourth article of that law, which led to such controversies that the text was eventually withdrawn, was not very different from the paragraphs that encouraged the teaching of slavery in the Taubira law. The first paragraph of article 4 asks that 'Les programmes de recherche universitaire accordent à l'histoire de la présence française outre-mer, notamment en Afrique du Nord, la place qu'elle mérite [university research programmes grant the place that it deserves to the history of overseas French presence, specifically in North Africa].[18] The formulation is vague and it is hard to decide whether the legal text is saying too much (intruding into university programmes) or not enough (how is one to decide, legally, what exactly constitutes the right place?). Perhaps the text would have been treated as one of the memorial laws and objected to as a matter of principle had the rest of the paragraph not demonstrated that the legal Code is a double-edged sword: the same tool that can help France construct a national narrative that includes long-forgotten slaves can just as easily be used, by other representatives, in the very same democratic process, to suggest that colonization should not be condemned:

Les programmes scolaires reconnaissent en particulier le rôle positif de la présence française outre-mer, notamment en Afrique du Nord, et accordent à l'histoire et aux sacrifices des combattants de l'armée française issus de ces territoires la place éminente à laquelle ils ont droit.

[Curricula recognize in particular the positive role of France's overseas presence, especially in North Africa, and grant the prominent place that they deserve to the history and to the sacrifices made by the French soldiers who came from these territories.]

t is difficult to read this paragraph without noticing that the word 'positive' resonates so loudly that it distracts our attention from the other specific and limited details of the formulation. In fact, any mention of colonization is avoided, replaced by the more neutral 'presence', but this paragraph suffers from what we could call a reiteration disease. If we refer to this article, we are probably going to translate it, to add words that are not actually used in it. It is not stable. French presence, in this context, immediately sounds like and then becomes repeated as 'colonization'. I am not suggesting that this is a misinterpretation or even a betrayal, rather, that no narrative can control its own transmission and that it is a good rule of thumb to remember when we look for the reparative. Critics of the law were right to be offended by what can be summarized as a reactionary apology for colonial times. And the 'sacrifices' that this text is supposed to recognize and valorize are contaminated by the implicit self-congratulatory tone. Once again, the law says too much or not enough, tries to be a general frame and chooses to focus on specific aspects whose status is not clear: are dead soldiers examples of France's 'positive' presence? Was the role of France 'positive' in general although so many people died? What is the connection between 'the history' and 'the sacrifices'? Is one reducible to the other? Are sacrifices the most obvious part of that history?

Or is it the case that such texts should precisely not be closely read because what matters is the signal they send about what the majority of a democratic country accepts as an implicit historical canon. And should we conclude, because the uproar generated by this particular text was such that the law had to be modified, that the implicit and explicit narrative was so unacceptable that the legal text's attempt at infiltrating other domains (education, history books, the general public) failed?

In this particular case, the argument against the principle of memorial laws reinforced strong criticism against what I have to recognize as a political interpretation of what is then presented as historical truth. And such moments of history raise (rather than solve) obvious questions about our tactical or ethical reactions to such situations. We cannot tell whether people who reject all memorial laws (including those that make anti-Semitic Holocaust denial illegal) wish to be free to express the views that are proscribed, or rather wish to protect themselves against a state that would hypothetically condemn such behaviour. In other words, the same stance may be a rejection of the specific content of such laws (regardless of whether the opponent accepts the state's right to intervene), or a refusal of the principle of state intervention. But even the choice might be tactical or principled. In other words, I may have strong views about whether the state should or not interfere, and in one specific case fight for or against a certain legal disposition because I consider that the moment is right, for example, to change educational programmes or modify pension plans designed for African veterans. What constitutes a reparative reading of such legal texts is therefore always re-definable and there is, precisely, no definitive reparative canon or overall strategy. Like the narrative itself, all positions are unstable; they depend on the power of certain words. Some circulate easily, some get hold of the collective imagination, and some are forgotten or ignored. Controversies draw our attention to certain aspects of legal texts that we might otherwise ignore. Each intervention modifies the overall narrative by emphasizing or de-emphasizing some of its parts and the critic's identity or legitimacy depends on his or her ability to reach a wider public via public media.

'Working Through' the Past

What seems to be at stake, today, is the use that individuals and nations make of memory. When I decide to search for the reparative in memorial narratives, I make a conscious decision to accept what some could call an instrumentalization of narratives that function at the intersection between memory and history. Although the difference between memory and history has become a commonplace theoretical starting point partly because of the widespread influence of Pierre Nora's work, some narratives develop in a space that blurs the distinction between them or rather perform a type of cultural work that cannot be accommodated by an either–or logic. The search for the reparative treats historiography and the memorial in narratives as two equally important manifestations of a certain type of intervention. Historians, from this perspective, provide one type of account. Their books are one of the narratives that delineate what is at stake when the present is redefined, because of the ongoing debate about the place of something called the past. Individual testimonies and state interventions bring another set of stories to the table.

What matters today, then, is the past, its impact on the present, but also, and much more importantly, what Theodor Adorno called 'the meaning of working through the past' (Adorno, 1998, 89). As the translator Henry Pickford points out, it is important to keep in mind that the phrase 'working through' is potentially ambiguous. One of the German words that Adorno uses is *Aufarbeitung*, which implies 'working through in the sense of dispatching tasks that have built up and demand attention, such as catching up on accumulated paperwork etc. It thus conveys the sense of getting through an unpleasant obligation, clearing one's desk etc.' (Adorno, 1998, 337–38). If we agree that the 'memory fever' demonstrates that France, in general, and most of the cultural agents whose voice can be heard have given up on amnesia and silence as the best way of locking the colonial past into an irrelevant closet, it opens up a new issue: how then, do we, they, I deal with this 'working through'? Working through the past is both a practice and something between a politics and an ethics, something that could be called an agenda. The *Aufarbeitung* option is obviously undesirable in Adorno's text but 'working through' also means something else. Pickford writes: 'At the outset of the essay, Adorno contrasts "working through" (aufarbeitung) with a serious "working upon" (verarbeiten) of the past in the sense of assimilating, coming to terms with' (Adorno, 1998, 337–38). What one does as one 'works through the past' must be carefully translated, and the images that the translator uses (going through paperwork, assimilating) cannot solidify all the aspects of a given practice of memory but they give us a sense of what type of involvement is at stake.

The constellation of practices and concepts that come together when I use the word 'reparative' in conjunction with memorial narratives takes into account the ambiguity of what we do when we 'work through that past'. Remembering, historicizing, making one's account public, at least to oneself, demands a continuous act of translation. And each translation or retranslation adds, to the original formulation, a layer of metaphors or examples that indicate that the practice of memorializing is not a goal in itself. What we do with the memorializing process cannot be cut off from the process itself.

The past is always rewritten or retold because it was already once before written and told. Even a strict ethics of neutrality suggests that we know that camps existed or exist and that stories are already organized according to whose interest is served. And each ambition to tell the truth, even or especially if it is a sophisticated practice that includes one's own subjectivity, is a form of instrumentalization, if by instrumentalization we mean that it falls closer to the first or second definition of 'working through the past'.

When I remember, rewrite, retell the past, the new past turns my present into a narrative environment that becomes a type of norm, a constraining and enabling frame that defines what I will need to oppose, celebrate or defy. The act of translating, from one discipline to another, from one linguistic or cultural environment to another, actively participates in the memorialization process. The search for the reparative in narratives cannot be done if 'working through the past' means relegating it to inexistence or irrelevance. As Adorno puts it:

> One wants to break free of the past: rightly because nothing at all can live in its shadow, and because there will be no end to the terror as long as guilt and violence are repaid with guilt and violence; wrongly, because the past that one would like to evade is still very much alive. (Adorno, 1998, 89)

Concentrating on the reparative in memorial narratives is the opposite of 'breaking free from the past'. Or rather, it is a deliberate attempt to function as a to-and-fro shuttle between the two points that constitute Adorno's seemingly aporetic geography of time (mandatory break, illusory break). Some stories know that it is impossible to live in the past *and* impossible to break free. Still, they attempt to live in the past and to be free from what, in the past, turns the present into a terrifying repetition of endlessly reconfigured guilt and violence. They do not seek to 'evade' anything but they are looking for a different type of freedom. Their focus is on the past but only because the present does not 'live in the shadow' of the past. Instead, the present is the choice of the story that we make of the past.

Each translation, each moment of 'working through', has an opportunity to function as a reparative moment and to engage in a reparative performative story. One very specific example comes to mind. The English title of the published translation of Eric Conan and Henry Rousso's *'un passé qui ne passe pas'* is *Ever-Present Past* (Conan and Rousso, 1998), which emphasizes the past-in-the-present logic: the past does not become the past. Just like 'working through', however, the 'passé qui ne passe pas' is ambiguous or rather polysemic. Time is not 'passing' but another meaning of 'ne passe pas' is that something does not 'go through'. Something cannot be swallowed, it is indigestible. There is a blockage, something like a traffic jam. A different translation could have highlighted this second layer of Conan and Rousso's title: we cannot break free of the past. And in that configuration, not only is the past very much 'alive' in the present but clearly it functions as a pathology or at least a danger. We might choke on it.

I am not suggesting here that the two meanings of 'working through' in Adorno and the two possible translations ('ever-present-past' and something like 'stuck in your throat') can be exactly superimposed. The richness of Conan and Rousso's formula rewrites Adorno's mandatory impossibility. In Conan's and Rousso's case, the idea is that without 'breaking free', we can treat the past both as something that can be life-threatening (nothing lives in its shadow) and something that we always live with (it is ever present).

I am suggesting that what I call the reparative in narratives blends the two implicit agendas. The goal is to invent or perhaps to recognize and celebrate, where it exists, a new type of 'breaking free'. It does not have to be a breaking free 'from' the past but a recognition that living with the ever-present past is unavoidable, that, therefore, the present is this so-called past of violence and guilt, but also that a welcoming of that heritage does not mean that we must reproduce it. And this is not a three-stage dialectic process but a constant articulation between these positions.[19]

One of the theoretical hypotheses that I propose to test is that if a story that we make of the past has the ability to hurt, then there is no reason to assume that it could not do something else. t may not 'repair' (it will not be a reparative narrative), but the knowledge that we have that it might have an effect is the first step in the direction of imagining how it could be reparative for whom and how.

Why 'Reparative'?

Exploring how the reparative interconnects with Adorno's working through the past does not, however, explain very effectively why this particular word was chosen and what type of 'working through' I am proposing to analyse. Where, you may ask, did the notion of the 'reparative' come from and why did I find it useful to add what seems like yet another metaphor to the series of available images that Adorno and his translators have provided us with? Doesn't the reparative promise a quick fix? Why not Adorno's freedom, or his translator's administrative tasks or assimilation and digestion as in Conan and Rousso, and why not haunting?

As has already become obvious, the word 'reparative' that will be used in conjunction with 'narratives' is far from a perfect tool. It could be thought of as a weak concept whose meaning gets fuzzier and fuzzier when it is used in the context of memorial recovery. The intuition that something about the past needs to be repaired does not explain what exactly needs repairing, what it will take to repair, who will do the repairing and who will be able to assess the repairs. Yet I am willing to gamble that such uncertainties make the reparative difficult to grasp and quantify, not irrelevant.

If I wish to explain why I chose 'reparative' as the inappropriate and unsatisfactory adjective that describes the cultural work I am looking for, one narrative comes to mind. The notion of the reparative 'comes from' (although the metaphor of origin needs to be questioned) the work of Eve Sedgwick and more specifically from a chapter called 'Paranoid Reading and Reparative Reading' in her book *Touching Feeling*. As I try to find out more about how France's colonial past is constructed and how it is now linked or disconnected from our (also constructed) present, I often remember Sedgwick's warning about the dangers of paranoid critique or of critique as paranoia. I welcome her suggestion that we find ways of

> moving from the rather fixated question Is a particular piece of knowledge true ... to the further questions: What does knowledge do – the pursuit of it, the having and exposing of it, the receiving again of knowledge of what one already knows? *How* in short is knowledge performative, and how best one moves among its causes and effects? (Segdwick, 2003, 124, emphasis in original)

In a theoretical world permeated by performativity theory, it may not take much to convince readers that there is more to the 'true or not' response to a given statement. When I read history, I am aware of constantly negotiating the theoretically fuzzy line between the idea of what a fact is and the knowledge that facts are also an effect of certain types of mediation. This consciousness coexists with the conviction that sometimes, perhaps most of the time, it is more urgent and ethically desirable to engage in rather than postpone a conversation about why it is that reality and the real can and must still be claimed. But Sedgwick goes one step further. She meticulously articulates the dangers of paranoid readings: paranoia is 'anticipatory', generating a 'unidirectionally future-oriented vigilance' (130), which means that the backwards-forwards hope that reparative narratives might produce will never develop as long as we are constantly on the lookout for the necessarily bad surprises that we want to avoid. Paranoia is 'reflexive and mimetic' (131); it is a 'contagious tropism' (131). Sedgwick warns her reader against the generalization and quasi-naturalization of paranoid paradigms:

> Subversive and demystifying parody, suspicious archaeologies of the present, the detection of hidden patterns of violence and their exposure: as I have been arguing, these infinitely doable and teachable protocols of unveilings have become the common currency of cultural and historical studies. If there is an obvious danger in the triumphalism of a paranoid hermeneutics, it is that the broad consensual sweep of such methodological assumptions, the current near profession wide agreement about what constitutes narrative or explanation or adequate historicization may, if it persists unquestioned, unintentionally impoverish the gene pool of literary-critical perspectives and skills. The trouble with a shallow gene pool, of course, is its diminished inability to respond to environmental (e.g., political) change. (143–44)

The first difficulty with that almost dangerously compelling paragraph is that it makes us quasi-systematically paranoid of our own probably paranoid reflexes (to the point of forcing us into an unproductively deconstructive relationship with paranoia: it takes one not to be one). Moreover, it does not tell us much about what we might possibly do if we wish to free ourselves from the delicious trap of paranoid readings.

Sedgwick's critique of the hermeneutic of suspicion and of the exclusiveness of paranoid critique constitutes one of this study's analytical horizons. But horizons are not tools that you pull out of a box to fix a neatly identified problem. It would be naïve to assume that once we have identified paranoid approaches as dangerously solipsistic, a perfectly symmetrical solution (non-paranoid readings) will magically reveal itself. If readers, convinced that it is urgent to look for a better way of reading, go back to Sedgwick's chapter in search of a repertoire of tactics and critical moves, they will probably be disappointed.

The value of this kind of trouble is that it invites us to recognize just how seductive Sedgwick's critique is and to heed her own ironic advice: don't do as I tell you. Earlier in the chapter, she had alluded to one of the bumper stickers that 'instruct people in other cars to "Question Authority"' (125). 'Excellent advice', Sedgwick notes wryly, 'perhaps wasted on anyone who does whatever they're ordered to do by a strip of paper glued to an automobile' (135). In a sense, the paradox serves us well: paranoid readings are not bad acts from which we can or should virtuously abstain. On the other hand, even if we (in)consistently succeed in not taking a perverse delight in our paranoid readings, we have only found a position from which we may start looking for what exactly a 'reparative reading' or 'reparative critique' could look like.

In this study, the search for the 'reparative' includes reading and writing and goes beyond literature to include cinema, theatre and political or legal discourse. But the cultural analysis of what the reparative can do is also limited to a certain type of project. While I have no ambition of ever reaching a perfect definition, clearly the paradigm constituted by the reparative in narratives leaves untouched whole areas of the broad semantic field occupied by the notion of reparation. If by 'reparations' we mean the type of financial compensation owed to the descendants of slaves or the heirs of Holocaust victims, this book is almost irrelevant unless we consider the reparative in narratives as what may produce the profound symbolic and cultural changes that need to take place before governments, states, associations or individuals can agree on what must be negotiated and by whom.[20]

Let us posit, for now, that the reparative is an energy, a process, a specific set of narrative choices that propose to offer a conscious or unconscious strategy to a double process of recapturing and recovering: as Maeve McCusker suggests, 'any attempt to recover collective memory will also, by definition, be an attempt to recover *from* that very memory, a paradox of reluctant anamnesia' (McCusker,

2007, 9). The reparative evokes but does not completely overlap with the notion of restoration that suggests a teleological pattern of memorial activity: often, a moment of amnesia is metaphorized as a loss, a gap, something that must be made whole again, and the moment of anamnesia restores the community to a previous state of 'plenitude'.[21] In other words, the reparative is an urge to participate in a journey for the sake of the journey rather than out of a desire to reach an illusory end point. What happened in the past, what the past did to (some) of us and therefore to all of us, is irreparable. The reparative in narratives is not a cure but it may help us reread the metaphor of a diseased past as a problematic construction. The reparative in narratives does not pretend to fix something. But just as the issue of forgiveness makes all the more sense in the context of unforgivable acts,[22] irreparability can function as a given and as the motivation to accept the discomfort of an apparently contradictory critical stance: how is it possible to both, on the one hand, renounce denial, forgetfulness and amnesia and, on the other hand, to give up on the illusion that once we have looked the past in the face, once we have 'worked through' it, our present will be free from its traumatic legacy?

The focus on narratives also implies that I agree to renounce the paradigm of lived memory that more or less privileged the notion of immediacy and presence. The following chapters are studies of stories made of words or images and do not imagine their reliability as the result of present, immediate events.[23] The reparative aspect of such narratives accepts that memory is a product of certain types of mediation and that recovery implies constructing, in the present. This study is about what it means to tell the story of a traumatizingly violent past, without having to choose between a principle of healing (the past cannot be healed) and a principle of perpetuation (not knowing the past will lead to repetitions). The books, films, performances and discourses that will be treated as the main objects of study were chosen because they nurtured my hope that it is not only possible to make a sane story out of a mad history, but that it is theoretically feasible to identify the specific narrative techniques and strategies used by subjects who have managed to do so. Very simply put, then, the reparative, when it works, is what makes us understand, believe or imagine an alternative out of a seemingly doomed double alternative: either I should know the past because it is the only way of not reproducing its horror in the present (the 'never again' grand narrative), or I should live in the present to make sure that past horrors do not infect us. Both postures have, or claim to have, the same ultimate goal in mind. It is in the name of a better present that both history and memory are implicitly recruited.

What is reparative about some narratives is that they accept giving up on repairing the past. The harm is done. We have to work through the trauma. But although working through the past is not going to systematically produce reparative effects, it does not follow that we should therefore stop working through the past. The past will not be repaired. What is reparative about a memorial narrative will always be limited and imperfect, sometimes undecidable and eminently fragile. The following chapters are not a repertoire of reparative narratives because I do not know which ones are (or are not) and for whom. Neither do I wish to police that border. On the other hand, the search for the reparative in narratives and the narrativization of the reparative enable me to suppose that in each narrative context, it is possible and desirable to make some choices, sometimes small, imperceptible choices, pushing in one direction rather than another, emphasizing one aspect at the expense of another.

The search for the reparative requires a focus on the productivity but also on the limits of narratives. The issue is not to reassess the difference between fiction and reality but to analyse what happens when the narrative is aware of being a narrative involved in the production of truth and values. If we conceptualize both the past and the future as what we construct through our narratives and if we recognize that a narrative grammar is not so different when we remember the past and imagine the future, it becomes urgent to scrutinize the type of theory that we deploy when we produce or analyse reparative or paranoid readings.

When the figure of the backward-looking pessimistic historian is invented to condemn those who are interested in sorting out the colonial archaeology, the implicit suggestion is that looking back is regressive and that it is necessary to focus on what is ahead of us, in the future. That we confuse the past with something that is 'behind' us is of course one of the ways in which narratives and fictions of a certain type are naturalized.

The reparative aspects of the narratives that we are about to read are to be found in those articulations that allow us to move from whether or not we must or can remember to more specific, difficult and perhaps frustratingly laborious processes of evaluations. Among all the narrative techniques that enable subjects to talk about the past or talk about the necessity to talk or remain silent about the past, which ones manage to look back productively? That is, which ones look at the past and welcome it as the present while still avoiding potentially devastating effects? Each narrative has, as one dangerous horizon, the possibility of participating in a cultural war and of re-establishing, in the present moment, the divisive social formations that characterized the violent era that we seek to remember. And a second risk is to assume, over-optimistically, that once the past is remembered whatever might have been traumatic disappears, as if the power of storytelling were predictably therapeutic, both on the individual and on the national or community level.

The reparative in narratives is less an object (a type of narrative) or even a practice (reparative reading) than the encounter between the two. Although authorial intentionality has not been a particularly productive category in post-structuralist critique, I propose that the mutually performative effects that narratives and subjects have in the presence of each other sometimes produce effects that resemble what we used to call authorial intention. In this context, the interest of assuming the performativity of narrative as subject-forming moments or places and also as effects of the subject's attempt to give an account of themselves is to reframe the debate about the use, abuse or abusive (re)construction of national pasts.

The discovery of what happened does not have to be reduced to the acquisition of knowledge. As Sedgwick remarks in the context of HIV, figuring out whether or not the virus was intentionally or inadvertently released out of some laboratory may be less important than understanding why the desire to trace the origin confirms our (paranoid) knowledge that some social categories are not considered as what Judith Butler would call grievable lives (Butler, 2004a, 19–49; 2004b). Confirming that colonized bodies were institutionally reduced to cannon fodder or deprived of their citizenship, parked in segregated cities and tortured by the army of a democratic republic can be done over and over again in a way that will, each time, reach a new public, but not necessarily produce any new political or ethical effect. What is important, Sedgwick suggests, is what we do about and with that type of knowledge. Answering such questions will naturally lead to privileging certain areas of research rather than others and will present the search for the past as a multifaceted type of questioning.

Each of the following chapters represents one particular narrative technique or cluster of narrative strategies that are offered here as the beginning of a critical reparative alphabet. The first chapter is devoted to an Algerian humorist and actor who lives in exile: Fellag. That his main objective should be that we also laugh with him does not make his subject matter any less tragic. His work addresses the traumatic traces of the colonization not only in France but also in Algeria, and the systematic recourse to humour is the opposite of escapism. Fellag does not break free from the past but pursues, in a messy present, what resists oblivion and senseless reproduction. His fascination with issues of multilingualism, with mistranslations and misinterpretations, forces us, the audience, to adopt a meta-perspective on what is said, to whom and why. Fellag uses words to write history but he also suggests that we should not ignore what history has done and continues to do to words. Sometimes, the reparative entails the decoding of tensions that could very easily remain unheard, of conflicts that would remain unnoticed if the humorist did not choose to highlight what, in a conversation, can be traced back to old patterns of domination and violence. No 'community' is immune but it is not the case either that perpetrators and victims are stuck in their positions. In fact, one of the ironies of Fellag's reparative tactics is that he alerts his public to the fact that some of 'us' may be incapable of even identifying the moment when the power to inflict violence or to exclude the other from one's community has changed hands.

The next chapter will not give the reader much cause to laugh or smile. As we move from comedy to the novel, we encounter an author whose visibility owes very little to postcolonial studies. Like all the young men who came of age during the Algerian war, Nicolas Ehni was directly involved in the conflict and his current work bears witness to the fact that a whole generation is now struggling with the memory of atrocities, with the issue of forgiveness and with the consequence of a past that now defines the way in which he views his own national genealogy. His beautiful and terrible book, *Algérie roman*, was written in 2002. It is perhaps even more obvious to Ehni than to any of the other artists studied in this book that nothing will repair the past. If I dare offer this work of art as part of a collection on the reparative, it is not because I am convinced that this idiosyncratic tale offers any kind of response or solution but because here is a text written from the point of view, not of the victim who wishes to see his or her past recognized, but of one of the torturers who agrees to wonder about forgiveness, about the relationship between violence and the nation, without hoping to be himself forgiven or repaired. The issue raised in this novel is whether it is possible to write a sane story about history gone mad.

The following chapter is devoted to recent films that address France's colonial past, and focuses more specifically on Michael Haneke's *Caché* and on Rachid Bouchareb's *Indigènes*. The role occupied by Haneke's hero could be seen as the dark side of Ehni's narrator. At first, *Caché* seems to provide a perfect counter-example to what I am calling the reparative in narratives. Here is a middle-aged man who absolutely refuses to take any responsibility and mobilizes every possible strategy to prevent a story of personal involvement in state violence from telling itself. And yet a comparison with *Indigènes*, made specifically to bring the past back into the present, suggests that nothing is ever simple and that authorial intention does not miraculously generate reparative tales. *Indigènes*, which documents the role played by North African soldiers during the Second World War, had a direct political, legal and economic impact. *Caché* and *Indigènes* seem to respectively exemplify the *Aufarbeitung* and *Verarbeiten* Adornian poles, and yet the way in which each film instrumentalizes history offers the audience two radically different theories of what a given moment of memory can achieve. Contrary to what we may think at first, *Caché* may offer us more opportunities to imagine and practise an individual and ultimately collective reparative memorial process than *Indigènes*, which aims to be a ready-made or ready-to-consume reparative narrative.

The final chapter returns to textual environments that mix autobiography, history and legal issues. It is devoted to the work of a lawyer who, very early on, knew what the Algerian war meant. No period of silence or ignorance was ever part of Gisèle Halimi's trajectory. Looking back, for her, means giving an account of her life-long confrontation with violence. For Halimi, the past is a long list of successful or at times tragic and exhausting battles against injustices. Armed with words and her expertise as a (young) defence lawyer, she defended the victims of torture during the Algerian war. And it is no coincidence that one of the most famous of these cases involves a woman, Djamila Boupacha, whose fate at the hands of the paratroopers would not be effectively narrated if gender issues were left aside. Halimi, whose role in the legalization of abortion was crucial in the 1970s, invites us to reflect on the difficulties that emerge if the reparative appears in a complex narrative that crosses several apparently distinct threads. Her political autobiographies weave an intricate and sometimes disturbing web of historical, legal and personal elements. In her books, she presents a whole gallery of characters or figures who can only meet productively in Halimi's texts. By letting the tortured body of an Algerian woman cohabit with a mother who never loved her daughter, a father who could not admit that a girl had been born, a little brother burned alive in front of Gisèle's eyes but also the memories of a botched abortion that exposes the sadism of European doctors, she helps us reflect about the role that colonial values play in the definition of the universal, of the (gendered and ethnicized) body and on the definition of what it means to defend a plaintiff and to ask for justice.

CHAPTER I

Algerian Humour

'Jay Translating' Words and Silences

The hero of this chapter is Fellag, a famous Algerian humorist, a 'comic, clown, mime, and performance artist' as Ruth Weiner calls him in her review of one of his shows (Weiner, 1999, 470). Fellag is a public speaker and a published author. He believes in the power of words and stories and in the inextricability of autobiography and politics. Fellag is originally from Kabylia and grew up during the war of independence. He started his career as a performer in Algiers, where his parents moved when he was a child (a first cultural and linguistic displacement), but he had to resign himself to exile in the middle of the 1990s, at a time when unspeakable violence made his country especially dangerous for public intellectuals and artists.[1] For Fellag, tragedy was never set in another time or another place.

Yet there is one obvious difference between Fellag and all the writers analysed in the other chapters of this book. Humour, and a very specific form of verbal play, are his trademark. For Fellag, laughing is a strategy, the reparative energy that enables him both to confront the unbearable and offer his audience a way out of despair. But not just any kind of laughter will do. Fellag chooses very specific types of tactics that I propose to observe in this chapter. Exactly what type of humour is powerful against despair is one of the questions that Fellag grapples with. Commenting on *Delirium*, the show that opened in Tunis during the darkest hours of the Algerian civil war, Fellag pointed out that laughing is not enough to alleviate despair. '[*Delirium*] played a year in Tunis and 20 times in France, but it was too harsh. People laughed a lot but they left in despair.' Despair, he said he quickly realized, is a dead end: 'It's better to leave them laughing and then let them work it out later. The public works on what is unsaid' (Blume, 2005).

Fellag reaches a large and multicultural audience. Before leaving Algeria, he had become a star in his own country thanks to the popularity of shows such as *Les Aventures de Tchop* (1986), *Cocktail Khorotov* (1990), *SOS Labess* (1991) and *Babor L'Australia* (1991). His tender satires of Algerian daily life have been just as successful in France where *Djurdjurassique Bled* (1999) and *Le dernier chameau* (2004) met with popular and critical acclaim.[2] His theatrical alter ego, a clown in red braces and a polka-dot shirt, has become a familiar figure, and he is now part of the relatively small group of successful Maghrebi artists who make their multicultural audience laugh about the relationship between France and the Maghreb or about what goes on in the Maghreb in people's everyday life. Unlike other famous humorists such as Smaïn and Djamel Debbouze, he is not identified as a 'Beur' and he arrived in France relatively late in his career, although he has worked with Beur filmmakers such as Malik Chibane (he appeared in *Résidence Mozart* in 2005) and Yamina Benguigui (*Inch'Allah dimanche* in 2001). His career as a performer and actor is comparable to Gad Elmaleh's, except that Fellag is not from Morocco but from Algeria and more specifically Kabylia, which directly influences not only what he chooses to talk about, but also his unique relationship to his three languages, Berber, Arabic and French.

In all his texts and performances, Fellag draws our attention to moments of multilingualism that some of the protagonists do not perceive as such and that could easily result in incomprehension, friction or even open conflicts. In this chapter, I propose to focus on the way in which Fellag represents often brief but complex linguistic and cultural encounters, in order to explore the specific tactics that he invents to come to terms with potentially volatile situations. In his stories, words often fail, generating misunderstandings or hostile silence that Fellag's humour tries to describe in a way that provides us with an antidote. The first two subsections are thus devoted to an analysis of how Fellag (mis)translates or 'jay translates', when he refuses to move from one language or one culture to another but stays, instead, in the seemingly impossible and messy space between languages and cultures. The end of the chapter examines what, perhaps, constitutes an extreme case of linguistic in-betweenness, the representation and articulation of encounters that we experience as moments of silence and noise, because the other's words are incomprehensible or self-censored.

Maghreb, East and West

Fellag's texts are always impossible to translate from one language to another because what we normally think of as the original text is already multilingual. One of the distinctive facets of Fellag's humour is his idiosyncratic multilingual idiolect. He constantly and unpredictably mixes French, Arabic and Berber. Words are both the obstacle and the means by which the obstacle is dealt with, transformed into an uncomfortable yet funny in-between space that the performer occupies and shares with his audience. Language does not flow naturally, or rather the interruption makes us aware of the fact that there is nothing natural about the relationship between the speaking subject and the language(s) that historical and local contingencies impose. He claims: '... je m'arrête sur un mot et je m'amuse à le triturer, à le retourner et à inventer d'autres sens' [I spend time on a word (literally I stop, I interrupt myself on a word) and I have fun manipulating it, turning it inside out, inventing other meanings] (Caubet, 2004, 55). Sometimes, the literally 'arresting' power of Fellag's work is extreme because it creates new and therefore alienating knowledge. At other times, he slightly disturbs the relationship between a word and its most common meaning, reminding us of the forgotten and complex transformations that a linguistic unit typically undergoes as languages come into contact.

His play with the word 'Maghreb' is one of the most representative examples of what happens when 'stopping' on one word interrupts the ideological flow of monolingual dialogues. On the one hand, Fellag does not hesitate to link his origin, his quasi-national identity, his ancestors with 'the Maghreb', yet, in the same text, he points out that even the name to be given to his (trans)national heritage is problematically polysemic although usually treated as self-evident. n English and in French the word refers to the North African region that covers several independent nations, Algeria, Tunisia and Morocco. But in our imagination, the Maghreb overflows its geographical and political parameters: the word continues to evoke the Orient, which, on a map, should be East. Of course, in Arabic, the word *maghrib* means both Morocco and the West. Maghrebians, in Arabic, are Westerners. For most postcolonial studies scholars as well as people said to be of Maghrebi origin, the double and transnational meaning of the word is well known, but like many supposedly well-known facts, the equivalence between 'Maghrib' and the 'West' does not have enough symbolic power to counteract the stereotypical associations between the Maghreb and the Orient.

In one of his published texts, *Comment réussir un bon petit couscous* [How to cook a great little couscous], Fellag adds a crucial element to the linguistic ambiguity. Published in France during 2003, *Comment réussir un bon petit couscous* is a collection of amusing and thought-provoking stories, anecdotes and comments on what it means to live in France when you are from the Maghreb. The first part is written as a monologue addressed to a Francophone audience and his first-person narrator is a fictional version of Fellag as performer. 'Comment réussir un bon petit couscous', the first story, is followed by another text whose title reads like that of a pseudo-philosophical essay: 'Manuel bref et circoncis des relations franco-algériennes' [a brief and circumcised/circoncised manual of Franco-Algerian relationships].[3]

At the beginning of the monologue, Fellag addresses the issue of what the word 'Maghreb' means and he points out that we should not overlook the affective – rather than semantic – aspect of the issue: 'Les Maghrébins *n'aiment pas* qu'on les traite d'Orientaux. Et pour cause! Les premiers vrais Occidentaux, c'est nous! En arabe, le mot Maghreb signifie 'Occident'. Maghreb, Occident – Maghrébin, Occidental! Alors que Français ne veut dire que Français.' [Maghrebians *do not like* to be called 'Orientals'. No wonder! We are the first authentic Westerners! In Arabic, maghreb means 'the West' – Maghreb, the West – A Maghrebian, A Westerner! Whereas French means nothing but French.] (Fellag, 2003a, 30; my emphasis).

Like most of Fellag's jokes, this passage is a combination of light elements and of potentially controversial and conflictual allusions. Given the context (the goal is to entertain and amuse), it would be reductive to assume that the point of Fellag's story is mainly pedagogical or linguistic. He does not (only) wish to teach a non-Arabic speaking audience the 'real' meaning of the word in Arabic. I doubt that he believes that the ambiguity of the word makes Maghrebians superior to the French ('French means nothing but French'). After all, the word 'French', contrary to what he claims, also means something if we remember its history.[4]

Fellag often plays similar games, acting as if the primary goal of his stories was to teach a French audience rudiments of Arabic. He may ask the audience to repeat words after him, at first simple words such as 'hit' (for wall) and then suddenly complete sentences that of course no one will be able to master unless they already know Arabic.[5] But the Maghreb/West discussion is slightly different. After all, what exactly would change if we stopped thinking of 'the East' when someone says 'Maghreb' and started calling Moroccans 'Westerners'? What is at stake is not the accuracy of the translation between 'maghrib' and 'maghreb' but the possibility for monolinguals and multilinguals to communicate, especially when 'likes', 'dislikes' and a sense of national superiority are superimposed over the opposition between East and West.

Fellag's achievement is not to replace an incorrect translation (Maghrebi means Oriental) with another (Maghreb means West) but to inaugurate a new way of thinking about what we normally call translation or multilingualism. The images that the word 'orientalism' triggers will not simply disappear once we find out that 'maghreb' also means 'the west' in Arabic. Fellag's stories build a linguistic and cultural universe where the word 'maghreb' means both East and West. Europeans do not so much learn Arabic as (re)discover that the Arabic root of the word Maghreb has always been occulted.

Algerian authors such as Assia Djebar or Rachid Boudjedra like to remind their francophone readers of the forgotten Arabic origin of so-called French words. Djebar lists 'Algebra', 'zero' and 'chimie' [chemistry] in *Les Nuits de Strasbourg* (Djebar, 1997a, 216). Boudjedra sometimes inserts dictionary entries into the fabric of his novels: in *La Vie à l'endroit* (1997, 164, 213), he explains the meaning of 'assassin' or 'mesquin' [mean]. Fellag's tactic, however, is different. He does not so much go back to the linguistic origin as create a zone of comfort and discomfort where the likes and dislikes of monolinguals and multilinguals are kept in mind.

His humour is the kind of discursive, narrative and poetic tactic that is required of cultural agents who desire to stay in this ambiguous linguistic space even if it is uncomfortable. Fellag's story is not aimed at restoring the truth of some etymological archive, neither is it about finding a better translation for the word 'maghrib'. The story would not be funny if he were simply arguing for a more accurate and erudite use of the original. Instead, he makes us recognize that apparently incompatible meanings of the 'maghreb' coexist and that it takes a certain type of story for the public to keep hearing both sides at once. The story about the maghreb must be performed again and again. Like a coming-out story, it will never be told once and for all, in one language, one space and one word. Fellag shows us how to move within and between languages when we choose to have it both ways, to have East and West at the same time, and in at least three languages or even four if we wish to heed Djebar's suggestion that we should also add body language to our repertoire.[6]

Renouncing the comfort of a word-for-word translation means accepting the risk of what Edouard Glissant calls 'opacity'. For Glissant, opacity is highly desirable and he even insists that it should be a 'right for all'.[7] When one subject refuses to function in the language of destination, when another one accepts not understanding the other and the other's language, the protagonists are confronted with 'opacity', and even if we intellectually understand why this is desirable, we may still experience the situation as one of frustrating alienation.

I am suggesting that one of the reparative facets of Fellag's humour has to do with the fact that he proposes new ways of imagining such possibilities. His texts propose a new approach to the issue of translation and migration. Rather than worrying about the equivalency between words or even ideas, Fellag's stories bridge the gap between people who have access to two systems and those who, being less knowledgeable, are powerful enough to impose their own unselfconscious monolingualism on the bi-cultural and bi-lingual individuals who migrated and settled in what the monolinguals think of as 'their own' country. That unbridgeable chasm, or rather the dangerous road that cannot be crossed, is the tension between the sensitivity of bilinguals who 'do not like' being called Easterners and the ignorance of monolinguals who are not even aware of their breach of etiquette. Fellag's texts provide us with a new metaphorical road, not between languages but between people who have a different relationship to languages. His implicit theory of translation goes beyond words and factors in an emotional reaction that tends to be left out of linguistic studies.

Where translation normally occurs, we find, in Fellag, the representation of an embodied practice: multilinguals cross over to meet monolinguals and they are changed by the process. I suggest that Fellag creates new 'roads' between speakers because his intervention forces us to reconfigure the naturalized metaphors that make us think of translation as the passage of words from one language to another and the translated statement as a self-contained unit produced in the language of 'destination'.

Translation as Jay-Crossing

propose to call Fellag's linguistic and cultural strategy 'jay translating' because his practice has everything to do with jay walking, that is with crossing not only one but several intersecting roads (or languages), walking in the middle of traffic (linguistic traffic) and occupying a space (the middle of the crossroads) that you are told to stay away from, for your own safety and that of others.[8]

Just as the word 'maghreb' opens a messy mental passage or secret tunnel between East and West, jay translation occurs when a subject refuses to obey street signs and ventures where there is no legitimate path, creating what is sometimes referred to as 'lines of desire' across lawns, across unmarked fields.[9] Fellag's relationship to his linguistic raw material is unusual: he is not interested in looking for a lost vernacular language whose recovery would be the goal of his experiment. He is not claiming that his art seeks to resurrect the tongue of his ancestors; he is not 'berbériste' even if he obviously defends the right of Berbers to their cultural identity. He does not yearn to recapture the mother's or even grandmother's tongue like the narrators of Assia Djebar's *Oran langue morte* (Djebar, 1997b). Neither does he set out to collect traditional folktales as Mouloud Mammeri or Jean Amrouche did before him (Mammeri, 1989; Amrouche, 1989). Although he acknowledges his debt towards traditional storytellers, he also emphasizes the differences between his texts and old folktales. In an interview granted to Dominique Caubet and published in her *Les Mots du bled* [Words From Back There],[10] Fellag states: 'En général, les conteurs maghrébins sont les gardiens de la morale sociale: ils confirment les interdits qui existaient déjà dans l'esprit des gens; ils les reproduisent avec des effets grossissants qui leur donnent encore plus de poids pour les auditeurs. Tandis que moi, je remonte la morale à contre-courant ...' [Generally speaking, Maghrebi storytellers are the keepers of moral order: they re-enforce taboos that already existed in people's mind. They reproduce and magnify them, which increases their influence on their audience. I, on the other hand, go up against the moral flow ...] (Caubet, 2004, 36). Fellag knows that claiming an identity they taught (him) to despise, to borrow Michelle Cliff's title, is not an inherently progressive gesture (Cliff, 1980). The 'flow' of morality and the 'flow' of his words follow a direction that is not predicted by existing genres or codes.

By positioning himself in the middle of the road, or by going against the flow of the traffic, Fellag gives us an opportunity to follow in his tracks, to emulate his tactics. Rather than translating from one language to another, he invents a (relationship to) language that we may learn to imitate. But this is a rather unconventional form of language acquisition. Caubet writes:

> Fellag emprunte certes des expressions à la rue, et les retravaille largement (comme il l'explique dans les entretiens), mais la rue reprend également les siennes, parées désormais d'une forme de légitimité ('ki ma qal Fellag …' 'comme disait Fellag …'). Il ne s'agit pas d'un simple aller-retour, mais d'un véritable processus de transformation. (Caubet, 2004, 15)

> [Fellag borrows street language and then radically reworks the expressions (as he explains in the interviews). But on the street, people then re-appropriate his words, which are now endowed with a form of legitimacy ('ki ma qal Fellag …' 'as Fellag put it …'). It is not simply a two-way street but a genuine process of transformation.]

When someone picks up a nicely turned phrase and adds a tag such as 'ki ma kal …' followed by a name, the enabling precaution reveals the existence of what I am calling 'jay translation': instinctively, the speaker knows that it is not enough simply to use the word, and that it is prudent to place it behind a sort of symbolic marker to protect the new and fragile usage against the 'flow' of legitimate words.

Another manipulator of words, an Algerian linguistic craftsman, has provided me with an adequate metaphor for the type of reparative safeguard that is necessary to nurture the emergence of a new (tri)language. His name was Boussad Abdiche. Like Fellag, his trademark was humour and, like him, he was fascinated by flows, by crossing and by surreptitious passages, and by what happens when a person walks across a busy Algerian street, interrupting the flow of fast and furious traffic, under the relative protection of a pedestrian crossing. One of his favourite themes was the typically chaotic Algerian traffic which Abdiche had renamed 'circus'lation' ('circus'lation, ki ma qal Abdiche …').

Who was Abdiche then? Like Fellag, he was from Kabylia and, as a journalist, he tried his hand at various genres but excelled as a satirical writer. In the 1980s he published several book-length collections of social commentaries or chronicles and 'billets' (short position pieces) before being killed in a terrorist attack in December

1996 in Algiers. The book called *Circus'lation* is a series of satirical fragments written by an Algerian author who humorously criticizes his compatriots' driving etiquette or lack thereof (Abdiche, 1986). The bilingual title fuses the French word 'circulation' (traffic) and the English word 'circus', an effective signal that the tone is going to be humorous. Many of the drivers, pedestrians or road builders mocked by Abdiche are clowns. At the same time, we would not be wrong to suspect that the reference to the circus hides more serious undertones. Slightly freakish performances are to be expected. Sometimes, clowns are cruel, or pathetic or both. After all, circuses have always played with a certain stereotype of the monstrous, etymologically what is shown (*montrer* in French).

The possible presence of monsters, or at least of ambiguous clowns whose antics might amuse as well as frighten us, is worth keeping in mind, especially if we notice that for the author, traffic, the way in which people move about, is already a metaphor. In this compilation of jokes, anecdotes and quotes, traffic stands for what has gone horribly wrong in post-independence Algeria; it represents the social ills that plague the country. The circus'lation of cars and people is already a transfer, we might say a translation, of what the author thinks about the polis, and about his compatriots' cultural practices. The satirical short pieces denounce Algeria's woefully inadequate road system, but also what the author calls the Algerians' 'detestable mentality' and their disregard for rules and public space. Talking about traffic enables Abdiche to move from the car and the driver to the nation and the nationals' shortcomings. He bemoans the absence of proper highways and blames it on corruption; he laments the incessant traffic jams that interrupt the flow of cars and clog the system, physically but also symbolically since the lack of fluidity generates tensions and anti-social practices. When drivers get stuck (and they are always stuck), solidarity and equity disappear. Everyone tries to cheat, developing individualistic practices to get around the problem. Instead of waiting for their turn, drivers sneak up to the front of the line. Neither fair play nor regulations play a role in this system where the most audacious and the most corrupt always win.

Like ancient Greek fables or their seventeenth-century equivalent, his 'billets' sometimes spell out the moral lesson that they wish to teach us. On 7 April 1983, Abdiche writes: 'Lorsqu'on parle du non-respect de la priorité, on pense généralement au code de la route.

Mais dans la conduite des affaires publiques, nous trouvons aussi de mauvais conducteurs qui ouvrent à certains des voies en principe réservées à d'autres, favorisant ainsi des dépassements dangereux' [When we talk about people who disregard the right of way, we usually refer to drivers. But in the conduct of public affairs, we also have bad drivers who allow some to take roads that are, in principle, reserved for others, and encourage dangerous overtaking] (Abdiche, 1986, 39).

In such a perversely unpredictable system where the right of safe passage has disappeared, itineraries become chaotic and it is impossible to conceptualize how best to travel from point A to point B. Only anarchy and individualistic tactics subsist; the system of signs that the code represents is replaced by incomprehensible chaos. Language is noise. Because transportation and movements become haphazard and unpredictable (there is no etiquette, no protocol), the land and the territory lose meaning. No one knows which movement is safe, which is unsafe. No one knows how to read the map and it ends up disappearing. The difference between public and private is eroded by people who appropriate the street and turn it into their parking space, or conversely build extensions to their houses that occupy public space, or add obstacles such as road bumps that slow the traffic. What is proper, propriety, is replaced by a mad understanding of private property that is never shared by the community at large. Pedestrians are just as guilty as drivers:

> Bien des piétons s'imaginent qu'à partir du moment où ils traversent dans les clous, ils sont protégés par un rempart invisible.
> Aussi, vert ou rouge, ils foncent sans regarder. D'où cette réflexion acerbe d'un automobiliste qui a heureusement de bons freins: 'Ce passage, ils le considèrent tellement comme le leur, que s'ils le pouvaient, ils l'amèneraient à la maison'. (Abdiche, 1986, 9)

> [Many people imagine that they are protected by an invisible wall if they cross at a pedestrian crossing.
> Regardless of whether the light is green or red, they march across the street without another look. A driver, whose brakes were fortunately in good shape, remarked bitterly: 'They are so convinced of their right of passage that if they could, they would take the pedestrian crossing into their homes'.]

What Abdiche describes is remarkably similar to what Fellag does when he moves between and within languages and cultures. The practice requires humour but also virtuosity, it is dangerous and potentially lethal both for the literal pedestrian and for the figurative conversation between cultures. Like the pedestrian who crosses a street, a translator who must transform his or her language in order to bring words home to someone else must interrupt the traffic of fast everyday language that does not necessarily pay attention to his or her lateral move. In the realm of print culture, a certain type of commodified circulation of books assumes that success means that the largest number of copies will make their way to their reader (or owner/buyer) as quickly as possible.[11] Consequently, the translator goes across that metaphoric high-speed lane and interrupts the traffic of goods. He or she needs some sort of protection that guarantees that the seemingly slow and lateral (transnational and also transgressive work) will not be killed by a fast car.[12]

Abdiche does not criticize the principle of the pedestrian crossing but he objects to people who forget that they are in a vulnerable position. Similarly, it is probably a good idea for translators to remember that they are not safe. The vision of someone actually bringing the pedestrian crossing into their own home is obviously absurd, but the desire to do so signals a selfish appropriation of something that belongs to all. Part of Abdiche's critique is that Algerians try to offset the absence of safe public space with individualistic tactics that backfire lamentably. In this particular case, however, what is especially laughable is the notion that the sort of right of way that a pedestrian crossing provides can actually be removed from its context (the street) and kept active in one's own house. When one is at home (within one's own language, within one's own borders and protected by the laws that define private property), one has already contained the flow of traffic. The safety provided by the four walls of the house is not increased by importing a symbol that shields us from a deadly collision with otherness that only happens when we take the risk of crossing over to another side. Safety comes at precisely that price: inside, we no longer encounter the other (languages) that might threaten but also inspire us. If jay translators are the people whose role is to take the risk of going across the traffic, the monolingual who speaks only one language (or who thinks that it is possible to 'have' a language, if we think of Derrida's *Monolingualism of the Other* [Derrida, 1998]) is the one who stays at home. And if the translator needs some help in the difficult task of interrupting the norm (Venuti, 1998), the monolingual subject, on the other hand, is in need of less safety and of more reasons to venture outside. Ultimately, what is ironic about Abdiche's vision is that the person who acts as if he wanted to take the crossing home is in fact the same person who crosses the street without even being aware that a danger exists, as if that subject did not even know that caution is in order when one goes across cultures ('regardless of whether the light is green or red, they march across the street without another look'). A driver did stop because his brakes were in good order, but that does not mean that the pedestrian did not risk his life.

In Fellag's shows, the audience is often suspected of being in the shoes of the reckless pedestrian and part of the clowns' function is to expose their absent-mindedness. The colonial past makes us imagine the postcolonial migrant as the formerly colonized individual who writes in French (the 'Francographe' subject as Djebar would put it) and whose responsibility it is to make French monolingual subjects understand the other tongue. That logic should put Fellag in the shoes of the perpetual translator but his imaginative rewriting of that position redefines translation as what we (the 'ignorant' public) should be doing more consciously.

Fellag is not the migrant worker whose non-European language must be translated so that the majority audience can understand him. His exile was also motivated by the fact that his choice to also use French and Berber in Algeria was a dangerous stance to take against those who want to standardize the traffic of words in order not to be interrupted and contradicted. Talking about the imposition of 'classical Arabic' as the official state language after 1962, Fellag says 'l'état écrivait des textes et faisait des discours politiques dans une langue que personne ne pouvait contredire parce qu'ils ne la comprenaient pas' [the state wrote texts and delivered political speeches in a language that no one could contradict because no one understood it] (Caubet, 2004, 40). That type of opacity is the opposite of what Glissant envisages: it is the totalitarian assumption that no translation should be attempted because every language is going to be an inferior copy of the original. State language masquerades as a sacred tongue.

Instead, Fellag's stories create a type of opacity that comes from the fact that what he calls 'MA' langue is a constantly evolving mixture of Arabic, French and Berber. 'Quand je pense, c'est vraiment les trois. Quand je travaille, c'est vraiment les trois. Quand je m'amuse comme ça dans ma tête, à inventer des choses, à me faire un petit monologue, ça passe vraiment par les trois langues aussi.' [When I think, the three are really there. When I work, the three are really there. When I have fun dreaming up something, inventing a little monologue, it really takes all three languages too.] (Caubet, 2004, 48). Because Fellag uses all three languages simultaneously, the result is a heterogeneous combination that cannot be translated because different bits belong to different languages. Translating the whole text into one single language would be the equivalent of taking the pedestrian crossing home. It would feel safe, but the reader would precisely lose the experience of what happens when one is confronted by this flow of words, some of which remain incomprehensible although the show as a whole is not. This level of non-translatability does not have to do with the meaning of each word but with the rhetorical decisions that motivate the cohabitation between the three languages. By agreeing to threaten some of the spectators, Fellag reveals the potentially dangerous consequences of messing with the flow and traffic of signs. Political interventions that try to treat certain languages as correct and others as marginal and unauthorized idioms are a good symbol of the type of systemic violence that any scene of translation may well trigger. Something is interrupted by Fellag's practice and it may be described as the illusion that translation can pacify the encounter between subjects whose languages are fundamentally always opaque to one another.

The presence of trilingualism invents new solutions to the problems discussed by Gayatri Spivak in her famous essay on 'The Politics of Translation' (Spivak, 1993). Talking about what constitutes 'safe' translation practices, and more specifically about her own experience as a translator of eighteenth-century Bengali poetry, she advocates 'surrendering' to the text, a word that evokes vulnerability but also violence or at least danger. She argues against what would constitute 'safe' translation practices:

> First then, the translator must surrender to the text. She must solicit the text to show the limits of its language, because that rhetorical aspect will point to the silence of the absolute fraying of language that the text wards off, in its special manner. (Spivak, 1993, 183)

n Fellag's discursive universe, this 'absolute fraying' spills over into encounters between subjects who sometimes do not even know that they are not speaking the same language or rather who must be made aware, thanks to Fellag's layer of commentary, of what is at stake in the moment of fruitful misunderstanding between the migrant who speaks French with an accent and the French people who do not even know that they are guilty of ignorance.

How does Fellag manage to translate his own sense of opacity, the protective yet messy and unrecognized mixture of languages that sometimes are not even called languages, without 'taking the pedestrian crossing home'? Why am I suggesting that his jay translation accepts a level of risk that is a calculated reparative tactic? One of Fellag's typical gestures as a jay translator is to refrain from staying at the level of exchangeable words. He does not replace one self-contained system with another as if the transfer exhausted the traffic of cultural signs. Instead, he either mixes languages or, when he does not, he relentlessly draws our attention to a flow of signs that we may not even be aware of. In other words, he reminds us that the pedestrian crossing is not foolproof, that the business of translation is never finished, that we are still at risk of not understanding, of misunderstanding.

For example, Fellag systematically highlights moments of intercultural dialogue that normally get neither translated nor interpreted because they fall into the category of silence, of linguistic non-events. He listens to silences and teaches us how to interpret what is not said, what is not heard, those untranslatable nodes of multilingual powerlessness and ignorant power, resignation and resistance. Silence is not necessarily censorship, or amnesia and repression. Silence is a language too, and whether we are talking about the past or about the present, our interlocutors challenge us with different forms of opacity. Fellag's stories invite us to learn the intercultural art of decoding silence, a crucial skill without which the same wrong gets perpetuated in our dialogue. Knowing how to work with silences, or at least recognizing that it is a desirable skill to do so, is part of the reparative reader's toolbox. It is a way of 'working through'.

How to Translate Silence

In *Comment réussir un bon petit couscous*, Fellag shows that a jay translator must pay attention to *how* silence signifies, because ignoring it would be similar to finding oneself at a busy intersection where multilingualism and ignorance meet disempowerment or empowerment. In the following scenes, casual interpretive practices are shown to have potentially serious consequences. After explaining to his audience that the French appreciate couscous, he tells us a story of what, at first, appears to be a non-conversation. The non-dialogue occurs between what the French call 'l'Arabe du coin' (the Maghrebi owner of their local convenience store and a stereotypical figure of contemporary France) and a clueless customer who has come to buy what will turn out to be second-rate couscous. What Fellag jay translates is a moment during which there is apparently nothing to translate because the characters do not talk to each other.

> Le grain industriel se vend dans n'importe quel espace commercial, mais on peut aussi l'acheter dans sa rue, chez 'l'Arabe' du coin, qui est le plus souvent un Berbère marocain. Il n'a rien contre les Arabes, bien au contraire, mais ça le fait chier qu'on l'appelle par quelque chose qu'il n'est pas et il considère que c'est une grave atteinte à son intégrité identitaire. Il ne dit rien parce qu'il respecte la France et ses lois, ainsi que l'ignorance et la légèreté de ses habitants. (Fellag, 2003a, 22)

> [You can get industrial couscous in any shop but you can also get it on your street corner, from the 'Arab's' store. Most of the time, the 'Arab' in question is a Moroccan Berber. He does not have anything against Arabs, quite the contrary, but it bothers the hell out of him to be called something that he is not and he considers that it is a serious attack against his identitarian integrity. He says nothing because he respects France and its laws as well as its inhabitants' ignorance and superficiality.]

From one point of view, since the grocer says nothing, there should be nothing to translate, there appears to be no traffic at all. But Fellag's jay translation of the cultural encounter has to do with the identification of a moment of silence as the proliferation of invisible signs. Saying 'he says nothing because ...' identifies the moment of silence (thus interrupting it and replacing it with words). Fellag reads this silence for us and interprets it as a self-conscious decision, a thought-through political gesture involving the recognition of something called France, the law and the French. Fellag chooses to interrupt the man's silence with a story. His explanation reveals the presence of a flow of signs that needs decoding. Just as he makes his audience (or 'them' in the audience) repeat words in Arabic, he teaches us how to distinguish between silence and nothingness.

And Fellag goes even further. He reveals the man's position of power and his deliberate decision to remain in control of the conversation by choosing silence as one of the options rather than as the result of constraint, fear or submissiveness. Fellag's rhetorical trap lies in his use of the word 'respect'. Saying that the reason for the grocer's silence is a form of respect seems, at first, to pacify the exchange: the cultural translator protects the flow of information from threats that we normally associate with misunderstandings. The reader suddenly realizes that something was there that he or she did not perceive, and the word 'respect' is like a pedestrian crossing. Something was coming at us that we had not seen but we are safe. The fast car was in fact a demonstration of respect. The readers or a portion of the audience, to whom the lesson is addressed, are after all the same men and women who would witness the man's silence without understanding it. Pointing out that they mistook a sign for meaninglessness and nothingness makes them aware of their incompetence. They appear bad readers. On the other hand, if the sign that they missed was a mark of respect, what Fellag adds to the context is a benevolent and generous explanation and addition. The grocer is not paranoid, the reader need not be. The audience understands more and what is understood is likely to improve the atmosphere of the dialogue. Note that this is achieved (or at least so we think at first) at the expense of the man's 'integrity' and dignity: he must swallow his irritation and the trade-off is his 'respect' for something called 'France' and its laws.

Of course, even that proposition should be greeted with suspicion: if we think about it, no French 'law' requires that a Berber grocer should remain silent when mistaken for an Arab. Yet the connotations of the trade-off are clear. The grocer makes the sacrifice of his identitarian integrity (the phrase sounds just as strange in English as in French) by placing himself in the subservient position of the migrant who assimilates and respects the country's 'laws'. Fellag implicitly refers to and seems to condone the pessimistic vision of the anti-repentants: let's not look too closely at the reasons why the French are ignorant. Silence is better.

Up till then, there is no humour in the sentence until the supposedly safe crossing of signs provided by Fellag is abruptly terminated when he equates 'France' and its 'laws' with the French's 'ignorance' and 'superficiality'. The migrant's silence is now revealed to be a form of superior knowledge that far exceeds the type of condescension or paternalism that we expect of the majority. The word 'respect' barely hides the fact that the man allows the silly protagonist to get away with his ignorance and to preserve a feeling of superiority. This comfortable position is what Fellag shatters when he describes the grocer's silence as 'respect for the French's ignorance and superficiality'.

The next scene goes even further. If the grocer's silence can be interpreted as the removal of a symbolic pedestrian crossing, the next episode is the equivalent of a pedestrian being warned too late that a truck is about to run him or her over. In the passage, silence is replaced by threatening sounds that do not count as translatable language until Fellag intervenes.

> Quand vous arrivez à la caisse, soyez patient si l'épicier palabre au téléphone … S'il devient tout rouge, gesticule, transpire et crache des sons bizarres en vous fixant droit dans les yeux, n'ayez pas peur. Primo: pendant qu'il vous fixe, il ne vous regarde pas. Il prend juste appui sur vos yeux pour se projeter jusqu'à son village natal et dire à son cousin ce qu'il pense. Secundo: les mots rugueux, acérés et remplis d'âpres consonnes qu'il mâchonne dans sa bouche avant de les envoyer dans le combiné ne sont pas des insultes. C'est du berbère.
>
> Il jure que, depuis trois jours, il n'a vendu qu'un misérable pot de harissa et que le premier client qu'il voit depuis la veille, c'est un 'infidèle' qui se tient devant lui, en ce moment même, comme un dadais, un paquet de couscous à la main. (Fellag, 2003a, 24)

> [When you get to the cash register, be patient if the grocer is talking on the phone … If he is red in the face, gesticulates, sweats and spits out weird sounds as he looks straight at you, don't be scared. First of all, he is staring but not looking at you. He is bouncing off your eyes to project himself back to his native village so that he can give his cousin a piece of his mind. Secondly, the rough, sharp words full of acrid consonants that he chews before spitting them into the phone are not insults. He is speaking a Berber language.
>
> He swears that for three days, he has sold nothing but a lousy tube of harissa and that the first customer he has seen in two days is an infidel standing in front of him like an idiot, a pack of couscous in his hand.]

Once again, the system of address explicitly asks the reader to put him or herself in the customer's shoes (the text is addressed to 'you'). Fellag uses the same tactic of one-upmanship or overbidding as in the previous passage and then goes one step further. At first, he pretends to act as the knowledgeable mediator who will make sure that a misunderstanding due to linguistic incomprehension will not result in a painful and conflictual dialogue. What is literally misunderstood or not understood should not lead to a dispute. The customer who, as we have already established, is potentially an 'ignorant' and 'superficial' reader, is confronted with aggressive noise (the man 'crache des sons bizarres' [spits out weird sounds]). The grocer sounds like a foreigner and a barbarian. But Fellag's intervention allows 'us' to cross, supposedly unharmed, this barrage of 'bla-bla' which, as Kristeva reminds us, signals the presence of the barbarian because it is not understandable (Kristeva, 1988, 75). As Fellag describes it, a 'Berber language' is almost an oxymoron, it sounds like inarticulate and barbaric noise.

Fellag's intervention turns noise into language. He describes the sounds in a pseudo-scientific manner that disconnects meaning from the words but places them in a linguistic universe: they are 'rough, sharp words full of acrid consonants'. They cannot be ignored as parasitical nonsense. But just as Fellag is pointing out that the customer is in the presence of meaning, of 'words', he also immediately spells out the nature of the fear that the customer may experience in the presence of the unknown and strange language. What we do not understand could be interpreted as threatening, as a form of violence directed against us in particular. Fellag first pretends to protect the reader from such misunderstanding, and he feigns to reassure: these are not insults. And at the same time, when he does interpret the situation as a whole, we discover that the words are indeed insulting for the customer, not because the grocer curses him, but precisely because he talks about him as if he were not there. As if he ignored his presence in the middle of the busy street, as if he were a non-entity. The man is not being insulted by the words, or even by the fact that he is described as an idiot (the word 'dadais' in French is in fact rather mild). What is insulting is that the owner does not even address him. The 'ignorant' and 'superficial' customer is not likely to understand that he is being insulted because he is being treated like someone who is not worth talking to, but only about.

If the man's goal was to insult his customer in Berber, then his speech act failed lamentably since the meaning of the word for 'dadais' [idiot] gets lost in the space between languages. The performative effect that typically accompanies an insult, at least if the aggression is a felicitous speech act, is completely neutralized in this story. As Judith Butler reminds us in *Excitable Speech*, hate speech does not always work and words can 'misfire' even when a subject deliberately directs a slur at another (Butler, 1997, 19). But in this case, the system of address makes it impossible for the word 'idiot' *dadais*) to affect the potential victim since the curse is proffered in a language that he cannot understand.

In this strange case of what Austin might have called 'hollow' or parasitical speech (after all, it does sound like static on the line, meaningless background noise),[13] misunderstanding does not mean that the violence of the insult disappears, nor is Fellag trying to deny the frictions and tensions of the dialogue. We could argue that, as a storyteller, far from repairing the threads of the dialogue, he casts oil on the fire and re-introduces the word's venom by providing a French translation of the grocer's tirade. But even in the absence of a translation, his account of what happens between the two men is enough to reveal the offensive quality of the phone conversation, which relegates one of the potential interlocutors to the place of the excluded and silent third. What constitutes the most serious insult here is the fact that the grocer denies his customer his identity as a man worthy and capable of sharing words and ideas.

Jacques Rancière's model of 'mésentente' (disagreement but also mishearing) provides us with the beginning of an interpretive grid of this moment, provided we redistribute the roles played by the characters along lines of power that would normally make us assume that the dominant subject is the French customer. This exchange is a specific type of 'mésentente' (disagreement) where the subject who normally is supposed to be in a position of power experiences the encounter from the point of view of the 'sans-parts' as Rancière calls them: those who are never counted as parts of the community.

> Car le problème n'est pas de s'entendre entre gens parlant, au propre ou au figuré, des 'langues différentes', pas plus que de remédier à des 'pannes de langage' par l'invention de langages nouveaux. Il est de savoir si les sujets qui se font compter dans l'interlocution 'sont' ou 'ne sont pas', s'ils parlent ou s'ils font du bruit. (Rancière, 1995, 79)

> [The problem is not for people speaking 'different languages', literally or figuratively, to understand each other, any more than it is for 'linguistic breakdowns' to be overcome by the invention of new languages. The problem is knowing whether the subjects who count in the interlocution 'are' or 'are not', whether they are speaking or just making noise.] (Rancière, 1999, 50)

As Jean-Louis Deotte points out, this definition of 'mésentente' insists on the fact that one of the protagonists' words are denied the status of human 'logos': according to Rancière,

> the most radical misunderstanding is the one that divides two speakers – when the first cannot understand the second because, according to him, words do not belong to articulated language, to *logos*, but rather to an inarticulate voice, to *phôné*. That voice, which, according to Aristotle (in *Politics*), humans have in common with animals, can only express feelings, pleasure or pain, in the form of a cry, contentment or hate, and by cheers or booing in the case of a group. If some people cannot consider others as speakers, it is simply because they do not see them, because they don't have the same share within the political partitioning of the sensible. (Deotte, 2004, 78)

A conventional interpretation of Rancière's model would lead us to assume that the grocer is one of the 'sans part'. We usually assume that the marginal migrant, reduced to powerlessness by the majority, will occupy the place of those humans whose language is reduced to the level of noise and who are thus silenced within the dominant history of the polis. When we say that someone has a foreign accent, we have already forced him or her to operate within our area of competence, our native language and even a local or class-inflected manifestation of it. That subject's linguistic knowledge (of his or her mother tongue) is often dismissed as noise and even overlooked or left unread. One of the first Beur novels, Farida Belghoul's *Georgette!*, has provided scholars interested in this pattern with a paradigmatic example of such encounters between the ignorant schoolteacher and the misinterpreted pupil. When the child's father opens her notebook and writes a letter in the Arabic alphabet that the daughter's teacher cannot read, he does not know that the first page will still look 'blank' to the teacher because even the most basic assumption about which side of the notebook constitutes the front and the back is not shared (Belghoul, 1986).

Fellag's portrayal of *mésentente* modifies the paradigm in a reparative and original way. In Belghoul's novel, the migrant logos and even written words are reduced to the level of absence and meaninglessness whereas, in Fellag's scene, those roles are reversed. The customer and the grocer are locked in a moment of disagreement/ *mésentente*: they cannot talk to each other because one subject does not recognize that the other is endowed with language. But the man reduced to a silent and patient silhouette is the national and the fact that the 'stranger' talks to him in a language he does not know disempowers him because he cannot impose his own language.

The grocer does not even 'see' the other and uses him as a means of transportation: 'Il prend juste appui sur vos yeux pour se projeter jusqu'à son village natal' [he simply uses your eyes as a stepping stone to project himself to his native village]. His only raison d'être is to provide an excuse for the message that the grocer wants to deliver to the cousin (who called to ask for money). The customer only represents the man's difficulty in making ends meet. He is not there as himself, a man who wants to buy couscous. He is interchangeable, he is a metaphor, both what stands for something and what etymologically transports, allows the other to go somewhere.

I suggest that this passage offers a reparative rewriting of one of the most famous postcolonial myths, that of Caliban. The hero of Shakespeare's play and of so many rewritings has provided us with the exemplary hero of postcolonial criticism, a model for those who need to re-appropriate languages to reclaim their dignity. We invoke Caliban (another diasporic Algerian and also a second-generation immigrant) when we want to analyse the process of writing back to the Empire. Caliban is the rebel who says 'You taught me language, and my profit on't Is, I know how to curse' (*The Tempest*, I.ii.362–63). In Fellag's story, it is much more difficult to identify who occupies the position of Caliban, and the same ambiguity obtains if, as readers, we try to recognize ourselves as grocer or customer.

Fellag invites us to imagine what it means to be a subject who stands there like an 'idiot' without knowing that he is being called an idiot. He teaches us to recognize such situations and provides both sides with a new insight into what seemed to be a failed dialogue. Fellag's reader does not have to say, like Caliban, 'You taught me language, and my profit on't Is, I know how to curse', but he or she can say something like: 'although you have not taught me the three idioms that you speak fluently, you have taught me how to jay-translate. I now know that I am being cursed even if I don't know your language.' On the other hand, if we identify with the grocer, we learn something different about languages and translation. The grocer can now say: 'I know that you know that I might be insulting you'.

No one, in Fellag's scene, speaks directly to the other stating 'you taught me language'. The migrant may be from a formerly colonized nation, but he makes no effort to speak the colonizer's language, what has sometimes been called, in a Maghrebi context, the 'langue adverse' [the antagonist's language]. But the logic is not simply reversed either. The grocer obviously knows how to curse but he does so in his own language and his insults are precisely not meant to have a performative effect. The curse is not a malediction. He does not try to threaten his customer with a deadly disease and the only 'red' plague in this story ('The red plague rid you For learning me your language' [*The Tempest*, I.ii.363–64]) is a harmless tube of harissa.

Fellag's stories can hardly be claimed by those interested in building a new common national myth. They continually cross the often invisible, unmarked and therefore unprotected passage that opens up within the word Maghreb when we agree to have it both ways and to listen to at least two languages simultaneously. Like many contemporary artists who tend to be identified with popular culture[14] and with satirical dissidence, Fellag's system of address forces his audience to take risks as we agree to accompany him on a journey that is neither the equivalent of an emigration nor a return to the native land. He is implicitly asking us to cross a powerful flow that is sometimes called the Mediterranean, or sometimes Arabic, sometimes Maghrebi culture. Positioning oneself in the middle of this current reveals the resemblance between what we call a language and a nation, a genre and a register. What matters is not so much the result of this crossing (the translated unit) or even the process (the translation itself). After all, we may be less interested in the perpetual delay of the translation process than in the transformative, creolizing effects that such a journey has on us readers, the audience, the public at large, speakers of Arabic, French and Berber, and perhaps eventually ideologues who have been known to control the linguistic scene especially in Algeria since 1962.

Loving Couscous and Loving 'Us'

Silence, however, is not only on the side of dislikes and insults. What is not said could, after all, be a token of affection, as the first-person narrator tries to convince us in another, interestingly symmetrical scene. This time, the story implicitly mocks the deceivingly cheerful title of the collection (*Comment réussir un bon petit couscous*). The promise of a recipe could have fooled the reader into believing that Fellag's humour would be less political than usual. A recipe for a 'bon petit couscous' (a nice little couscous) suggests a relaxed and laid-back conversation between friends. But the reader soon realizes that in spite of the belittling qualifiers, 'a bon petit couscous' is much more than a simple meal. Fellag describes couscous as a national treasure, as his 'Maghrebi ancestors'' national dish (Fellag, 2003a, 9). The title hides the fact that couscous is the cultural object that the narrator chooses as a pretext to talk about the more controversial and problematic issues explicitly addressed in the second part of the book, about 'franco-algerian relations'.

In the following scene, Fellag comments on a passage from a magazine and, once again, chooses to decode something that was not said or more exactly not written.

> J'ai récemment lu dans un magazine très sérieux un sondage qui affirme que le couscous est aujourd'hui le plat préféré des Français. Vous imaginez ma joie et ma fierté en apprenant que le peuple qui a porté au sommet de ses possibilités l'art et le raffinement, mettait en tête de son panthéon culinaire « LA » création de mes ancêtres maghrébins. (Fellag, 2003a, 9)

> [Recently, in a very serious magazine, I read a poll whose conclusion is that couscous has become the French's favourite meal. Imagine how happy and proud I felt when I read that THE creation that we owe to my Maghrebi ancestors was deemed to be the crowning piece of the culinary Pantheon in the nation that had brought art and refinement to its highest level.]

Fellag's insistence that the magazine is 'very serious' sets the tone, because the adjective sabotages the claim. The narrator is already overcompensating for the fact that his source, a 'magazine', is bound to be dismissed as non-serious, and adding that the publication is 'very serious' only confirms our doubts. Just as a 'scientific' journal tries to protect its articles and authors from the supposedly less interesting characteristics of the genre of the journal as a whole, so is the 'magazine' too closely associated with the quotidian and the ephemeral for its contents to systematically count as knowledge. When Fellag announces that he will talk about a poll found in the popular press, and when he implicitly defends himself against accusations that have not yet been formulated, he reinforces the contract already promised in the title of the book: this is going to be 'un bon petit couscous', prepared with humour and levity. Advice about how to 'préparer un couscous' could be a serious affair, a chapter in a coffee table book of canonical or exotic recipes. But 'un bon petit couscous' has no ambition except that of graciousness and casual hospitality. The humorist announces in the same breath that he is serious and that he is ironic about the importance of being serious.

The obvious presence of irony, however, does not tell us much about how to decode the rest of the paragraph. Here, Fellag resembles the Roland Barthes of *Mythologies*, who reads *Paris-Match* at the barber shop and reads the photograph of a 'jeune nègre vêtu d'un uniforme français' [young Negro in French uniform] as the myth of France's imperial glory.[15]

> ... je suis chez le coiffeur, on me tend un numéro de *Paris-Match*. Sur la couverture, un jeune nègre vêtu d'un uniforme français fait le salut militaire, les yeux levés, fixés sans doute sur un pli du drapeau tricolore. Cela, c'est le sens de l'image. Mais naïf ou pas, je vois bien ce qu'elle me signifie: que la France est un grand Empire, que tous ses fils, sans distinction de couleur, servent fidèlement sous son drapeau, et qu'il n'est de meilleure réponse aux détracteurs d'un colonialisme prétendu, que le zèle de ce noir à servir ses prétendus oppresseurs. (Barthes, 1957, 223)

> [... I am at the barber's, and a copy of *Paris-Match* is offered to me. On the cover, a young Negro in French uniform is saluting, with his eyes uplifted, probably fixed on a fold of the tricolour. All this is the *meaning* of the picture. But, whether naively or not, I see very well what it signifies to me: that France is a great Empire, that all her sons, without any colour discrimination, faithfully serve under her flag, and that there is no better answer to the detractors of an alleged colonialism than the zeal shown by this Negro in serving his so-called oppressors.] (Barthes, 1972, 116)

Like Barthes, Fellag observes the way in which magazines represent contemporary French culture and pinpoints obvious contradictions. He acts as a cultural critic and helps us draw conclusions about the ways in which we are expected to conceptualize the relationship between the French and a Maghrebi 'we' that he constructs as both included and excluded. Unlike Barthes, however, he immediately casts doubt on the scientific value of his own analysis. Barthes takes *Paris-Match* seriously enough to use its cover as the object of his analysis but not seriously enough to grant the magazine as much weight as his own critical discourse. Regardless of which myth he analyses, he remains the expert, the one who knows about mystification and demystification. What we learn from *Mythologies* is that we are duped by the image and that we should know better than to like it, whether we are black or white (though the assumption is that 'we' are not the young black man of the picture).

Fellag (and the difference is crucial) does not want to be in the position of the expert. He opts out of the role. What he knows does not empower him as a scholar or even as a native informant. When Barthes denounces the arrogance of a colonial regime, he splits his public into (French) colonialists and (French) anti-colonialists. n that sense, whatever reparative impulse is at work in his text is limited by the system of address, even if we, the group to which he belongs, represent the anti-colonialist community.

Fellag identifies with a 'we' that is both included and excluded from the audience: the 'vous' (you) represents the French, and France as a whole.[16] Both Barthes and Fellag thus occupy interestingly different positions on the national and cultural chessboard. Fellag comments on the culinary taste of 'the French' as a member of a community that sees couscous as 'theirs'. Barthes, on the other hand, criticizes an image but treats the colonized body as a 'he' with which he cannot identify. The young black soldier cannot be 'I' or even 'we'. Barthes refuses to condone the political and ideological myths smuggled through a supposedly positive image of the black body. He denounces the implicit hypocritical praise but does not create a space that would allow him to be part of the same community as the soldier. He is still the insider. Fellag, on the other hand, chooses to represent his own 'I' as a member of a community of others. He is the stranger, the migrant, who feels judged (liked, disliked, hated or loved) by a whole nation. He thus makes readers aware of their own positioning and of the fractured postcolonial social fabric.

What does it mean for the French to appreciate couscous, what is the exact nature of this 'taste' that Pierre Bourdieu has taught us to interrogate as a category that establishes distinction, and therefore hierarchies and exclusions (Bourdieu, 1979)? In Fellag's text, the French's 'preference' for couscous is treated a cultural issue, as if the author agreed to culturalize his vision of the national. The French's culinary expertise is not dismissed as a stereotype but taken seriously and therefore identified as knowledge and part of a larger set of aesthetic practices. Taste is here synonymous with good taste and France symbolizes art and refinement. And to the extent that everybody's 'favourite dish' is linked to where we came from and to childhood and the land of origin, we will probably not realize that Fellag casually slips from the idea of a favourite dish to that of a national dish.

The national preference revealed in the survey is symbolically problematic. Although Fellag claims that he is delighted to discover that the French like 'couscous', he explains their preference in terms of their specifically national knowledge. They are international and universal experts when it comes to judging cuisine. In other words, their 'preference' is not a matter of individual choice revealed by innocent statistics. The fact that a majority likes couscous democratizes the French's preference. Fellag treats the result of the questionnaire as evidence of a rational decision. Couscous is part of a culinary canon that the French can rank because they know about the 'culinary pantheon'. An old grand narrative about cuisine meets the newcomer's dish. The French prefer couscous, or rather they have skills that allow them to rank and compare dishes, and their judgment is based on a competence that Fellag admires. Their preference is a form of knowledge and Fellag, who identifies with couscous from a national perspective,[17] receives the news with 'pride' and 'happiness'.

What is curious in Fellag's reaction is that he is not satisfied with the compliment, even if he describes it as 'exceptional'. Obviously, the expert's rational judgment is not enough. No sooner has the narrator admitted how proud he is than he immediately starts looking for what the compliment hides, what is 'behind' the preference, what it really means for him and his ancestors.

> Derrière ce compliment exceptionnel à notre plat national se cacherait-il une déclaration d'amour? N'est-ce pas une manière pudique et détournée de nous dire que vous nous aimez enfin? (Fellag, 2003a, 9)

> [Is a declaration of love hiding behind this exceptional compliment addressed to our national meal? Is this not a shy and roundabout way of telling us that, finally, you love us?]

The narrator reads the compliment as a screen, it 'hides' something else. But why does he suspect that something is not said? Why must he look 'behind' a statement that obviously pleases him? Is he a paranoid rather than a reparative interpreter? For a reader to adopt the position of the detective looking for clues behind the message, some hermeneutic energy must have been triggered. Fellag suspects the existence of words whose meaning is not immediately transparent. But how does one know about something that may not even exist? How do I understand that I am in the presence of an absence? The question is both theoretical and political and it is an issue both for the narrator and for the reader of Fellag's text. The idea that words 'hide' behind words may be immediately recognizable in certain types of psychological or psychoanalytical discourse, but for the narratologist, it is a metaphor rather than an interpretive grid. How is a critic expected to deal with a reference to what has not been said?[18] Have decades of poststructuralism not trained us to repeat that there is nothing beyond the text and that it is naive to treat a narrative as the superficial layer of some sedimentary structure of meaning, without acknowledging that the image itself is part of our critical vision? Yet, if it is not a proper scholarly gesture to ask what's hiding behind words, should the critic systematically refuse to address silences, pauses and what, in a story, constitutes structuring absences? Are they not part of a textual performance that our critical tools can help us decipher?

Could we, like Fellag, welcome silence as if it were a text and read it with the same attention as words? Can we have a reparative dialogue with silence and do silences expect to be heard, understood and answered? Susan Lanser suggests that the presence of what we look for or what we find, of what we invite or disinvite as relevant or irrelevant object of analysis, cannot be scientifically determined. n other words, the goal is not to demonstrate that what we read pre-exists our critical reading. Instead, our approach grants the object of our attention a degree of validity. And our selection or 'preferences' (as is the case for food) is not only determined by our competence as experts but also by the energy that we deploy as desiring subjects:

> What we choose to support, to write about, to imagine – even in the scientific realm of narratology, is thus also as much a function of our own desire as of any incontrovertible evidence that a particular aspect of a narrative is (im)proper or (ir)relevant. (Lanser, 2004, 135–36)

When we suspect that something is hidden, a type of desire is at stake even if, later, our investigation relies on scientific methods. We analyse, as narratologists, silences that our desires detect. If Fellag writes that the survey 'hides' something, it may be less important to ascertain whether something 'hides' than to analyse the effects of what he thinks he found.

As cultural critics, our own desire may be to understand just which pedagogical, reparative or imaginary effects the narrator produces when he claims to believe in the presence of hidden words. How then, can we describe Fellag's interpretation? He states: 'Derrière ce compliment exceptionnel à notre plat national se cacherait-il une déclaration d'amour? N'est-ce pas une manière pudique et détournée de nous dire que vous nous aimez enfin?' [Is a declaration of love hiding behind this exceptional compliment addressed to our national meal? Is this not a shy and roundabout way of telling us that, finally, you love us?]. The first striking element of his reaction is that, 'behind' the compliment, Fellag does not find another statement but a question. And his question will remain unanswered so that what he adds to the story and what he calls the secret are his own doubts.

We discover that what the narrator is looking for, what he wants and desires, is a 'declaration'. An expert's compliment is not enough. The narrator's yearns for affection. In retrospect, it becomes obvious that through the notion of 'exception', 'preference' and later 'creation', Fellag was already leaving the territory of knowledge. If couscous is a 'creation', then we are in the domain of art and it is not so easy to rank and judge according to purely quantifiable norms.

Moreover, using words such as 'exception' and 'preference' is not politically innocent in a French context. The phrase 'exception culturelle' evokes the struggle of artists against forms of globalization that only recognize the law of commercial exchange and reduce every object to its price, to a number.[19] As for 'preference', when used in a context that defines nationalism, it evokes an extreme right slogan that proposes 'préférence nationale' as a response to immigration.[20] It is another type of hierarchical ranking that is used to exclude those whose relationship to the nation is not considered legitimate.

When Fellag describes couscous as his ancestor's 'creation' and when he notes that it is now the French's 'favourite' (*préféré*) meal, his text cleverly mobilizes two notions that appear in radically opposed political discourses. He is not appealing to our democratic reason. His pleasure, pride and subsequent doubts do not lead him to argue in terms of knowledge and rights. He takes us to a place where the expert is not the only authority. Even the first paragraph, which pretends to acknowledge the French's proficiency, is already contaminated by an implicit critique of rationality and objectivity.

Moreover, when Fellag looks 'behind words' he writes the text that will end up revising and repairing the original paragraph. Although he gives, at first, the impression that he accepts the French culinary superiority, he also creates the condition of a resisting reading. He suggests, to an imaginary French audience, that he lacks their national arrogance. Even if the judgment is positive, it now appears perhaps less desirable than what the narrator is looking for behind the poll.

The trouble is that if the result of the survey is perfectly clear, what the narrator has detected behind words is far from explicit. The presence of a declaration of love is uncertain: is something hiding …? ['se cacherait-il …?'], is this not a way of …? ['n'est-ce pas une manière …?']. Fellag presents his interpretation as a hypothesis. It is up to us to decide whether these are pessimistic rhetorical questions (of course the French do not love 'us'), a veiled request, or a prayer I wish they would). A few paragraphs later, he even suggests that the declaration is a 'subliminal message'. He spends as much time commenting on the genre of the declaration as on the declaration itself. The meaning of the survey thus depends on the genre of the dialogue.

But why would it be so important for Fellag to believe that the poll talks about love? And how does Fellag want to discover the lover hidden under the expert? The passage answers the questions, reminding the reader that the French have been hostile to the narrator's community, to 'us' as Fellag puts it ('… vous nous aimez enfin' [finally, you love us]). Besides, even if the feeling exists, it does not manifest itself very loudly. The declaration is so veiled and indirect ('pudique' and 'détournée') that we wonder if Fellag's interpretation is not an expression of his own frustrated and naïve desire. For the French, it seems, are not inherently shy. Are experts expected to be so tentative after all? Their discretion is not a form of refinement or delicate sentimentality. France makes a collective declaration of love 'à quelqu'un qu'on a méprisé assez longtemps' [to someone they long despised] (Fellag, 2003a, 10). The French's 'pudeur' (if it exists) is not a national trait, it is a form of guilt says Fellag, who manages to accuse them of something that they have not acknowledged.

Of course, we could object that the hypothesis about love, about discretion, about guilt only exists within Fellag's text and not in the space where he detects a silence. I would argue, however, that this interpretive energy is what makes his intervention reparative, regardless of whether 'the French' accept his interpretation or not. Perhaps Fellag invents a love that is not there but he does manage to recapture a new position of power as an expert. For when he suggests that the French are discreetly declaring a love that Maghrebians have finally inspired, he does not do so from the position of the supplicant. He does not beg. His way of asking for love is very cleverly and counter-intuitively articulated as evidence of his own expertise: Fellag explains that as a Maghrebian, he is an expert in that domain. The French may know a thing or two about cuisine but in the Maghreb, Fellag insists, 'we' are great interpreters and 'we' are especially adept at recognizing two types of protocols and genres: 'we' can decipher encrypted discourses and 'we' know all about etiquette and politeness (i.e. about discretion and understatements).

> Nous sommes issus d'une culture où la parabole et la métaphore sont des modes de communication naturels. Message reçu. Nous savons décoder. Merci. (Fellag, 2003a, 10)
>
> [We are from a culture where parables and metaphors are natural means of communication. We get it. We know how to decode. Thank you.]

The reparative twist has to do with the reversal of the expert's position. Maghrebians are communicators. They know about rhetoric and genres. When Fellag now states that the French are indeed discreetly declaring their affection, he mobilizes his own quasi-national expertise: he is adept at detecting codes and etiquette, discursive practices that enable speakers to 'hide' their feelings and wrap them in diplomatic understatements.

Two national traits are thus implicitly compared. The French have a 'culinary pantheon', but Fellag's Algerian ancestors are said to master a rhetorical knowledge, which should prevent us from suspecting the narrator of an excess of (naive) interpretation. Fellag invokes a collective and cultural expertise ('Nous savons décoder' [We know how to decode]). The French would therefore be sadly mistaken to assume that when Fellag identifies a subliminal declaration of love ['déclaration d'amour subliminale'], he is only expressing an individual desire to be loved. He is a knowledgeable decoder. He reads the expression of the French's hidden affection in a scientific way, just as he was able to recognize that the French's preference for couscous was not irrational but an effect of their cultural superiority. Just as French teachers have taught generations of students that, in *Le Cid*, Chimène's 'Je ne te hais point' must be understood as a trope, that is, as a discreet and roundabout way of saying 'I love you', if we trust Fellag's claim that he is an expert at decoding what hides between or behind words ('nous savons décoder'), our role as readers or spectators of his critical approach is to recognize that what may have looked like a compliment addressed to the ancestors' culinary flair is indeed a declaration of love. The expert's approval (you are good) should be read as a lover's discourse I love you).

We have moved from the fanciful 'bon petit couscous' to issues that have to do with painful historical situations, with the tragedy of overt or covert racism and collective contempt. Fellag's 'merci' is addressed to a 'you' who has despised 'us' for a long time. Fellag is giving the French the benefit of the doubt or, rather, performing, for them, a strong affirmation that he is loved. Here, the reparative is performative as well as possibly ironic. The will to project this model of interpretation and attribute it to the French treats them as a benevolent partner in a potentially tense dialogue. Paranoia or justified fears are equally rejected and the tactic is deliberate.

Another perhaps obvious but much more pessimistic reading of the poll is thus avoided, its absence legitimized by the allusion to Fellag's ancestors' specific know-how. In the story, one interpretation of the survey is never considered: that it is possible for the French to love couscous without loving Maghrebians. The hypothesis is simply not entertained that a people could appreciate couscous as the others' exotic dish without feeling any affection or even respect for their creators. As readers of *Mythologies*, which suddenly appears very pessimistic after all, we could suggest that Fellag is in the same position as Barthes 'young Negro in uniform'. His 'zèle' or eagerness to expect the best could be interpreted as a postcolonial symptom. Is the Algerian clown a victim of what is called, in France, nostalgeria? Are fundamentalists right to suspect him of a pro-French, i.e. pro-colonial, attitude? This expert decoder does not even mention the possibility that loving couscous could be a form of culinary exoticism. The connection between appreciating couscous and loving Maghrebians, which some readers may find incongruous and arbitrary, is presented as self-explanatory and obvious.

In this context, humour repairs apparent contradictions. That the expert in 'decoding' should miss the possibility of a more pessimistic interpretation is, in itself, an interpretive issue. Either his skills are after all not so remarkable or they are, on the contrary, so developed that he is making another (reparative) point. I would suggest that humor, in this passage, is the built-in antidote against a rational argument. The point of the story is precisely not to convince. Behind that rhetorical shield, Fellag is allowed to flaunt a form of trust that redefines naivety as a reparative tactic. Refusing to entertain the possibility of a paranoid reading (they do not love us after all), Fellag doubly legitimizes the survey of a 'serious' magazine and his own optimistic interpretation by claiming that two national discourses of truth back him up: experts in cuisine and experts in metaphors both agree. The French finally love 'us'.

He would rather not know better and he opts out of writing back to the Empire. Fellag renounces the effectiveness of the postcolonial tactic that consists of pointing out blind spots and of uncovering what, in the contradictory aspects of a story, masks forms of latent racism or (unconscious or conscious) nostalgia for domination. When Barthes reads *Paris-Match*, he highlights for us the metropolitan French reader's hypocritical self-satisfaction. He teaches us how to recognize that the black soldier's 'pride' and 'joy' come at a price. Fellag could of course be perceived as the exact equivalent of this 'young Negro' when he sees 'pudeur' and 'love' where history should have warned him to read contempt.

But Fellag's humour is precisely a form of 'pudeur' which allows him to read reparatively without losing his dignity. His attention to what is not said reminds us that what 'hides' behind compliments could cut both ways. Silence goes well with 'pudeur' but it also goes hand in hand with shame. And once we add words to a text that supposedly 'hides' another text, a structure of infinite regress opens up in front of the critic.

The expert in decoding and parables does not count on the gullibility of a naive reader to claim, with dignity, the affection and respect that his ancestors are entitled to. He pretends to believe that the French are shy [*pudiques*] and that they would rather express their affection indirectly, hiding it under a form of expertise that no one denies them. But this is a deliberate tactic and it is obvious that Fellag is very much aware of what he does. He even has a name for this type of decoding. He calls it a form of politeness or more exactly 'la politesse du désespoir' [the politeness of despair]. In *Djurdjurassique Bled*, Fellag had already explained the principles of his 'Algerian' humour. The following passage is, in a sense, the theoretical equivalent of the couscous episode.

> L'humour algérien repose sur l'autodérision. Nous sommes des humoristes ambulants et cruels. Nous avons tant de problèmes que l'humour est le seul moyen de les exorciser.
>
> Les Algériens rient énormément, dans la rue, dans la vie, dans la misère, dans la tragédie. Si le rire est 'la politesse du désespoir', le peuple algérien est très très poli. (Fellag, 1999, 150)

> [Algerian humour is based on self-derision. We are all walking cruel humorists. We have so many problems that humour is the only exorcist.
>
> Algerians on the street cannot stop laughing. If laughter is 'the politeness of despair', Algerians are very, very polite.]

A despair so intense that it needs to be encoded as 'politeness', the politeness of humour, is also 'hiding' behind the joy and pride that Fellag wants the French to imagine that he experiences when he reads the poll as a declaration of love. His questions and ironic remarks about two people's cultural skills (the French are culinary experts, his ancestors are masters of metaphors) suggests that he is very conscious of how to construct falsely symmetrical statements that would give both parties equal power. After all, even the survey itself is one of the fictional ingredients in Fellag's story. It has the same value as his own analyses. All the elements in his narrative underline the fact that the original source that he examines (the results of a poll about couscous) must be (over)interpreted if the goal of the story is to state that the French finally love the Maghreb.

'La politesse du désespoir' [the politeness of despair] consists in pretending to discover a hidden declaration of love instead of formulating a question that could well lead to yet another rejection. That Fellag should choose to see, behind the culinary expert, a discreet lover, and that he should validate his own interpretation as a cultural skill (Maghrebians are experts at decoding) allows him a double sleight of hand. He opts out of the negative interpretation but he also implies that it might still exist if he, the clown, were not so 'pudique', if he did agree to formulate his fear: so you still do not love us after all? We tend to equate naivety with innocence and its etymological absence of knowledge. But Fellag's naivety is precisely not the type that a critic can dismiss as an absence of knowledge. His Algerian 'politesse du désespoir' is a deliberate, non-ignorant and generous naivety. The clown's pride is to perform an excess of politeness (he is 'très très poli') rather than (or as an expression of) an excess of despair. His story is the parable that he is capable of addressing to 'us' and 'them', it is a plea that does not need a pleading agent, a reproach that does not even admit that he needs to blame. He claims the affection that he craves as if it had already been granted and he gracefully and generously points out that it is a rhetorical coup de force that, as readers, we can always dismiss as a form of naivety.[21]

CHAPTER TWO

René-Nicolas Ehni

Matricide and Deicide as Figures of Unforgivable Violence and Redemption during the Algerian War of Independence

L'important aujourd'hui n'est plus de dénoncer ou de dévoiler des secrets. Il est de comprendre et plus encore d'accepter. Non pas se résigner, mais accepter que ce passé, et peut-être plus encore la manière dont il a été géré après la guerre par la génération qui l'a subie, est révolu.

(Conan and Rousso, 1994)

[Today, what matters is not to denounce or unveil secrets but to understand and above all to accept; not to resign ourselves but to accept that the past and perhaps more importantly the way in which it was processed after the war by the generation who experienced it, is behind us.]

Forgiveness is not, it should not be, normal, normative, normalising. It should remain exceptional and extraordinary, in the face of the impossible: as if it interrupted the ordinary course of historical temporality.

(Derrida, 2001, 40)

René-Nicolas Ehni is not Algerian. He was neither a *harki* nor a *moudjahid*. He was never a *pied noir*. He was not one of the French 'porteurs de valises', who helped the NLF in Europe. And he is not a child of Algerian immigrants. As a result, his novels and plays may well have remained invisible to critics interested in the way in which France remembers the war that led to Algeria's independence. Yet, at the beginning of the twenty-first century, two reasons may be invoked to justify Ehni's inclusion into a reconfigured postcolonial canon. And interestingly, they may well seem contradictory at first.[1]

The first argument that I wished to test, though it proved relatively weak, is that we should read Ehni because he was one of the half million 'appelés' (conscripts), young French soldiers who had to do their military service in Algeria and whose collective voice is, or seems, less audible than that of the other communities involved in the conflict.[2] The specificity of the young drafted soldiers' experience has perhaps not been sufficiently explored because, unlike groups who had a collective identity before the war and retained it after the end of the conflict (Algerian and Europeans settlers for example), they were only temporarily and artificially united by their mission. Besides, they are veterans of a war that did not exist at the time and the singularity of their collective experience was part of the overall silence. Given that the war of independence as a whole remained taboo until the beginning of the 1990s, it is not implausible to assume that the memories of young conscripts were silenced and that even after the voices of historians, writers and filmmakers managed to lift the veil, the representation of that particular group should not have been a priority.

Soldiers during the War of Independence: A Specific Sub-genre?

But were soldiers utterly powerless and incapable of articulating their position publicly or collectively? Is it the case, as Claire Mauss-Copeaux argues as late as 2002, that their words were 'confiscated' (Mauss-Copeaux, 2002)? By definition, a drafted soldier does not have a choice and does not have to have an opinion about the war but that certainly did not stop some *appelés* from resisting. In the metropole, there were clashes between groups of men who refused to go to war and the riot police (Evans, 1997). And in the case of those who went to Algeria, the issue was not so much that they did not have a clear collective position to articulate but that what they had to report was so painful that even finding a way to formulate it was sometimes impossible. Even the arguments over colonialism and anti-colonialism in general were highly volatile at the time, but what conscripts had to say, in their letters to their family or when they came back on leave, was almost of the order of the unspeakable:

that they witnessed and sometimes participated in acts of torture. And as soon as the word 'torture' appears, the debate is bound not only to transcend the experience of any particular group but also to influence the ways in which the issue is going to be addressed. Torture was an ethical, philosophical and political tragedy that affected the nation as a whole. In that context, the focus was not only on the military, but also on the state. Paradoxically, conscripts were both directly involved and not the main interlocutors. So many prominent intellectuals publicly intervened at the time that even if attempts were made to censor their voices, their names are now easier to remember than those of the thousands of anonymous young men who could have told similar stories had they had access to similar platforms. Jean-Paul Sartre, Simone de Beauvoir, François Mauriac and Gisèle Halimi, who were all involved in anti-war activism, were sometimes able to act as relays and echo chambers.[3] Some conscripts did testify, eloquently, and very early on. Robert Bonnaud's 'La Paix des Nementchas' (Bonnaud, 2002), a testimony published in 1957 in the journal *Esprit*, could hardly be a more explicit denunciation of torture. But the introduction to the reprinted issue points out that Pierre Vidal-Naquet, a prominent historian and public figure, had intervened. He had urged his friend to testify and promised to talk to the editors of *Esprit* to make sure that the story would come out (Roman, 2002, 9). That said, soldiers also availed themselves of other channels of communication. Georgette Elgey suggests, for example, that the campaign against torture went well beyond the circles of public intellectuals. Testimonies of returning soldiers profoundly affected what is known as 'la France profonde':

> Ce sont en effet des jeunes du contingent, qui, à leur retour en métropole, horrifiés de ce qu'ils ont vu en Algérie, en parlent à leurs confesseurs – la France est encore un pays rural et catholique. (Egley 2007, 59)

> [Young conscripts, horrified by what they had seen in Algeria, talk to their confessors on their return to the metropole – France is still a rural and catholic country.]

And to be fair, the idea that conscripts have not testified seems difficult to substantiate as soon as one looks long enough at this alleged void of memory. It is true that the figure of the First World War 'poilu' endlessly rehearsing heroic deeds to blasé grandchildren has no equivalent for the war of independence, but given the number of books by and on conscripts available to the trained researcher, it is perhaps more relevant to try and understand why the presence of this material coexists so happily with a discourse about its absence. The analysis of what conscripts had to say, but also, and now more importantly, of what the French did or did not hear, and also of which types of stories they or others were able to construct to tell their tales, belongs to the history of decolonization and to our present postcolonial condition.

Even memory has a history and the memory of conscripts also depends on whether historians can be heard. If we regularly read Benjamin Stora, whose interdisciplinary historical works cover so many facets of the war, including its representation in film and literature, we will be aware that he devoted a whole book to *Les Appelés en guerre d'Algérie*. The date of publication, 1997, could be read as a landmark of its own. The visibility of the scholar's name produces effects that change or at least become an integral part of what constitutes the memory of the war. The publication of a book by Stora can, in itself, be considered as the beginning of a new period to the extent that the famous historian lends his own visibility to the object of his research.[4]

After 1990, autobiographical texts written by or about conscripts, letters(Lemalet, 1992), testimonies(Matéos-Ruiz, 1998) and documents (Bergot, 1992) appeared more or less regularly. Some were published by mainstream Parisian houses (Bergot, 1991; Vittori, 1997), many by small independent companies or associations of veterans (Laurini, 1995). After 2000, the number of testimonies further increased as if a tipping point had been reached. The number of publications was beginning to add up to what historians and literary critics consider a critical mass, although the fact that they were published by small presses, often in the provinces, and that they were not widely reviewed may have contributed to an artificial fragmentation of the corpus. For example, Michel Le Cornec's *Appelés en Algérie* (2000), Michel Verdier's *Bandes de brêles: les appelés en Algérie. Quand violence et torture deviennent banalité* (2002), Pierre Olaïzola's *Algérie! Nous aurions dû tant nous aimer* (2002) and Michel Froidure's *Où était Dieu? Lettres de révolte et d'indignation d'un appelé en Algérie (1956–1958)* (2006) were respectively published in Monaco, Louge-sur-Maire, Anglet and Metz. Aléas, in Lyons, has published a cluster of comparable testimonies in their 'history' collection: Albert Nallet's *On n'efface la vérité: Guerre d'Algérie, Grande Kabylie* (2004), Ugo annucci's *Soldat dans les gorges de Palestro* (2001) and Paul Jay's *Des années sans cerises* (2005).

At first we may therefore be tempted to place Ehni's *Algérie roman* within the sub-genre that was in the process of constituting itself, even if it was not perceived as such by the general public. But there are several fundamental differences between Ehni's book and the titles mentioned above. First of all, this book is published by Denoël, one of the most prestigious Parisian companies. Secondly, as its title indicates, it is a work of fiction rather than a memoir or an autobiography.[5] Finally, Ehni's novel is less about memory than about guilt and forgiveness. As such, this text asks and answers questions about the potentially reparative value of a tale written more than forty years after the war.

The most remarkable feature of Ehni's text is that it constitutes a radical point of discontinuity in terms of narrative intervention. Ehni breaks with a double tradition. Not only does it interrupt years of silence (as we have seen, Ehni is no longer unique in that regard) but it also moves away from an aesthetics and politics of confession, revelation and denunciation that appeared the most effective rhetoric for storytellers who tried to deal with the issue of torture. To dare say that it even existed, and to denounce the unacceptable (or in some rare but well-publicized cases, to justify its use[6]), could a story be asked to do much more? When the difficulty is to testify at all, the search for a reparative narrative is obviously premature or simply unthinkable. From that perspective, Ehni represents, or perhaps inaugurates, a new era, the choice of a specific narrative strategy, the exploration of storytelling practices to produce a reparative effect. He shares with Halimi or Michael Haneke an interest in issues of remorse and impossible forgetfulness.

Let me first concentrate on three important characteristics of Ehni's work and discuss the consequences of each of these aspects in terms of the memorial work that *Algérie roman* can be expected to accomplish. First of all, the fact that *Algérie roman* appeared in a well-distributed and well-publicized collection and that Ehni's name is far from unknown (at least in intellectual circles) puts his text in a different category from those of former soldiers who were writing their first and perhaps last book-length project. More often than not, their publishers did not have much more than their integrity and passion to ensure that the testimonies would circulate. Ehni, on the other hand, can hope to reach readers who are not already personally fascinated, obsessed or traumatized by the Algerian conflict.

In itself, however, this remark is not sufficient to explain why I would choose to concentrate on Ehni. If I wished to study stories that reached the largest possible public, then visual narratives would have been more appropriate. For not only are films and television more popular than the type of testimonies written by conscripts, but they also provide contemporary audiences with a complex layering of fiction and non-fictional work. I suggest that the fact that Ehni writes fiction is significant because readers mobilize different criteria when they approach a novel rather than a testimony. Fiction tells a different historical truth, and even if Ehni is not unique in his decision to stay away from the genre of the memoir, it is worth examining the consequences of his literary choice. The word 'novel', added to the title, makes a point to the extent that the text gives us interpretive guidelines and seeks to avoid confusion. This story is not meant to be read as an autobiography, as a testimony or as a memoir even if Ehni could have played on the ambiguity of his narrator's position and insisted on the text's autobiographical aspect.

The coexistence of fiction and non-fiction, however, is not unique to the printed world, and in the past ten years documentaries on the war of independence and especially on the experience of soldiers have gradually morphed into popular fiction. Even spectators who have never seen or have forgotten the films made in the 1960s and 1970s[7] were given many opportunities to remember or discover what soldiers went through during the 'dirty war'. *Les Années algériennes*, the three-part documentary prepared by Bernard Favre and Benjamin Stora, constituted a memorial turning point. Shown on the France 2 network in 1991, it coincided with, or rather symbolically marked, the thirtieth anniversary of Algeria's independence. Since then, many fiction and non-fiction films and mini-series have been added to a memorial archive, telling a story that is slowly being woven into national consciousness.[8]

The three versions of *L'Ennemi Intime* are a good example of the current dissemination of knowledge through different genres. In 2007 a film intended for the largest possible public and entitled *L'Ennemi Intime* told the story of soldiers who were directly involved in acts of torture and barbarity. Although the story is based on archival research, critics recognized the importance of the fact that it is not only fiction but a typical action film, which can be compared to American war movies about the Vietnam War.[9] Florent Emilio Siri's film, however, is the third version or rearticulation of a narrative that appeared as a book five years prior to the making of the film. In 2002 Patrick Rotman had published the first *L'Ennemi intime*, a series of harrowing narratives told by soldiers who were barely in their twenties when they committed atrocities. Then the book became a three-part documentary that was shown on France 3 on three consecutive nights in March 2002. That version of *L'Ennemi Intime* reached between 2 and 3 million French spectators[10] and received similar reviews in newspapers as different as *Le Monde*, *Libération* and *Le Figaro*. All the films, TV series, documentaries, testimonies and historical analyses cited above share two characteristics. They relativize or at least complexify the notion that conscripts have no words to talk about their experience, or that the French public could not or at least cannot, today, have access to their stories even if they wish to do so.[11]

In other words, the first hypothesis that it was urgent to read Ehni to give conscripts a voice is not particularly compelling. Even the fact that his novel is a fictional account does not in itself constitute a reason to single it out. Instead, I propose to analyse the reparative potential of Ehni's specific narrative techniques and to see how he may influence the parameters of the whole debate about memory and national identity.

Reconfiguring France's Postcolonial Condition

Ehni's voice contributes to a relatively new but increasingly audible chorus that rejects the idea that only a few well-defined communities were affected by the war of independence. The same current of thought insists that the memory of colonization must be reinserted into the national myth, not as a peripheral phenomenon but as a fundamentally Republican issue and that the war of independence cannot be separated from a long history of violence and conflicts that concerns and even defines France as a whole. In his *Postcolonialism: An Historical Introduction*, Robert Young goes as far as saying that the war without a name serves as an explanatory matrix for the end of the twentieth century, including the whole poststructuralist movement (Young, 2001). Benjamin Stora, rejecting the idea that the war of independence was a 'a tragedy on the margins' (Stora,

2005, 60) that only affected soldiers, *pieds-noirs*, migrants and *harkis*, asks himself:

> Pourquoi ... subsiste-t-il la sensation diffuse que le reste de la société française ne se sent pas 'touché' par cette histoire coloniale? Est-ce que les groupes précités ne sont pas, précisément, isolés dans la société française? Et non seulement isolés dans la société, mais isolés entre eux? Dans le fond, ce refoulement de la guerre d'Algérie si souvent évoqué, n'a-t-il pas été possible justement parce que le coeur de la société française n'a jamais véritablement intégré la cquestion coloniale? En fait pourquoi la guerre d'Algérie apparaît-elle toujours comme extérieure, *périphérique*, dans l'histoire générale de la France contemporaine? (Stora, 2005, 60)

> [Why ... do we have the vague feeling that the rest of French society is not 'touched' by colonial history? Are the groups I just mentioned not, precisely, isolated within French society? And not only isolated from society but also isolated from each other? In the end, was the so-often mentioned repression of the war of Algeria made possible by the fact that the heart of French society could never truly integrate the colonial question? Why, in fact, does the War of Algeria always appear as external, *marginal*, within contemporary French history?]

I suggest that Ehni's work does not offer answers to Stora's questions but actually performs the reparative position that he implicitly advocates. For Stora, the idea that colonial values have played a fundamental part in the construction of each French citizen's subjectivity is still far from self-evident. To imagine the colony as the margin of the metropole and postcolonial migrants as the tail end of a long-gone era allows citizens of European origin to think that whatever is left of the colonial past only affects the margins of a system of thought otherwise dominated and governed by radically different categories. The end of 'silence' does not necessarily solve that problem.

The history of peoples' cultural memory, however, is also the history of how such assumptions evolve. *Algérie roman* contributes to (both reflects and makes possible) the slow evolution of mentalities: contemporary France may now be envisaged as a country shaped by its postcolonial condition or its postcoloniality.

Algérie roman is a relevant manifestation of the reconfiguration of the postcolonial debate in France which enables us to reread both this book and the rest of his oeuvre through that critical lens. Looking back at Ehni's literary productions from a reconfigured critical perspective provides us with a reparative vantage point. Our backward glance benefits from a context in which some taboos have disappeared so that when we look back at Ehni's early publications, the obvious yet oblique significance of the war of independence clearly emerges as one of the crucial elements of his imagination. As early as 1964, the hero of his first novel, *La Gloire du vaurien*, is radically changed by his experience in Algeria where he found himself to be a reluctant witness and an accomplice. Criticizing the 'camp' aesthetics of the novel, Robert Maples reads the character's tendency to confuse 'art and life' (Maples, 1966, 669) as the result of his powerlessness to denounce unpunished crimes.[12] From that perspective, there is a clear link between the early work and the recent *Algérie roman* published in 2002. But this aspect of Ehni's work is rarely mentioned in narratives that focus on the beginning of his career. Before leaving France and settling in Crete, Ehni made a name for himself in the 1970s among the European intelligentsia, but he is mostly remembered as an *enfant terrible* and provocateur.[13] He was close to Jean-Paul Sartre and Simone de Beauvoir, whose anti-colonialist positions are well known.[14] Eric Dussert points out that he was a close friend of Pier Pasolini and Elsa Morante and that he was also involved in the so-called 'Beat generation'. But he also worked with two authors who recently re-entered the postcolonial canon through the back door: Jack-Alain Léger and Pierre Guyotat. The first author is better known under the pseudonym Smaïl whose *Vivre me tue* started a heated controversy about whether an author had the right to adopt a fake Beur identity (Smaïl, 1997). As for Pierre Guyotat, Ehni is said to have declared that he 'hates' him (Dussert, 2000). The narrator of *Algérie roman* accuses him of never taking advantage of his position at *France-Observateur*[15] to denounce torture (Ehni, 2002, 39–40) and in *Babylone vous y étiez nue, parmi les bananiers* Ehni severely criticizes Guyotat's literary rendition of the conflict (Guyotat, 1967; 1970; 1972). Ten years later, he is Gisèle Halimi's political ally during the difficult campaign for the legislative election that she describes in *Une embellie perdue*, and in which Ehni appears as one of the protagonists.[16] Even the fact that he is of Alsatian origin will not seem irrelevant to readers familiar with Assia Djebar. They will remember Alsalgérie, the imaginary country created by the characters of *Les Nuits de Strasbourg*.[17] The relationship between Ehni's Alsatian origin and the war of independence cannot, however, be directly extrapolated from what history books tell us. Ehni was not born into one of the families that had to leave Alsace-Lorraine during the Second World War for example. And yet Alsace is significant to the extent that Ehni constructs many of his heroes as nomads or outcasts, exiles who know exactly what it means to belong to a culture whose hybridity is frowned upon. Ehni insists that he is a 'gypsy' and he does not hesitate to reappropriate derogatory adjectives to describe himself as a 'tzigane enjuivé' [a jewified gypsy] (Dussert, 2000). In short, Ehni's anti-colonial and anti-war position is nothing new and *Algérie roman* is not an exception to the rule. The novel is not riding a marketable or literary fashion wave, but contributes to the reconfiguration of France's postcoloniality.

The Memory of a Murderer:
The Killing of Aïssa

Algérie roman's reparative contribution is to stage the way in which such a story can be told today. The ethical and political stance that Ehni wishes to adopt requires a new type of narrative and a new position of enunciation. One of the most significant characteristics of *Algérie roman* is that the hero is not one of the victims but one of the executioners, and that he agrees to take responsibility for what he has done. At the same time, the narrator's willingness to talk is the problem rather than the solution. The difficulty is to find a type of story that can mediate the truth about horrifically violent events. The novel is the self-reflexive search for that tale, a fictional and theoretical exploration of the limits of the testimony.

The originality of Ehni's position is that he does not assume that there is something unspeakable about the type of violence that he wants to narrate. Instead, *Algérie roman* seeks to articulate an impossibly contradictory imperative: the war of independence makes testimonies both absolutely indispensable (we must tell, it is possible to tell) but also useless (witnessing will not change anything, cannot justify, cannot explain what happened). And still, the story as a whole avoids falling into a self-destructive loop. The double imperative does not lead to aphasia and new forms of silence but to a new type of writing that is part testimony, part novel, part prayer, part theoretical reflection on what it means to write such hybrid texts.

The novel is constructed as a superposition of narrative tactics that grapple with three difficulties. How do I speak as a murderer? How do I resign myself to the fact that, even if I want to remember, my tale is not reliable? How do I then construct my story if I want to take responsibility and write from a position of enunciation that participates in a collective work of mourning rather than in the perpetuation of victimization? The rest of this chapter is devoted to an analysis of how Ehni answers the three questions. I will first concentrate on the novel's relentless reiteration of the encounter between the 'I' and his victim. I will then move on to the analysis of a passage that stages the story's double constraint (it is impossible to remember, it is imperative to tell) before focusing on the formulation of a (disturbing) reparative narrative frame that the narrator coins a 'paramyth'.

When the story starts, not only has the worst already happened but the narrator has already confessed. The hero and first-person narrator describes himself as a murderer. He admits that he has killed a *fellagha*. But the idea is not to finally come clean and to plead guilty. The man's death is not told once but repeated many times, in many different ways, sprinkled throughout the novel like the dots on a pointillist painting. At first, the reader may be confused because the story fails to provide a clear linear plot. The narrator's tale is constantly interrupted by a traumatic memory that is told, over and over again, from many different angles. The 'fact' that is thus endlessly re-mediated is a murder. When the narrator was drafted and sent to Algeria, he participated in the arrest, torture and killing of a *moudjahid* whom he pushed out of a helicopter.

On the other hand (and this is one of the contradictions that make the novel so interesting, because the reader is confronted with two apparently incompatible threads within the same story) many passages talk about the victim as a man for whom the narrator had enormous respect and even a 'sort of' friendship. The very first page of the book states that they were 'comme des amis' [like friends] (9). The goal of the novel is to finally weave these apparently contradictory threads together in an attempt to find an answer to the following question: now that the 'livre du crime' [book of crime] (34) exists, who will use it and for what purpose?

The confession, in this novel, is not presented as a performative religious ritual that will, of itself, have desirable effects. The perpetrator is not interested in revealing what he has done but rather in defining the act so as to make amnesty impossible. The dead man is never reduced to the position of Giorgio Agamben's 'homo sacer' because to the state logic that has the power to turn the prisoner into an anonymous casualty, a body without a grave, the narrator opposes his will to name, to remember and honour him (Agamben, 1998). He is not even the enemy whose cause is respected and understood (as when we choose to call someone a resistant rather than a terrorist). He is not even sacrificed to the Gods of the community, and he is not the scapegoat who will restore the cohesion of the group. He is God himself. The originality of Ehni's approach is that he deliberately describes his hero's misdeed as the worst possible crime, not even against humanity but against what is, for him, the most sacred, the idea of God. The narrator recognizes that he is guilty of what could be called a war crime but he does not use that type of vocabulary. When he starts his narrative, his point is that what he did constitutes, for him, the worst possible deed. This orthodox Christian, whose faith borders on mysticism, accuses himself of an unforgivable sin for which there is no human or divine statute of limitation. He has tortured and killed his God, who had come to him in the body of a *fellagha*, just as a humble stranger knocks on a door to test a mortal's hospitality.

Ehni writes: 'La rencontre avec mon Dieu eut donc lieu pendant cette terrible guerre appelée pacification' [I encountered my God during the awful war known as pacification] (155). As he is about to push the tortured *fellagha* out of a helicopter, he asks for his name, and the man answers: 'Aïssa! … Jésus comme vous dites!' [Aïssa! … Jesus as you put it!] (155). Unlike many texts on the war of independence, *Algérie roman* relies neither on the myth of the enemy brothers or on the figure of estranged lovers, two grand narratives that have haunted Franco-Algerian literature from Mouloud Feraoun and Jules Roy to Kateb Yacine or Assia Djebar.[18] Refusing to oppose Christians and Muslims, and therefore eschewing the age-old rivalry that might justify and legitimize a conflict against the archetypal historical enemy, the narrator talks about the war of independence as if it were a re-enactment of the Passion of Christ. The death of (his) God functions as the scene of origin.

The description of the moment when Aïssa is pushed out of the helicopter intertextually recalls the image of the 'Creation of Adam' that appears on the ceiling of the Sistine Chapel, except that the index finger, in this scene, is used to kill and not to give life. Ehni's narrative succeeds in painting Aïssa not as a powerless and passive victim but as a subject who recognizes and reads the torturer's signal. He is not reduced to a sub-human status; instead, he transcends his condition by preserving his agency to the end: 'Je n'ai usé que mon index pour le pousser afin de lui indiquer que c'était le moment de sauter. Il sauta.' [I used only my index finger to nudge him to let him know that the time had come to jump. He jumped.] (153). Ehni is not trying to put the blame on the *fellagha* or to suggest that he consents to his fate, but he still describes him as an active participant who is the subject of the sentence: 'Il sauta'. That the narrator no longer needs force, at that particular moment, reflects the overall level of brutality that characterizes the war. Just as the use of the word 'pacification' cannot hide a horrific conflict, the index finger stands for the level of violence that defines the relationship between men like the narrator and men like the *moudjahid*. Yet the man is not killed by an anonymous war: the first-person narrator takes full responsibility, he does not claim to be executing a direct order and there is no mention of some national interest that would, if not exonerate him, at least frame his act within a broader ethical frame.

The man who dies is sacrificed. He is a divine figure whose last gesture is to give the murderer a copy of a sacred book: 'Il fouilla dans sa poche et en sortit son saint livre Coran. Il me le donna après l'avoir vénéré. C'était si beau, entre nous aucun schisme. J'ai conservé le Coran comme on garde près de soi un corps angélique.' [He went through his pocket and pulled out his holy book, the Koran. He gave it to me after worshipping it. It was so beautiful, no schism between us. I kept the Koran as one keeps an angelic body close by.] (156).

The staging of the gift is rather unrealistic: how could a *moudjahid* about to be thrown out of a helicopter have been able to keep his sacred book? But within the economy of the story, its presence enables a principle of transmission and forever links the two men together. Aïssa does not disappear even in the absence of a proper burial. There is no grave but a new *lieu de mémoire* is created, which is both abstract and concrete. It is made of words that function as an angelic body, and whose proximity constitutes a perpetually renewed act of witnessing. The physicality of the Koran stands for a presence-absence that guarantees that the man's death is not the equivalent of a disappearance.

Forever, the relic testifies. Ehni's novel exists as evidence that no legal statute of limitation exists, that no state amnesty has the power to suppress the angelic body. The narrator cannot forget, cannot forgive himself, cannot hope to redeem himself, and still he worships the trace, the Book that symbolizes his crime.

Ehni's book is not about memory, or about the imperative to remember, nor even one of those novels where history and fiction mutually enrich or critique each other. It is the self-reflexive story of an attempt to turn writing into the special form of text that could be used to ask for forgiveness. The book starts from the premise that such a genre does not exist. It would be a sort of prayer, a performative liturgy that conventionally falls outside the realm of literature. Ehni's narrator and the novel as a whole represent the desperate but eventually successful attempt to use words to invent the literary equivalent of a prayer for forgiveness.

At first, the narrator finds himself up against two obstacles. First of all, the desire to ask for forgiveness is disallowed by a culture of amnesty, which deprives the narrator of an adequate discursive theatre: his act has no obvious public. The narrator was a soldier who became a murderer in the absence of a responsible witness. He was never brought to trial, never even accused or even suspected. He was never asked to tell his story or to confess. In Halimi's texts, the space of a public trial becomes the theatre where words are used to denounce and impose the idea that justice and the legal system cannot be destroyed by the logic of the conflict. Here, no lawyer intervenes and the novel is the only space that can refuse the type of exoneration that the state implicitly imposed. The principle of amnesty functioned as the impossibility of taking responsibility, of even being imputable. No mourning could ever take place because the narrator's memory had to be content with the vacuum of legal amnesty, which, as many thinkers suggest, is the opposite of forgiveness: in 'Amnesty: Between an Ethics of Forgiveness and the Politics of Forgetting', Peter Krapp writes:

> It is crucial to distinguish between certain modified forms of recollection or of forgetting that come into play in politics and in jurisprudence, before raising other questions regarding forgiveness and amnesty. The latter, which can be understood as mutual forgetting, stands almost diametrically opposed to the former, insofar as forgiveness in its long monotheistic tradition conjures up the past to the extent of making it present again, repeating the injury, opening the wound, so that its full extent may indeed be forgiven. (Krapp, 2005, 190)

Similarly, Paul Ricoeur insists on the constraints that institutional amnesty adds to the issue of forgiveness:

> The institutions of amnesty are not at all the institutions of forgiveness. They constitute a forgiveness that is public, commanded, and that has therefore nothing to do with what I described earlier as a personal act of compassion. In my opinion, amnesty does wrong at once to truth, thereby repressed and as if forbidden, and to justice, at it is due to the victims. (Ricoeur, 2005, 10)

Algérie roman does not use the trope of the secret discovered by chance and no diegetic or even implicit detective is here to accuse the narrator. There is no revelation in this book and the reader is configured not as the recipient of new knowledge but as a historical subject who is already fully aware of what happened in Algeria and shares the narrator's vision. This construction of a knowledgeable reader is an interesting strategy because it implicitly makes us responsible for finding out whether we fit in that category or not.

In *Algérie roman*, the issue of forgiveness is central. The narrator takes for granted that it is indispensable to be forgiven. And such a premise is crucial if we situate the book within the current French context in which the idea of acknowledging guilt and taking responsibility for the past is a political, historical and cultural question. Ehni's narrator agonizes about *how* to ask for forgiveness, never about whether or not it is important to do so. And he acts as an individual, not as the representative of a nation or a community. This way of approaching forgiveness is radically different from the model that has gradually become the norm among politicians, journalists and historians who are asked or required to talk about France's involvement in past tragedies (the Vichy period, slavery and colonization). As we saw in the introduction, it is significant that the word 'repentance' should now be used to refer not, as in English, to the feeling of regret for having done something wrong but to a supposedly dangerous tendency to systematically dwell on the nation's past errors. President Sarkozy is not the only one to deny any distinction between forgiveness in general and a supposedly pathological symptom that endangers the nation as a whole (Paoli, 2006; Lefeuvre, 2006). The authors of such manifestos or pamphlets are just as passionate as those who argue that the state has a duty to acknowledge its responsibility even and especially when historical events include what President Chirac has called 'the irreparable',[19] i.e. genocides, torture, and generally speaking a betrayal of Republican ideals.

This way of framing the debate opposes two camps whose representatives both pursue the same goal but disagree on how to reach it. It is in the name of less division and more harmony that some speak up against 'repentance'. They argue that the focus on the past pits communities against each other and destroys the cohesiveness of the nation. But like them, thinkers who insist on remembering the dark periods of French history are concerned with the harmful effects of wilful amnesia. Wars of memory are fuelled, rather than healed, by a nation's refusal to take responsibility. What Marc Ferro calls the 'Black book of colonialism' (Ferro, 2003) is not only an indictment of colonial violence. His subtitle ('from extermination to repentance') suggests an evolution. Asking for accountability is not incompatible with the desire to work towards more harmonious cohabitation between people whose history cannot be combined until a complex narrative helps all the actors of former conflicts come to grips with the historical importance of colonization.

What distinguishes the terms of this controversial examination of 'repentance' from Ehni's take on forgiveness is that *Algérie roman* is not explicitly interested in whether the French nation will benefit or not. The issue is not whether or not 'repentance', in general, is desirable or undesirable in its cultural and national effects, or whether any attempt to dwell on past tragedies will have a divisive impact on the community. That the novel should treat forgiveness as an imperative situates Ehni in a current of thought that welcomes the opportunity to take responsibility both at the individual and at the national level. But for the narrator, the era of repentance has not even begun, let alone progressed to a point where we should 'en finir' [be done with it] (Lefeuvre, 2006). Like the main protagonist in Michael Haneke's *Caché*, he is confronted with his own guilt. Unlike Haneke's hero, he refuses to subsume his own need to repent with the duty of the state or the government.

The murderer does not believe in the possibility of rationalizing what happened and the purpose of the story is to stage such rhetorical gestures as examples of bad faith. Not only does the narrator refuse to justify what he did but he rules out the principle of explanation by successively testing a few familiar narratives to better deny that they have any value. The reader is presented with an imagined dialogue between witnesses or drafted soldiers, or with quotations that we recognize as parts of often-repeated bits of discourse. Each time, the passage ends with a decisive 'there is no explanation', a litany that refutes all the attempts at exoneration.

For example, the story quotes 'un ancien' [one of the experienced soldiers] (69), who blames the officers for what happened. And for a while it seems as though his position is acceptable to the narrator who would find, in his peer's statement, a logic that would at least partly justify his actions. 'De ces jeunes citoyens sans expérience que nous étions, au lieu de nous éduquer comme des soldats de la République, ils ont fait des tortionnaires. Cela, je ne leur pardonnerai jamais. Nous n'étions au fond que des enfants malheureux.' [We were inexperienced young citizens and instead of teaching us how to become Republican soldiers, they turned us into torturers. I will never forgive them for that. We were but unhappy children.] (69). The novel as a whole manages to incriminate the soldiers' hierarchy but the narrator immediately refuses what, in the hypothesis, could be used as a redeeming factor for the young soldiers. Calmly and irrevocably, he comments: 'Je n'accepte pas, bien entendu cette explication' [Needless to say, I do not accept this explanation] (70).

Just as Ehni's book suggests that it is absurd to claim that we should be 'done with' repentance because the conditions that would enable individuals to even ask for forgiveness have not yet materialized, it also offers an implicit but forceful intervention in the contemporary debate about the place and status of victims. According to Benjamin Stora, one of the reasons that explain the 'fracture coloniale' in France (Bancel *et al.*, 2005) is the power of a national myth that separates the actors of the war of independence into discrete communities who all try to impose their own definition of the victim. Stora calls this phenomenon 'the war between victims' Stora, 2005, 66):

A propos de la guerre d'Algérie, les pieds-noirs s'estiment victimes du Général de Gaulle, les soldats se considèrent comme ayant été entraînés dans un engrenage cruel, les officiers croient en la trahison des politiques, les Algériens se voient en victimes des Français, les harkis vivent leur situation comme une trahison des autorités françaises … (Stora, 2005, 66).

[Concerning the Algerian war, pieds-noirs consider that they were the victims of General de Gaulle, soldiers think that they were sucked into a cruel vortex, officers believe that politicians betrayed them, Algerians see themselves as the victims of the French, harkis experience their situation as a betrayal by the French authorities ...]

The result, according to Stora, is that each community defends its own memorial narrative and that each competes for the status of 'la meilleure victime' [best victim] (Stora, 2005, 66). Ehni's narrator is not a victim, at least not in the sense of a subject who has lost agency and power. That role, in Ehni's book, simply does not exist, although his position is the opposite of a form of relativism that would have us believe that guilt is equally shared. If I suggest that even Aïssa is not a victim, it is because the novel makes sure that it is impossible to dismiss him, even inadvertently, as such. As for the young soldiers who became murderers, they are presented with the model of an individual who takes full responsibility for what he did. The story makes it clear that other discourses exist, and rejects them.

Algérie roman presupposes that the most difficult task remains to be accomplished. Convinced that he must ask for forgiveness, the narrator does not know how to do it. The state, his national myth and history as a whole have let him down, no narrative can help him. How do we look, he asks, for a text capable of bringing about forgiveness? For the second obstacle that Ehni's novel must overcome is that no pre-existing genre or type of story is suitable.

In *Algérie roman*, the frame of reference is obviously religious, bordering on the mystic, but the narrator still wants to tell a story whose purpose is to find a solution to the issue of forgiveness. The articulation between forgiveness and writing becomes an imperative because the way in which history and literature have dealt with the war have not provided an answer to that specific question.

The first temptation is to give up and to destroy the subject who cannot find an appropriate narrative of forgiveness. In this case, silence would be a recognition of ultimate powerlessness, the opposite of state or individual censorship: 'Si j'étais intelligent, je me jetterais dans le néant du vide (auquel je ne crois pas). Se tuer est la seule façon de dire l'Algérie ... Là est le seul devoir de tuer: se détruire. Autodestruction.' [If I were smart, I would throw myself into the nothingness of emptiness (but I don't believe in it). To kill oneself is the only way of talking about Algeria ... The only duty to kill is to destroy oneself. Self-destruction.] (72).

But what the narrator describes as an absence of 'intelligence' is also what allows his intelligence to mediate his death wish and force him to continue his search the reparative in a story. Self-destruction is relegated to the realm of the hypothetical ('if I were') and even rejected as a paradox. If 'nothingness' does not exist, what would be the point? Even killing oneself is a text or a spectacle addressed to others and to the self who would still need to be forgiven. Such a performance, though legitimate (the only duty) will not fulfil the narrator's desire to be granted forgiveness.

The question of how to ask for forgiveness is never solved, because it is the problem that the novel addresses and performs at the same time. According to the narrator, the time to 'ask' for forgiveness has come and gone, which means that he has no addressee. The difficulty as articulated by the murderer is that he is left alone to produce forgiveness in the absence of the victim who would have been the recipient of his text. Like a letter that is lost and can never be answered or acknowledged, the text that asks for forgiveness can never be read by its addressee and will never receive any response. The subject who could grant forgiveness is dead, killed by the same 'I' who would wish him to forgive.

> À qui peut-on demander pardon pour ses crimes, je vous le demande ? … On demande pardon aux témoins. Ils sont morts. Ils ne sont plus de cette mort que nous appelons la vie. Mais ils croyaient dans l'au-delà. C'est donc à l'au-delà qu'on demande pardon, car ici que des masques, que des masques. (36)

> [Whom can we ask to forgive the crimes that we committed, I ask you? … We ask for forgiveness from witnesses. They are dead. They are no longer part of this death that we call life. But they believed in the afterlife. It is from that beyond that we ask to be forgiven, for on this earth, masks, nothing but masks.]

Mom as Child, Raped and Killed (Maybe)

And the impossibility of addressing the testimony is only half of the problem. The narrator cannot rely on pre-existing discursive forms and, besides, he does not trust his own story. Ehni's narrator does not believe in his own reliability as a witness. The text both testifies and reflects on the limits of testimonies, in its attempt to articulate the relationship between writing and the hope of forgiveness, given the parameters of an imperfect genre. Even if the narrator is ready to take responsibility, he cannot accuse himself properly because the act of accusation is impossible to draft. In the novel, the staging of an impossible memory triggered by a photograph demonstrates his powerlessness. The narrator tells the story of his encounter with little girls in the area of Algiers. Amazed to discover that his mere presence terrifies the children, he asks a more experienced solider, his friend Guy: '"Qu'est-ce qu'elles ont, elles sont folles?" Il me rassura: "Elles ont peur de se faire violer."' [What is wrong with them, are they crazy? He reassured me: 'They are afraid of being raped.'] (35).

The verb 'reassure' could be read as evidence of the narrator's cynical irony (as long as the little girls are not mad, reason triumphs and the rationality of the narrator and of his tale is safe). But even that possible layer of irony is superseded by another irony. Reassurance is the result of Guy's one-upmanship. His answer sets aside the terrible hypothesis that his friend apprehends (they are paranoid). But he replaces it with an even worse scenario (they know). The little girls' madness is dismissed as implausible. But if the opposite of madness is to fear reasonably that every soldier is going to be a rapist, is that sort of reason the opposite of madness? The children are sensible (not mad) but only to the extent that they have every reason to be afraid of a world that is itself mad. Both the children and the soldiers share the same insanity. Both know that it is possible, even plausible, for a little girl to be systematically raped by other 'enfants malheureux' [unfortunate children] (69) sent by the metropole. The 'he reassured me' phrase is doubly ironic because what has become radically impossible is the very possibility of being reassured. Only the fact that he is responsible for the little girls' reasonable fear can be offered as a reassuring thought when the idea of the little girls' madness becomes insufferable. Reason (and words) may be safe only if the narrator recognizes that he lives in the middle of madness and violence, a place where reason itself is betrayed.

At this particular point, then, the reader could accuse the narrative itself of being mad, especially as the rest of the passage shows that even in the presence of recovered bits of archive, no story can be constructed. The narrator can neither remember nor forget. He has become a historian who must struggle to make sense of found documents, and the fact that the document belongs to him does not change anything. When he tries to share his interpretation of an object from the past, his reading remains fragmented and incomplete. Even in the presence of what could pass for hard evidence, a photograph, he cannot heal the story which suffers from the narrator's diseased and traumatized ability to remember.

The photograph that he describes represents one of those little girls whom he has learned to interpret as not-mad-to-think-the-world-mad. And here is how the narrator describes his re-encounter with the image and its legend:

> J'ai gardé une photo où l'on peut voir une toute petite fille, six ans à peine, s'avancer vers le photographe sous la menace du fusil de mon ami Guy, un alsaco du bled très indigénisé. Au dos de la photo: 'Copain Guy et la petite fille qui ressemblait à Maman enfant' Ressemblait? Est-ce que nous l'aurions tuée après l'avoir violée?
> … Bref, ce jour de patrouille je vis ma maman enfant qui avait peur de moi et j'en ai ressenti une grande fatigue. (35)

> [I kept a photograph of a very young little girl, she is barely six. She walks towards the photographer, she is held at gunpoint by my friend Guy, a fellow Alsatian gone very native. On the back of the photograph: 'My pal Guy and the little girl who looked like Mummy as child'. Looked like? Did we kill her after raping her?
> … To cut a long story short, on that day, I saw my mum as a child who was afraid of me, and as a result, I experienced an immense fatigue.]

The passage violently reframes a well-documented type of archive: the photograph of the Arab woman whose image is stolen by the colonizer, in a context that disempowers the object of the gaze and prefigures future violations. That genre has already been analysed and denounced by novelists and critics. Ehni's photograph is intertextually linked to a number of canonical postcolonial texts: it resembles the classic colonial postcards that Malek Alloula sought to return to the sender in his *Colonial Harem* (1981) or those that Leïla Sebbar comments on in the collection of portraits published in *Femmes d'Afrique du nord* (2006). It evokes the orientalist paintings that Assia Djebar reads in her 'Regard interdit, son coupé', the postface to *Femmes d'Alger dans leur appartement* (Djebar, 2002, 223–30). In *Algérie roman*, the violence of the gaze is only the prelude to the worst, and the worst must still be articulated, forty years later. The archive exists because the narrator has 'kept the picture' like a murderer who fails to get rid of the murder weapon.

But the document still does not make sense; the narrator no longer remembers the act but he knows that he is guilty.

The fact that the murderer and not the victim testifies seems to guarantee that the truth will be told and that witnessing will take place. When thinkers such as Agamben (1999) or François Lyotard (1988) wonder what type of language or 'idiom' is appropriate for the survivor who might be disqualified as a witness precisely on account on his or her having survived, they are trying to find a solution to the victim's plight. They are assuming that the executioner will deny, as, historically, they often have. Ehni's narrator is different. He has inflicted pain, he is the author of the wrong but he wants to bear witness. And still, he is also confronted with a different form of unspeakability, which will require the search for a new text. In *Algérie roman*, it is not the case that victims had to steal the image of the crime scene and risk their lives to contradict cynical torturers who insist that they are unreliable witnesses.[20] But the photograph can only demonstrate that it does not have the power to tell the truth.

In a story written more than forty years after the photograph was taken, the picture continues to be an opaque cluster of elements. As he looks at the portrait, the narrator's attention is drawn to what seems at first to be a detail but functions instead as what Roland Barthes calls the *punctum* of a photograph, that which hits you and establishes a unique relationship between the gaze and the object of the gaze (Barthes, 1980, 69). In this passage, however, the *punctum* is not part of the image but the effect of the confrontation between the image and the text that accompanies it. At the time of the event, a commentary was added to what we could have wrongly interpreted as unmediated reality so that the photograph does not make sense on its own and never did. It must be pulled out, observed, and the narrator must look at the back of the image, look away from the little girl, and read a text: 'On the back of the photograph: 'My pal Guy and the little girl who looked like Mummy as a child'. Looked like? Did we kill her after raping her?' (35). And even the legend is not immediately understandable. Just as there could be a *punctum* in the photograph, the *punctum* of this text is the grammatical sense of the verb that he used. He does not read the whole sentence, he focuses on what becomes a piece of evidence, evidence that even the testimony that the archive constitutes is a euphemism compared to what the narrator now imagines rather than remembering.

A little girl held at gunpoint and forced to walk towards the soldier who makes her mad with fear is already a horrific spectacle. But the vision that he revisits after so many years suggests even more terrifying spectacles. The narrator who pulls the photograph out of a drawer and studies it is in the position of Barthes' historian whose relationship to the object has to do with what he calls '*studium*' (Barthes, 1980, 69). Yet he experiences the pain caused by a *punctum*, the arrow that pierces and destabilizes. It is also an arrow that shows the way, that indicates a direction, tells us where to look, beyond what we see. And what the arrow points to is even more horrifying than the picture but still not completely unspeakable. What the legend of the image reveals is the men's responsibility, the fact that the picture is not an exception and that when such images were taken, they were routinely followed by atrocities, even if or precisely because this particular episode has left no trace in the narrator's memory.

Ehni focuses on the sinister and ambiguous imperfect tense (she *looked* like), that forces us to turn away from the picture and focus on what happened at the time. The 'looked like' brutally introduces the past into the present, contradicting the seemingly eternal presence of the image. Writing years after the episode, the narrator should use the past tense as a matter of course and if he had not stopped on the verb 'ressemblait' and therefore forced us to re-examine the meaning of his grammatical choice, the imperfect tense would probably have been unnoticeable. Instead, the narrator interrupts the rhythm of his story and of our reading when he repeats 'ressemblait' and finishes the sentence with a question mark. He makes us understand that he is not simply following grammatical rules of concordance and that he had used the past to talk about the present, which means that he had changed the linear course of the little girl's life. The tense of the verb is the trace, the mark left by the crime. And the narrator's focus on a seemingly banal grammatical choice makes us see the picture for the first time all over again.

'Est-ce que nous l'aurions tuée ...?' [Did we maybe kill her?] If the narrator asks the question, it means that he does not even need to remember to know that he was capable of killing her, or even that it is plausible that she should have been murdered. Adding 'après l'avoir violée' within the very same question also suggests that the story is not only 'plausible' but that the narrator is relying on his memory of what was then predictable, normal.[21]

We can only deduce, from the unanswered questions that the narrator asks himself, what happened to the little girl. But what he is saying is that men routinely raped, and killed, and that it happened so often that this narrator cannot remember individual acts. He kept the photograph, which makes him the guardian of a memory that testifies that what happened is worse than what is represented. Even the culprit cannot remember, but in Ehni's work this is precisely the reason why he should take responsibility.

The narrator does not mention whether he appears on the photograph, he does not tell us who took it, who held the gun, nor even if he was responsible for writing the text that he rediscovers on the back of the image. But even if we do not know exactly how, he is definitely involved. The whole event has everything to do with who he is, but also with where he comes from, as the horrific mention of 'Mummy as child' reveals. No matter what he did, and even if he can never remember exactly, he, as a grown-up but also as a child, is forever present in the scene that forever disjoints his chronology.

The confession is incomplete and does not bring about any relief. The picture triggers the memory of atrocious deeds but does not fill the holes in the narrator's story. It does not guarantee the possibility of anamnesis: even as he scrutinizes it, the narrator cannot recall what it represents. It triggers a series of very precise memories (the friend's name is Guy, we know where he comes from) but remains very vague as to what happened. Not only are past and present exposed as uncontrollably mixed up by the narrator's inability to remember, but his own identity borders are also endangered by his encounter with the photograph. The raped little girl is his own mother. The image of the little girl encapsulates a tragic combination of tenderness (for his own family) and a type of violence capable of annihilating the other as human being. The soldier (who could be the narrator or the photographer) faces a little girl and obliterates her when he replaces her with his own mother, or rather by a nostalgic image of his mother as child. Not only does he force the other's present to yield to his desire to perceive it as his own past, but he transforms the Algerian conflict and the little victim into a past that he, himself, cannot have known: when his own mother was a child, he did not exist. The return of this non-memory robs the little girl of her identity. She is turned into a ghost and loses all freedom except that of moving towards the photographer to go through this abject metamorphosis.

The powerless prey is expected to take the shape of the man's fantasized object of love and tenderness. The grown-up who threatens this little girl with a gun talks about his 'mummy' as if he were a little boy. He regresses and forces his own mother to anachronistically return to a past that was never his present and that he could only have gained access to through another photograph, another representation. Seeing the little girl as his 'mummy', which seems to reintroduce tenderness into the war, has in fact the opposite effect: he erases the little girl at the very moment when the film records the moment that makes 'us' guilty of an unredeemable crime: 'Est-ce que nous l'aurions tuée après l'avoir violée?' [Did we kill her after raping her?] (35). Comparing the little girl to 'mummy' could have functioned as a shield: the term of endearment could have imported or smuggled in tenderness and vulnerability, it could have provided an antidote to the script of the horrible scene of violence. But instead of protecting the little girl, the reference to 'mummy as a child' functions as an aggravating circumstance. The soldier is guilty not only of having murdered the six-year-old that the Raison d'Etat absurdly identifies as the enemy, but he has also killed the woman who brought him into this life.

Even more clearly than Rotman's *L'Ennemi intime* (2002), which explores a relatively classic 'evil in each of us' paradigm, Ehni manages to bridge a profoundly individual gesture and his community as a whole, starting with his immediate blood relative, his mother. That the narrator takes full responsibility for what he did could absolve the state, society and the nation as a whole, but this is not what the novel suggests. By proposing that he has met 'mummy as a child' in Algeria, the soldier implicitly refuses the idea that he has raped and killed the other. But he has not hurt himself either. or at least not directly. He is guilty of destroying his own nuclear family and, as a result, his own lineage and his own filiation. His own interpretation of his deed makes it impossible to separate it from the present, from his own social group. The victim is almost within him, but just far enough away for him to believe that he has not killed himself. Paradoxically, however, it is through a gesture that refuses all relief, in this chaotic interweaving of death and life, ascendants and descendants, victims and executioners, that Ehni will propose a form of narrative that restores hope and the possibility of going on in spite of the symbolic death of the mother-child, i.e. of what comes before and what comes after the crime.

The 'Paramyth':
The (Victim/Executioner)'s Son and his Story of A-filiation

The story of inextricability that Ehni proposes has a name: he calls it a 'paramyth'. Literary theory will not help us much if we ask ourselves what exactly a paramyth is and Ehni does not provide any explanation. We can only guess what the narrator means by a paramyth, try to understand, through some kind of mental bricolage, why he needs to coin such a word. Ehni needs to create a new genre and to distinguish it from pre-existing organizing principles. We all know what a myth is, at least intuitively, and we have to assume that a paramyth retains some of the characteristics of myth. We are not expected, for example, to confuse myths and truth, or, to put it differently, Ehni's story does not repudiate its own fictionality. On the other hand, a myth has to do with more than an individual; it is a narrative shared by a whole group that creates meaning and recognizes certain values. It is a point of reference for the community. But it is important that Ehni does not propose a counter-myth or a revision of a given myth. He does not replace one grand narrative with another but introduces a word that forces us to keep in mind that several myths already exist, and that his narrative intervention prefers to remain on the margins, at the level of the 'para', which is never as legitimate as the real thing. His creation exists side by side with other narratives that he does not wish to erase.

What Ehni, in this novel, calls a 'paramyth' is the result of his narrative quest for a type of writing that could ask the dead to forgive. The reason why the little girl is chosen as both unique and horribly representative has to do with the fact that, within the novel as a whole, the figure of the dead mother-child becomes the beginning of a solution. One of the 'paramythemes' proposed in the story is that, during the war, children killed and raped other children who looked like their mothers. This does not exonerate the killer children but it suggests that the war could have created an unthinkable transnational genealogy. Rather than separating nations (France vs. Algeria) or identifying sides (including victims vs. perpetrators), the story insists on the imaginary tissue of filiation that was both woven and unravelled by conflict. Identifying such connections enables the narrator to describe this madness without becoming himself mad.

The 'paramyth' works as a preface or as the frame of the whole novel and it is one of the most spectacular passages in Ehni's text.

f we remove this first page, the narrator's quest for forgiveness fails and what is left is a confession. For example, if we were to consider only the episode of the photograph or the relentless reiteration of the murder scene analysed above, no forgiveness is ever granted, the quest for what it could be remains open-ended. Instead, the beginning of the novel suggests that in the end an imperfect and fragile narrative solution was found. *Algérie roman* begins with the paramyth, with an 'I' who is not that of the murderer but that of his son:

'C'était en Afrique, quand la patrie de papa était attaquée par les Arabes, et papa était soldat. Et voilà que papa et les Français attrapent un partisan arabe. Papa parle avec lui mais il ne lui permet pas de s'évader. Cet homme s'appelle Aïssa, ce qui veut dire Jésus. Ils se parlent et deviennent comme des amis. Aïssa fait cadeau à papa de l'Evangile des Ottomans. Et puis les Français et papa mettent Aïssa dans un hélicoptère, ils s'envolent et quand ils passent par la montagne ils poussent Aïssa hors de l'hélicoptère et Aïssa tombe sur un rocher. Il est mort. Aïssa c'est mon grand-père, le papa de Myriam ma maman. Comme papa il était allé à l'école en France où il avait pris pour femme une Polonaise, ma grand-mère Catherine. Grand-maman attendait maman quand grand-papa Aïssa est mort. Papa a fini par retrouver maman et, plus tard, papa a demandé à maman d'être sa femme. Je suis né et aussi ma sœur Makrine et ma sœur Catherine.' (9)

['It happened in Africa when Dad's country was attacked by Arabs and Dad was a soldier. And Dad and the French catch an Arab rebel. Dad talks to him but he does not let him escape. The man's name is Aïssa, which means Jesus. They talk and become like friends. Aïssa gives Dad the Ottomans' Testament. Then the French and Dad put Aïssa into a helicopter, they take off and when they are above the mountain, they push Aïssa out of the helicopter and Aïssa falls on a rock. He is dead. Aïssa is my grandfather, the father of my Mummy Myriam. Like Dad, he went to school in France and he married a Polish woman, my grandmother Catherine. Grandma was expecting Mummy when granddad Aïssa died. Dad found Mummy eventually and later, Dad asked her to marry him. I was born and also my sister Makrine and my sister Catherine.']

As soon as the son's story is finished, the second narrator (the father and murderer of mum as child) calls it a 'paramyth'. The first pages of *Algérie roman* draw our attention to the fact that filiation is in crisis due to a historical catastrophe. As a result, words themselves are in danger of being orphaned. 'Dad's fatherland' is not the child's fatherland. In fact, he has no identifiable fatherland. The child's paramyth is the response to the unforgivable past. When a 'mum as child' is involved in a circle of violence that can only be incestuous, the symbolic link between father and son is radically affected. In *Algérie roman*, the relationship between ascendant and descendant turns into a horizontal relationship between two first-person narrators, two 'I's who are mutually engendered by the specific type of storytelling activity.

In the paramyth, the child is this non-space where the victim and the executioner are fused. The existence of this paramyth is one possible example of this 'mélange de mémoires' whose absence Stora continues to regret (Stora, 2001). The text constitutes a *lieu de mémoire* that is the result of a literary work of mourning. Here the figures of victim and culprit coexist forever. No one has forgotten, no one has accepted and time has not somehow miraculously or haphazardly led to indifference. History and collective memory are not some beneficent alchemy that would allow the descendants of both people to agree that there was violence on both sides and that both camps should be forgiven as a matter of course.

The paramyth creates a meeting point where two apparently incompatible principles coexist: filiation and affiliation. I borrow the terminology from Edward Said who points out that filiation and affiliation are usually perceived as mutually exclusive. Developed in *The World, the Text, and the Critic*, the analysis of the difference between the two principles explains the unique difficulties encountered by the migrant, the orphan or the exile. Identifying what he sees as two opposite paradigms in texts as different as Conrad's novels, T. S. Eliot's poetry or Georg Simmel's analyses of modernity (Said, 1983, 18–19), Said suggests:

> If a filial relationship was held together by natural bonds and natural forms of authority – involving obedience, fear, love, respect and instinctual conflict – the new affiliative relationship changes these bonds into what seem to be transpersonal forms – such as guild consciousness, consensus, collegiality, professional respect, class and the hegemony of a dominant culture. The filiative scheme belongs to the realms of nature and of 'life', whereas affiliation belongs exclusively to culture and society. (Said, 1983, 20)

I am not suggesting that Ehni replaces genealogy with the type of affiliation that resembles a social contract. He does not simply adopt the other's narrative (the war was just and independence was a worthy cause); he is not simply a dissident. Said himself insists that it would be a mistake to imagine that affiliation is systematically subversive or even progressive. Affiliation could easily mimic and perpetuate the type of power relationships and networks that filiation creates. For example, when institutions decide on a literary canon that must be taught to students, '[i]t should go without saying that this new affiliative structure and its systems of thought more or less directly reproduce the skeleton of family authority supposedly left behind when the family was left behind' (Said, 1983, 22). Sometimes, affiliation and filiation share the same structures, the same loyalties. But affiliation may also inaugurate a process that leads to the creation of new forms, in this case of reparative narrative configurations (Said, 1983, 24).

Ehni's novel constitutes the performative response to the new historical sensitivity that historians or cultural analysists express in non-literary contexts. In an article published in the communist newspaper *L'Humanité*, Charles Silvestre suggests that younger generations are searching for a way out of what he calls 'hypocrisy'. Like Ehni, he conjures up Pontius Pilate, one of the most famous mythic figures of non-responsibility.

> La jeunesse rejette l'hypocrisie qui consiste à oublier ce qui gêne – 'pourquoi raviver les plaies?'– et à jouer les Ponce Pilate sur les responsabilités: 'les crimes sont de tous côtés donc il y a match nul' ... Ceux qui ont vingt, trente, quarante ans, sans compter les autres, ont une vie à construire et peut-être un monde à rêver. (Silvestre, 2002)

> [The young refuse to hypocritically forget a disturbing past – 'why reopen the wounds?' – They do not want to act as Pontius Pilate: 'both sides are guilty of crimes, it is a draw' ... Twenty-, thirty- or forty-year olds, let alone all the others, have a life to build and possibly a world to dream.]

Ehni's strategy to 'dream a world' has to do with a search for a specific narrative that allows him to ask for forgiveness and testify while being convinced of the limits of the testimony. Pontius Pilate also appears in his text as a way to emphasize what happened to the body of Christ, tortured like Aïssa. In Ehni's story, Pontius Pilate is not above the fray. In his novel, he does not count on some sort of fraternity between peoples and never invokes the metaphors of heterosexual love that saturate many allegorical representations of the France-Algeria 'couple'. Forgiveness in *Algérie roman* does not need agency, cannot have agency. In this novel 'there is' forgiveness, as Paul Ricoeur puts it. In *La Mémoire, l'histoire, l'oubli*, he writes:

> L'expression 'il y a' veut protéger ce que Lévinas appelait l'illéité dans toute proclamation du même genre. L'illéité est ici celle de la hauteur d'où le pardon est annoncé, sans que cette hauteur doive être trop vite assignée à quelqu'un qui en serait le sujet absolu. (Ricoeur, 2000, 604)

> [The expression 'there is' is intended to protect what Levinas called *illéité* in every proclamation of the same sort. Here, *illéité* is the height from which forgiveness is announced, without this height being too hastily assigned to someone who would be the absolute subject.] (Ricoeur, 2004, 467)

Forgiveness is neither asked for nor granted but imagined. Ehni imagines the possibility of a forgiveness that could never be asked through the literary existence of this I-son-father who is the place where the impossibility to forget unites victims and perpetrators. The text invents a solution to what Ricoeur calls one of the dilemmas of forgiveness: we could all inherit the wrong suffered by your ancestors and as a result, the issue of forgiveness knows no bounds and no borders.

> ... le cercle des victimes ne cesse de s'agrandir, compte tenu des rapports de filiation, de l'existence de liens communautaires, de la proximité culturelle, et cela jusqu'à une limite qu'il revient à la sagesse politique de déterminer, ne serait-ce que pour se prémunir contre les excès de la tendance contemporaine à la victimization. (Ricoeur, 2000, 620)

> [... the circle of victims continue to grow, taking into account relations of filiation, the existence of community ties, cultural proximity, and so on up to a limit that political wisdom has to determine, if only to be in a position to confront the excesses in the contemporary tendency towards victimization.] (Ricoeur 2004, 479)

Ricoeur's dilemma often leads to what we could call a politicization of forgiveness, something that Jacques Derrida calls 'transactions', and although the philosopher is careful not to rule out the potentially valuable results of such gestures, he warns us against confusing them with forgiveness.[22]

The 'paramyth' that opens *Algérie roman* renounces the past as it is. The son's supposedly legitimate genealogy cannot be imagined as one of the circles since it already contains victims and perpetrators. The past, the land, or the father's blood cannot be claimed as the clear hegemonic line of lineage. What has happened turns the future into a space where forgetting and amnesty are impossible but where, on the other hand, communities are fused.

Instead of opting out of filiation, but also instead of preferring affiliation, Ehni starts his novel with a myth of (dis)continuity and rebirth that can best be described as 'a-filiation'. The legacy between father and son reshuffles historical cards. Continuity exists between the father and the child but also between the two historical sides that the principle of filiation threatens to organize along two parallel and incompatible historical paths. The obvious risk is that the sons of murderers and the sons of victims will reconstitute two people or communities whose memory cannot be reconciled.

Instead, the beginning of *Algérie roman* presents us with two narrators who belong to the same but reconfigured 'circle'. The first 'I' is not the one who will tell us, in the following chapters, about his war of independence. He is innocent. Yet this 'I' is not radically different from the second: the two 'I's share the same blood, they are father and son, or rather son (first) and father (later). The son's 'I' is in a direct relationship of filiation with the second 'I' who has literally but also figuratively engendered him: the first 'I' exists only because the second one has overcome his death wish. He has not killed himself in spite of his conviction that all words have become useless, now that the dead who could forgive have been killed while the only possible testimony should be addressed to them. nstead of committing suicide (a desire that haunts survivors), the 'I' married someone who, each day, reminds him of his guilt. The past is unforgettable, unforgivable and ever-present. The narrator had a son, a new 'I' who testifies, performatively, that something and someone has survived.

After that very first page, the first 'I' (the son's) disappears from the novel, to be replaced by the character who he has introduced to the reader, the second 'I' who, as we will realize later, has been forgiven at least by his own son, whether he knows it or not. The father's first intervention, after the son's short but powerful story, is to comment on the genre of this first page. This, he claims, is a 'paramyth', that is a 'mythe en puissance', a potential myth, a myth about to become myth (5). I am tempted to suggest that Ehni hopes to locate, or performatively identifies, an emergent grand narrative. We cannot immediately understand the significance of this unexpected rhetorical gesture, which insists on defining the type of story that the son tells instead of commenting on what he says. What the son says is so shocking and so hard to understand at first that the reader may be surprised by the distance that the father establishes between content and form. But the reader must take for granted, even before the father-soldier's testimony starts, that his son exists and knows about his dad's story. And the child's childish storytelling suggests that he takes his excessively tricky genealogy for granted. He is willing to recognize his filiation-affiliation as a form of lineage that we may deem abominable and that would indeed remain so if all we had, as readers, were the father's testimony.

At the end of the novel, we realize how crucial it was to have discovered, from the very first pages, that there were two narrators in this book, the son, who starts and frames the story, and the father, who takes over but only within the parameters that the other first-person narrator has opened up for him. Threatened by madness and mad memories, the father's story is protected by the son's sanity. The son is not mad. He is not a prisoner of the father's trauma. This child does not erase other children from his narrative; instead he names his family as a circle of people whose role is affirmed regardless of whether they came from Algeria or France, whether they were victims or executioners. As if to test the novel's sanity, the author checks that the child he has invented can speak as a child, can use language and not just inarticulate cries of pain. In Franco-Algerian accounts of the war (and in postcolonial novels in general), past traumas are often narrativized through the figure of the mad, orphan or permanently emotionally scarred child. And as a result, their stories are themselves mad, orphaned, diseased or even silenced. Authors resign themselves to declaring them mad, which means that they can no longer represent or imagine their language as words that we could share or listen to.[23]

The emblematic mirror image of Ehni's son is Boualem Sansal's eponymous figure, the mad child in the hollow tree. In *L'Enfant fou de l'arbre creux*, Sansal also tries to fictionalize what happens to the memory of two individuals whose nations were separated by independence but are still entangled in the same history of violence (Sansal, 2000a). The two heroes who meet in the infamous Lambese prison during the 1990s civil war could be archetypal enemies. Pierre, the Frenchman, came back to Algeria to look for his mother and Farid has been recruited by Islamists groups. And yet not only do the two men become friends and interlocutors (affiliation) but Pierre discovers, at the end of the story, that his mother was Algerian (unknown filiation). The book also insists on internal lines of fracture within the Algerian resistance, thus complicating the possibility of tracing a genealogical line that would contain only recognizable victims. But if Sansal's story is mildly optimistic about the possibility for the two grown sons to finally reread the past and therefore reorient a destiny that should have made them enemies, it cannot imagine the next generation other than as a mad child. Tied to a dead tree in the middle of the prison, the child is mad, aphasic and blind. In one of the interviews that he gave to the magazine *Lire*, Sansal suggested that the mad child, tied to a tree like a dog, is an allegory of Algeria as a whole.

> C'est [le visage] du peuple algérien dans cette immense prison qu'est l'Algérie. Un peuple infantilisé, aveuglé, enchaîné par le mensonge. Il a été amené à ce point où il ne sait pas qui il est, d'où il est venu ni ce qu'il veut. Il tourne autour de son arbre mort, il s'amuse avec un chien qui héberge toutes les maladies du monde, il n'a même pas conscience qu'il peut défaire la corde de son cou et s'en aller. C'est terrible. (Sansal, 2000b)

> [He has the face of the Algerian people in this immense prison that Algeria has become. Infantilized, blinded, shackled by lies, he was brought to this point but he does not know where he is, where he came from and what he wants. He turns around the dead tree, he plays with a dog that carries all the diseases of the world, he is not even aware that he can untie the rope around his neck and go away. It is horrible.]

Ehni's child is not mad, is not blind and knows very well where he came from. Perhaps more importantly, he not only speaks but he is capable of telling his tale in his own language. The paramyth mimics the characteristics of children talk. The first-person narrator refers to the parents as 'daddy' and 'mummy', his sentences are short and sometimes borderline agrammatical ('I was born and also my sister'), past and present are used in a rather approximative way and the absence of complex subordination enables the first-person narrator to by-pass causality altogether at the very moment when he would have to explain what is horribly unexplainable ('Aïssa falls on a rock. He is dead'). The rest of the novel describes the dreadfully shocking episode as an unforgivable, unforgettable and irreparable moment that recurs regularly, like a nightmare, throughout the father's story. Instead, in the paramyth, the child inserts the event into a simple genealogical tale where, as a matter of course, victims and torturers are all part of the same family, which means, for him, that all ancestors are men and women to be equally loved, dads and mums, grandmothers and grandfathers.

Just as the lack of distinction between 'mummy' and the raped little girl constitutes the climactic moment of the tale of violence, the ultimate level of reparative inextricability is achieved within the paramyth when the narrator revisits the story of 'mummy as child' after the son's birth, or rather, after he has met the woman who will become his wife. The passage in which the second narrator exhumes and displays the photograph occurs, for the reader, after the paramyth. In other words, analysing it, as I did earlier, as if it were a self-contained episode was slightly deceptive or at least not faithful to the overall logic of the text. Although the horror that we may have felt upon hearing the narrator's tale cannot be avoided, the way in which the narrator ends his analysis of the picture asks us to remember the beginning of the novel and the son's existence. After remembering what could have happened to the child in the picture and to all the little girls who were raped and killed, the narrator suddenly introduces the idea of an a-filiation based on what he calls a 'resemblance'. Saying that someone resembles someone else is another way of saying that our gaze perceives the other as the same, what is foreign as what is familiar, the stranger as one of mine, one of the members of my family. The narrator (and by now we know that he is only one of the narrators of the whole story) concludes this unbearable episode by superimposing the little girl of his (non)-memories over the mother of his own child. And by now, we know that this person is Aïssa's daughter, the woman who became his wife after he had murdered her father. Myriam is the mother of the other child-narrator, she is another 'mother-child', but this time she is a character in a different narrative: '... je signale que j'ai montré la photo à mon épouse Myriam qui, lorsque je la retrouvai, avait l'âge de cette petite fille et lui ressemblait comme deux gouttes d'eau' [... let me mention that I showed the picture to my wife Myriam who, when I found her again, was the same age as that little girl and looked just like her] (35). Like Frantz Fanon, Ehni knows that violence contaminates both the victim and the executioner, but in *Algérie roman*, he narrates the future of such entanglements through a deliberately (im)prudent and optimistic lyricism.

The victims and the executioners will never be separated, no distance will ever erect a real or symbolic wall between them. On the one hand, it is impossible to forget, but on the other, no judge will ever incarcerate the culprits (establishing a physical boundary between the victim and the perpetrator) or impose a principle of amnesty (which also imprisons the torturers within their traumatic past and forces the victims to share the sentence in a different space). *Algérie roman* invents a position of enunciation, a subjectivity capable of describing himself as the son of a murderer and the grandson of the murderer's victim. His daddy has killed his mummy's daddy and presumably many other 'mummies' who looked like children. The (para)mythical narrator is the result of the narrative that the other narrator makes, not of the war, but of his war.

In Ehni's novel, what is allegorized is not the figure of the child, as in Sansal's novel, but memory itself. In order to invent a future (i.e. here to have a child), the storyteller must fall in love with or more exactly make love to Memory. His (para)mythological tale is the offspring of his encounter with Memory, here figured as the Mother who will be capable of bearing children: in an enigmatically graphic and abstract gesture, the narrator declares: '... je veux pénétrer la mémoire, la connaître tel Zeus qui s'unit à elle pendant neuf nuits, en eut neuf filles ...' [... I want to penetrate Memory, to know her like Zeus who slept with her for nine nights and had nine daughters ...] (129).

The notion of 'disease' has not disappeared, however. Quoting Pasolini, the narrator calls the war a 'malattia' (34), a disorder that is both the cause, the consequence and the way in which the conflict manifests itself. Ehni suggests that the relationships between the metropole and the empire, but also between the bourgeoisie and the state, were incestuous and pathological. The father-writer is contaminated by that diseased filiation. It is an incurable and chronic disease that affects the ways in which he remembers and creates a narrative that gives meaning to his testimony. As we saw in the introduction, no one can 'break free' of the past (Adorno, 1998, 89). The disease does not disappear but disappears as disease in the son's story. Just as forgiveness is the opposite of forgetfulness but assumes the possibility of forgetting what, in the other's act, constituted an offence, the son remembers the a-symptomatic trace of the father's malady of memory. He could have been imagined as a monster, as the representative of a monstrous genealogy. Instead, he is the next generation's mythic solution to the father's eternal curse.

If the author's biography suggests that he preferred physical and therefore cultural and national exile to return and repatriation, his text opts for continuity. Symbolically, the son-father's birth coincides with and is made possible by the emergence of a revised Oedipal paramyth, the type of narrative that inaugurates a turning point in a potentially infinite lineage of violence. Ehni's novel provides us with an intertextual response to analyses of the war of independence in which the constitutive trauma of the war reappears as a murderous symptom from generation to generation.

In his *Postcolonialism: An Historical Introduction*, Robert Young suggests, for example, that Louis Althusser's tragic fate must be read in that context (Young, 2001, 291). He interprets Althusser's murder of his wife Hélène as an extreme manifestation of a diseased memorial myth. He claims that Althusser is a subject whose formation cannot be dissociated from the violence of colonialism, which he personally suffered at the hands of his father and grandfather. In Young's interpretation, a sick paramyth reveals that the violence that is both experienced and repressed is inherited and ends up resurfacing. It is beyond the subject's control and the 'I' finally exhausts himself in the manifestation of his diseased memory. For Young, history as a whole is murderous because violence is inherited and transmitted, without alteration. But the force of his rhetorical demonstration bypasses the differences that exist between the types of narratives used to mediate the past. Young does not propose creating a myth or a paramyth but seeks to uncover the truth, a well-guarded secret. Young invokes Sartre's authority to claim, about all the subjects who resemble Althusser without being aware of it: 'These children of violence were produced by the violent praxis of their fathers – which takes them back to the History from which they wished to escape' (Sartre, qtd. in Young, 2001, 295).

The originality of Young's approach is to re-interpret what history could have dismissed as an individual tragedy due to an individual pathology (Althusser was mad), and to reinscribe the episode as part of the French collective and national (repressed) memory. It is exposed as the missing link, the unavoidable and predictable consequence of the French-Algerian colonial past. Hélène is identified as one of the unknown soldiers of the war of decolonization.

The idea may seem bizarre at first but should not be dismissed as a curious rhetorical coup de force. It is reminiscent of the observations made by Fanon on the relationship between colonialism and madness in *The Wretched of the Earth*. He bitterly remarked that there was a tragic discrepancy between the medical progress achieved in the domain of psychiatry within the colonizing nations and the fact that this new knowledge had to be applied to help subjects whose diseases had been created by colonialism.[24] But such a theory is mediated through a historical narrative that Ehni's book invites us to scrutinize. This fictionalization of the effect of the French-Algerian trauma expresses a desperate fatalism that Ehni's lyricism and mysticism seeks to counteract. *Algérie roman* invites us to read Young's text as one other possible narration, one of the possible (para)myths of the war of independence. In Ehni's horrific story, the 'mother-child' is indeed murdered, but only once, not twice. The second generation does not repeat the pattern because it is not mad. The narrator does not marry Myriam in the hope of redeeming himself by allegorically re-uniting two enemy camps through the institution of marriage. His union is only confirmed by the wedding. The inextricable interpenetration between peoples, generations and nations already existed and it always was both the poison and the remedy. Not only does the couple bear a child (the union is not sterile) but the son is a full-blown subject who says 'I' and who is in control of the narration. He is fully aware of his own history and no secret haunts his memory. He is neither a colonizer nor a colonized victim. He is the heir and the guardian of historical violence but both as victim and as torturer. His destiny enables us to catch a glimpse of what could become history that neither pacifies nor renounces sanity.

The paramyth enables both reader and writer to agree on an imperfect historiographical protocol. The past is, forever, unforgivable and inexplicable. And yet, in spite of everything, 'there is' forgiveness, or at the very least there is imputability. The acknowledgment of guilt leads to a new definition of what it is to bear the burden of unbearable memories, to live with what should turn life into traumatized survival. In Ehni, the reparative critique of the war of independence consists in the possibility of inventing a unique genealogy. The narrator knows that it is mythical rather than biological: he does not hope that future generations will mix and forget. But he imagines a form of text, of genealogical myth, that enables him and the reader to project the image of a future that would be neither mad nor definitively affected by despair.

Even if the definition of the paramyth remains opaque to the reader, the fact that it exists and forces us to wonder about its potential effects is the result of a successful attempt at finding a new memorial narrative tactic. The killer and his victim can only be described as 'comme des amis' [like friends] once a reparative narrative solution has been found to put the unforgivable into words. Only because another first-person narrator intervenes (the perpetrator's son), can the story, *their* story, be told. Only then can a sane narrative tell a tale of madness and horror. Only then may a responsible postmemory (Hirsch, 1997) merge with memory to tell a tale that fuses torturer and victim without exonerating either one.[25]

CHAPTER THREE

The Truth of False Testimonies

False Brothers in Michael Haneke's *Caché*

This study of Michael Haneke's *Caché* tests some of the hypotheses formulated in the introduction about the different ways of instrumentalizing history. Is it possible to detect connections between moments of historiographical revision and the emergence of desirable ethical or political occurrences? Is the space between fictional historical rewritings and historical progress not always the site of an ethical dispute? Even if we decide to refuse, as paranoid, a definition of history as that which always sides with the powerful and the dominant, with the masculine or even the West, it would certainly be naive to assume that when discursive pressures change official history, the new narrative necessarily constitutes some sort of universal or universally accepted improvement. If historiography can make readers aware of history's canonical limitations and can successfully relay voices that were previously excluded from our textbooks, it is obviously capable of doing exactly the opposite. Counting on a natural historical progress of history would be a non-paranoid but definitely irresponsible form of trust and innocence. nstead, this chapter asks which reading strategies could help us look at moments of historical rewritings from a perspective that would be neither paranoid (each successive revision is a different type of exclusionary process) nor angelic (each revision corrects the past and finally does justice to the victims). At a very elementary level, those of us who are relieved to see that contemporary history no longer embraces a triumphant colonial mentality, or that Western countries are prepared to debate the impact of their colonial past, are probably quite aware that different forms of negationism have not disappeared and will probably never disappear even if they are made illegal.

Moreover, without analysing very carefully what we would be willing to recognize as 'progress', we may end up adopting whatever contemporary values are implicitly deployed in our new and improved stories, without realizing that we are now embracing a version of the 'civilizing mission' that we will, in a few generations, mock as obsolete and hypocritical. But what is the equivalent today of the 'civilizing mission' paradigm and how would we recognize it? Any attempt to answer the question raises an important issue that this chapter proposes to tease out in the context of Michael Haneke's 2005 film, *Caché*: what interpretive parameters do we use when we judge fictionalized historical narratives from a political and ethical point of view? Is there a difference between a historical fiction that enables political changes and one that forces us to consider the ethics of history in general (including what makes us judge historical events as infamous lies, irresponsible omissions or desirable rewritings)? Or is a political reading already necessary before we can sort out what, in a historical rewriting, we find ethical or not?

For example, how do we even select a narrative that we agree constitutes a progressive rewriting, but that we wish to analyse for hidden political or ethical agendas? In a book devoted to the quest for the reparative in narratives, and after a series of chapters committed to non-paranoid readings of what may be historically traumatic yet discursively sane accounts, a study of *Caché* may come as a surprise. Perhaps it is an unexpected object of study. When I watched it for the first time, shortly after it was presented at the 2005 Cannes festival, I immediately jumped to the conclusion that if it appeared at all in this volume, it would have to be cited as the perfect counter-example. And the film is not here to confirm a pre-existing thesis about its reparative qualities: after all, here is the story of a man who is forced to face the fact that something he did as a child resulted in a tragedy, and who still absolutely refuses to take responsibility, either for his past actions or for its present consequences. The issue of the main protagonist's accountability is all the more sensitive as the tragedy in question has everything to do with the colonial past in general and with the effects of the Algerian war in France in particular. The story unfolds against a structuring background of exacerbated manifestations of class, economic and racial discrimination that link the (un)forgotten past to a still traumatized present. It is therefore plausible to wonder if the only possible reading of this film is not that it confirms the worst about contemporary Europe: for all its talk about its colonial history, it is not recovering from it, mourning it, or finding ways of formulating its accountability. Instead, as Etienne Balibar puts it, it is involved in a process of recolonization[1] that the incessant debate about repentance conveniently masks. And that is what Haneke intends to show us, resorting to his usual and merciless tactic of making us complicit with the violence that he projects on the screen.

On the other hand, invoking Haneke's intentions in this context is important but doubly problematic. It is significant because when the director talks about how he learned about October 1961, the events that are the historical background of *Caché*, he presents us with a model of the reader of historical narratives who is sufficiently moved to turn his ethical interpretation into creative energy: he made a film about it.

In several of the interviews that he granted after *Caché* came out, Haneke explained that he was inspired to make a film after watching a documentary on the Franco-German network Arte (Toubiana, 2005; Porton, 2005). That night he learned about the tragic events that took place in Paris in October 1961. For the first time he heard about the demonstration organized by the National Liberation Front to protest against a curfew imposed on Algerians. He also discovered that the security forces, then under the authority of Maurice Papon, had engaged in such brutal repression that, in 2006, historians did not hesitate to describe what happened as 'the bloodiest act of state repression of street protest in Western Europe in modern history' (House and MacMaster, 2006, 1). Haneke discovered, at the same time, that a traumatic event had occurred and that he did not know about it.

But the consequences of this intervention are difficult to interpret. First, because we know better than to assume that the director controls his film and its meaning, which means that what Haneke says about history is yet another layer of analysable narrative,[2] and then because the way in which Haneke has talked about *Caché* directly contradicts the first pessimistic interpretation that proposed above, i.e. that the film is a disillusioned and violent perpetuation of the historical betrayals that constituted the director's inspiration. And to the extent that we cannot assume that Haneke's intentions are either completely relevant or irrelevant, nor that they are unambiguous and politically clear, it is worth comparing his own claims and the way in which *Caché*'s political, ethical and historical intervention can be articulated.

The documentary that Haneke watched on television framed his ignorance as an unavoidable part of his discovery by insisting that, for decades, 17 October 1961 was 'a day that went missing' [*Une journée portée disparue*].[3] *Une journée portée disparue* is the title of Philip Brooks and Alan Hayling's Franco-British film and it may well be the documentary that Haneke watched on Arte when he experienced this double shock of new knowledge and old ignorance.[4]

Contrary to what Haneke may have thought, however, that film was not an exceptional narrative at the time. In fact, it was one of the numerous cultural events organized in 2001, the fortieth anniversary of 17 October 1961, which, as Jim House and Neil MacMaster point out in their *Paris 1961*, 'reflected the unparalleled visibility this event had come to occupy within the French political landscape' (House and MacMaster, 2006, 319). That year a whole series of commemorative cultural manifestations were organized (Cole, 2003). Today it is easy, even for non-specialists, to find out about the event. Readers of fiction and non-fiction alike will have access to numerous publications that mention, narrativize or analyse what went on that day.[5] And around 2001, even those who never read would have found it almost impossible not to be aware of the large number of films, conferences and interviews relayed by the French media. The website of the association '17 octobre 1961: contre l'oubli' is a mine of information easily accessible to the general public.[6] In other words, 17 October is both what Pierre Vidal-Naquet called *Ce jour qui n'ébranla pas Paris* [the day that did not shake Paris] (Vidal-Naquet, 1989), and the object of what Benjamin Stora calls a 'flambée de mémoire' [flare-up of memory] (Stora, 2003). When Haneke discovered the documentary on the European network, the implied spectator was not completely ignorant. Historians agree that Papon's trial[7] constituted a turning point and Cole even suggests that a new 'consensus' emerged in the French media in the 1990s, at the time of the publication of Jean-Luc Enaudi's *La Bataille de Paris* [The Battle of Paris] (Cole, 2003, 24).

It may even be possible to talk about the slow creation of a collective European memory since, for the Austrian director watching television in his own country, the documentary functioned as a first but determining encounter with a historical event that he had never heard about. The director discovered, at the same time, the existence of the event and the fact that he had had to wait more than forty years to be told about it, not so much because there were no witnesses but, as usual, because those voices remained voices, were not stored as history or words.[8]

> I happened on it by accident while watching television one night in Austria and I was totally shocked that I had never heard of this event before. It's stunning that in a country like France that prides itself on its free press, such an event could have been suppressed for forty years. (Porton, 2005, 50)

So when, in another interview with Toubiana, Haneke explains, in French, that he made the film because he was 'shocked' by the documentary, he offers the critic a starting point: Haneke's individual reaction to what he discovers as a gap in national history is to construct a story about an individual whose relationship to national history is highly problematic. At the same time, his sophisticated visual narrative does not simply propose a more correct narrative but draws the spectators' attention to the ways in which stories can be legitimized, perpetuated, or, on the contrary, exposed as inadequate and replaced by a new version that different agents will recognize as acceptable.

When the film came out in France, the debate had already shifted from a demand for recognition of what happened to a discussion about which memorial events were appropriate, where and when. The film participated in this quest or questioning of what constitutes an appropriate way to remember such a tragic event in the public space, especially at a moment when the nation is forced to take into account the impact of a colonial past upon its uncertain present. The question that I will ask the film is part of this larger issue but has to do with a very specific aspect of this search for a proper form of national and public remembrance: is there a difference between the politics and the ethics of forms of memory and commemoration, collective and individual? Do we ask the same questions and provide the same answers if we analyse the political or ethical consequence of those acts of memory which, when they accumulate, end up changing the shape of a community's memory?

Moments of Memory:
Political and Ethical Events of Memory

Even before focusing on the articulation between the political and the ethical in commemorative narratives, it may be necessary to add, to Pierre Nora's classic *lieu de mémoire*,[9] an element of temporality that enables us to account for continuities and discontinuities in the processes of anamnesis or forgetfulness. The encounter between the director and the documentary on 1961 did and did not occur by chance. It was the manifestation of something that we could think of as a *moment* of memory. And *Caché*, which is the consequence of this moment of memory, also contributes to it, due to the spiralling rather than static nature of such moments.

The film itself plays a specific role within that scenario: I propose to call *Caché* an *event* of memory, historically situated with the moment of memory that makes 17 October 1961 a controversial but legitimate object of study. A moment of memory functions like a literary genre, enabling and constraining the range of what constitutes acceptable discourse about a historical event. It organizes the politics of verisimilitude, that is, the narrative or cluster of narratives that sound so true that they discourage the meta-question of the access to truth. The moment of memory is not reducible to one story but it opens up a scene of production and reception, it delineates the contours of a specific public during a specific time and place. It also produces effects of truth in the realm of what readers accept as relevant or irrelevant to an event, as connected or disconnected, and as being of individual or collective significance. Even if they are unstable, *lieux de mémoire* temporarily solidify as the manifestation of a moment of memory during which a public imagined as historically educated encounters a narrative canonized by the naturalization of a certain verisimilitude.

A moment of memory is thus inseparable from a public, from a collective narrative and also from a third crucial element: a system of representation that constitutes a relatively hegemonic means of symbolic circulation. Not every story is capable of contributing to a moment of memory. Haneke's film is representative of the type of stories that, at a certain historical moment, will or will not succeed in organizing (or performatively imagining) a public that shares, not the same memory of a certain event, but the same moment of memory.

Although a moment of history obviously has to do with temporality, each does not necessarily correspond to a given period. A moment of history does not necessarily include all the books or testimonies published at a given moment since what characterizes each moment is its ability to hear or ignore certain paradigms. In retrospect, we can describe specific moments of history by analysing what was left out. The books and testimonies that denounced the use of torture in Algeria and that were published in the 1960s belong to the moment of memory that started in the 1990s, and this seems paradoxical only if we do not distinguish between a historical period and a moment of memory. Similarly, the moment of memory that makes a film like *Caché* legible may or may not include other genres, other forms of testimonies or analyses. It may be that the definitive history book about 1961 has been written or is about to be written without participating in the moment of memory. *Caché* is the conduit of what we recognize as facts, in the absence of evidence to the contrary. A moment of memory may be as short-lived as the time during which a film remains visible, or last as long as the period during which a hegemonic regime controls historical discourse. What cultural critics may contribute to an analysis of such moments is a study of what conditions must be present for a moment to be a felicitous moment of memory that will change something in the national *lieu de mémoire*. Each moment of memory will change the shape of the community's or the nation's pre-existing *lieux de mémoire*, but there is nothing predictable about whether or not it will have any kind of performative power. Just as realist art movements wish to give the illusion of representing reality and make us forget that they are constructing it, moments of memory have a revelatory ambition and address a public that they are in the process of creating.

Moments of memory are not intrinsically didactic in the sense that the objective is not to explain who is wrong and who is right, but it is true that they will, if they are successful, provide subjects with a set of norms that they will then be able to decline, across disciplines but also according to what they imagine to be the point of their story. Each event of memory, within the moment of history, will deal with the norm and contribute to shaping and reshaping the current ensemble of *lieux de mémoire*.

It is the specific manner in which the *lieu de mémoire* will be changed that will help us distinguish between the ethical and political status of the event of memory. If a film's main contribution is to reveal a secret that was well guarded by the state or other collective agents, its historical intervention will be on the side of the political rather than on the ethical. If we listen to the director's interview, we might expect *Caché* to have been constructed as a political event of memory. Haneke apparently imagines two sides, those who want to censure and those who want to reveal, and he has clearly chosen his camp. He explains to Toubiana: 'J'étais choqué d'apprendre que cet événement a été caché pendant 40 ans et je voulais parler du 17 octobre' [I was shocked to discover that the event had been hidden for forty years and I wanted to talk about 17 October].

And yet I will argue in the next portion of this chapter that Haneke made a film that both undeniably belongs to a given moment of memory (that over- rather than under-commemorates 17 October) and also questions the norms that the current moment of memory sanctions. At the end of *Caché*, we have not been provided with a new repertoire of trustworthy facts, figures or interpretations of what 17 October 1961 represented, but we might be in a better position to identify our moment of memory and interrogate its limits.

A moment of memory delineates the parameters of conversations and obviously does not reduce them to a political and ideological content, but *Caché* suggests that this margin of freedom is relatively narrow. The norms that organize the legibility of what constitutes an event do not lead to the creation of monolithic units of meaning-fulness, but it would also be naive to assume that the setting up of a frame does not directly influence what we think of as the content of our cultural debates. By giving us the means to identify some statements as politically acceptable and to dismiss others as reactionary, a moment of memory contributes to the construction of a national consensus.

But even this norm can be questioned because any event of memory, if it is performatively felicitous, may have the power to open up a space of reception for narratives that are both recognizable as part of the new paradigm and impossible to contain within the progressive–conservative or dominant–dissident binary pairs. From a formal point of view, *Caché* only teases our detective instinct but never satisfies our potential desire for revelations, discoveries and definitive truths. *Caché* is not a documentary or a fictional war film, and it is a narrative that expresses doubts as to our ability to ever articulate the meaning of national memory and forgetfulness without first questioning the norms of the genre that has temporarily become hegemonic.

Indigènes as a Political Event of Memory

Before attempting to tease an ethical reading out of *Caché*, I propose to compare Haneke's film to what would be a more political and less ambiguous event of memory within the same moment of memory. *Caché* warns us against imagining that a clear connection exists between knowing the past and doing the right thing. 'Doing the right thing' is the formulation of an extremely naive and vague hope that something can be redressed, repaired, restored. The assumption is that we will not only know what that something is (we would recognize the appropriate translation of the historical narrative) but also that we have been given powerful instruments to participate in the construction of that 'right thing' (we will know what to do with the new narrative).

Caché does not believe in the solutions proposed by comparable works of fiction, produced within the same moment of memory and with the same overall desire to repair injustices. In that sense, it may be less politically effective than other recent films such as *L'Ennemi intime*, addressed in the previous chapter, or Rachid Bouchareb's 2006 *Indigènes*, one particularly representative example of how differently two films can deal with the same issue. *Indigènes* fiction-alizes what the spectator at the same time is expected to discover as what was repressed and remember as what should not have been forgotten. The message is that what is depicted should have already been known about the role played by colonial troops in the liberation of France during the Second World War.

It does not really matter if the film is really the first of its kind or if its revelatory power comes from its popularity. As Alec Hargreaves points out, there are precedents that can be read as comparable attempts. Not only are there intertextual links between *Indigènes* and the American tradition of recent war films (such as Steven Spielberg's 1998 *Saving Private Ryan*) but Bouchareb's work is also indebted to other historical filmic rewritings. The moment of memory accounts for the acceptability of a 'for the first time' rhetoric. Hargreaves suggests instead that *Indigènes* was not:

> … as the hullabaloo surrounding the movie led many to believe, the first feature film to depict colonial troops mobilized in the service of France. Almost twenty years earlier, in *Le camp de Thiaroye* (1987), Ousmane Sembene had highlighted grave injustices meted out to West African soldiers at the end of World World II. Pierre Javaux's

> *Les enfants du pays*, depicting a unit of *tirailleurs sénégalais* (West
> African colonial soldiers) in the Ardennes during the fall of France in
> 1940, preceded by five months the French release of *Indigènes* in the
> fall of 2006 but attracted little publicity. (Hargreaves, 2007, 206)

Indigènes, it is true, was a most successful cultural and political
intervention. The film focuses on forgotten colonial troops just as
Caché can be said to highlight the events of October 1961. But
the differences between the two films are more significant than
the resemblances. In *Indigènes*, the narrative is set in the past and
follows the tragic destinies of four North African soldiers who are
portrayed as the victims of history. Haneke, on the other hand,
does not tell us what happened to the two Algerian characters who
disappeared after October 1961 in his film. No detail is provided
and none of the images that function as flashbacks are meant as
the visual equivalent of historical archive. *Indigènes* is interested in
documenting a long and complex adventure that starts in the village
where the soldiers were recruited and ends with the last surviving
character visiting his friends' graves in a French cemetery. The film's
thesis is that these men who defended France against the Germans
were not recognized as war heroes and must carry out their own
lonely ritual of commemoration in the midst of general indifference.
Their heroic deeds were never recorded as part of France's history.
Their courage and abnegation were forgotten. Were it not for the
film, we, the implied public, would not know about these men,
which is of course quite different from the assumptions made by
Haneke's *Caché* about what we, the public, know about October
1961. From a formal point of view, *Indigènes* is relatively traditional,
relying on the conventions of realism and linearity.[10] The story
counts on our suspension of disbelief precisely to make us believe in
the extra-diegetic existence of the heroes. The point is that national
memory is guilty of not telling their story. In other words, there is
a remarkable coincidence or performative power in such a film: the
process of storytelling constitutes the historiograpic intervention
itself. Summarizing the plot of the movie leads to the revelation of
something that was, until now, unfairly ignored and forgotten. These
men were heroes and the non-reiteration or non-celebration of their
actions is, in itself, injurious. The film's ambition is comparable to
that of the documentary that Haneke watched on Arte. It belongs to
the same moment of memory that makes certain narratives audible
and believable. And it produces an effect of truth that spectators

are able to receive as the truth and not as fiction. Generic French spectators can now be expected to share the same narrative about the role played by Algerian colonial troops during the Second World War, whether or not their ancestors have been French nationals for one, two or twenty generations. Spatially, the history lesson belongs to *banlieues* as well as to urban centres; it is addressed to the unknown neighbour or to the imaginary national.

The film gambles that the individuals who watch *Indigènes* will agree to a number of mental steps. We are expected to treat the four North African heroes as representatives of a whole group that has, until now, remained invisible. We are expected to agree that the whole group has suffered from historical discrimination and to recognize that if we knew nothing about colonial troops, it is because the national narrative that French citizens share was flawed. In other words, the film hopes to revise one of the chapters of national history books by shocking the spectators out of their indifference or comfortable sense of historical knowledge.

Indigènes treats national memory as the sum of individual memories: once the incorrect narrative that forgot the role played by colonial troops is revised, then the group as a whole has solved the problem of forgetfulness. A better historical truth has replaced the inaccurate version. The story relies on an implicit notion of historical progress and, even if this stage is perceived as provisional, there is no question that it thinks of itself as an improvement. And these are narrative gestures that *Caché* never makes.

The type of narrative historical intervention exemplified by *Indigènes* could be described as political to the extent that it has a clear vision of what it wants to achieve by revealing a long-hidden truth and repairing the symbolic injustice that such silences constitute. But the film is not only credited with providing us with a counter-narrative, it is also perceived to have had immediate and remarkable political and economic effects. Commentators in France and abroad suggest that this work of fiction was the cause, or at least the catalyst, for the resolution of a forty-year-long dispute over African veterans' pensions.

Spectators who knew nothing about this controversial issue discover, at the end of the film, a text superimposed over the images of the military cemetery. The frame tells us that the pensions owed to African veterans had been frozen at the end of the 1950s. Since 1959, soldiers who, like the protagonists, had served in the French army were receiving a fraction of the sum paid to French veterans. Many protested the injustice that made individuals the victims of historic decolonizing processes. For decades, nothing was done. In 2001 the situation improved (for those veterans who were still alive). Their pensions were adjusted. But Africans were still penalized because the increase was aligned with the cost of living in their own country rather than with the rate of French pensions.

Finally, in what may appear a rather extraordinary and theatrical turn of events, *Indigènes*, a story made of moving images and sounds, a work of art, changed all that. As Emma Wilson puts it: 'The film's significant historical achievement, rightly vaunted, was in triggering Jacques Chirac in 2006 to bring the level of the pensions still paid to citizens of these nations in line with those paid to the French' (Wilson, 2007, 21).

What is, however, curious is the way in which the film is supposed to have produced its political effect, or more accurately the way in which its influence was described in the media. The film was a commercial success, it reached a very large audience and we might assume that the public would have been ready to mobilize and to put pressure on the government. However, when the film was released, it was already too late: Chirac had already intervened and, apparently, single-handedly solved the problem. In other words, when the spectators discovered the superimposed text about frozen pensions, the accusation was already obsolete. Pensions were finally going to be recalculated.

While there is every reason to celebrate the end of an injustice, it may be just as important to wonder about the strange journalistic myth that presented the political change as a result of a 'private screening' organized for President Jacques Chirac and his wife before the film was released. If the screening was indeed a 'private' affair, then isn't it the case that Jacques and Bernadette Chirac were there as ordinary French citizens rather than as President Elect and First Lady? And if a decision was actually made at the end of the screening, and on the basis of a film, how can we describe such a process? Does Chirac's apparently unilateral decision have a place within a democratic regime or does this look more like a sovereign's largesse? The story of how the Chiracs reacted to *Indigènes* quickly circulated and does not seem to have generated a public outcry or even questions about the seemingly direct connection between a private screening and a matter of public policy. It was also insinuated that Bernadette's (feminine) emotional reaction had influenced her husband, which paints an alarmingly individualized and vaguely sexist picture of the whole episode. Here is how an article published in the Communist paper *Libération* describes the scene:

> 'Jacques, il faut faire quelque chose!' L'émotion de Bernadette Chirac après la projection privée du film *Indigènes*, le 5 septembre, en présence de Jamel Debbouze et Rachid Bouchareb, a convaincu le président de la République qu'il fallait 'aller plus loin' pour améliorer la situation des anciens combattants coloniaux. (Merchet, 2006)

> ['Jacques, something must be done!' Bernadette Chirac's emotion, following the private screening of the film *Indigènes*, on 5 September, in the presence of Jamel Debbouze and Rachid Bouchareb, convinced the President of the Republic that he must 'go further' to improve the situation of colonial veterans.]

For 'Bernadette Chirac', the 'President of the Republic' is 'Jacques'. But for African veterans, Jacques is the individual who has the power, now moved by his wife and by a film, to change their fate. What is perhaps so disturbing about this historical fairy tale is the serendipitous aspect of the cluster of events that led to the new policy. Had Bernadette not been moved, had the film not been privately shown, had Jacques not listened to his wife, what would have remained of the so-called 'political' impact of *Indigènes*? Is it not a most depoliticized reading of the event to suggest that the fate of veterans depended on the president's wife's visceral appreciation of what critics described as a not-so-good film? The political result of this film can only be applauded but can its political power be just as equally embraced? What if the film had advocated the status quo or worse?

Towards an Impossible Ethics of History

The reason why *Caché* may help us distinguish between the politics and the ethics of such rewritings is that it occupies, structurally, a completely different place to *Indigènes*. I would argue, first of all, that *Indigènes* is the equivalent not of *Caché* but of the documentary to which Haneke reacted by writing his own film. And secondly, that *Caché* is the equivalent (but also the opposite) of the apparently direct and immediate connection that materialized when the film was shown to a political leader. *Indigènes* knew what it wanted, it dictated a response and the only possible reactions were either to do nothing or to do the right thing. *Caché* did not result in such spectacular effects and the lessons of what Haneke calls a 'conte moral' [moral tale] are far from clear and certainly not likely to induce optimism. Knowing, the film suggests, may well be irrelevant. Difference as knowledge, sometimes, does not make a political difference, which then raises the question of what kind of difference moments of memory make when they introduce discontinuity within history. *Caché* offers no such quick fix. Its way of dealing with a reconfigured national memory is radically different and its refusal to act as Chirac did can be downright infuriating, but also reparative.

Unlike films that wish to reveal a hidden story and whose implicit goal is to share, with spectators, a narrative to which they are not expected to have access, *Caché* starts from the original and startling premise that we already know about October 1961. We are not going to be treated as spectators whose ignorance can be understood and forgiven because they have been deceived by history, the history of the victors that became a national myth.

Viewers familiar with the film know that one of the main protagonists is a celebrity of sorts, the well-known presenter of a literary talk show. George (Daniel Auteuil) is the son of well-to-do farmers who employed Algerian workers in the 1960s, that is, during the war that did not have a name at that time. In 1961, responding to the NLF's call to protest, the Algerians left for Paris and never returned. They disappeared and seem to have left no trace in George's life or in the narrative that he must now reconstruct. But they left a son behind, and the orphan's presence on George's farm and, subsequently, in his life, in his dreams and in his narrative symbolizes the impossibility of making history go away and raises the ethical issue of individual responsibility. George's parents were willing to adopt Majid but their attempt to welcome him as part of the family failed because their six-year-old son, who resented the idea that he had to share his life with this new brother, kept making up incriminating stories. The combination that will prove (literally) lethal for Majid is that he is up against, on the one hand, a selfish petit-bourgeois who does not want to share his house, and on the other hand, an overwhelming array of historical parameters that saturate the characters' identity with extremely powerful markers (Algerians vs. French, employers vs. employees, demonstrators vs.

security forces). What will turn out to be a matter of life and death is, at first, the fib of a six-year-old creative thinker.

In other words, what connects *Indigènes* and *Caché* is that both films are about the political power of stories: if told by the right person in the right place at the right time and in front of the right public, narratives will have a direct impact on the lives of others. The tale acquires the status of a speech act although no identified pre-existing conditions precede the performance.[11] What distinguishes the films, however, is that the latter is not sure that the effect of the narrating acts is always desirable. At the end of *Indigènes*, the better, more accurate tale has led to a better and fairer political decision. In *Caché*, on the other hand, the child's story is just as powerful but has destructive and ultimately fatal consequences for Majid, and perhaps also for George's son or for the bourgeois couple themselves. And the story of that story is what the film is about, which means that the film is already warning us against whatever power it may have over us.

The most important difference between the two examples of historical rewriting is that, in the first case, the work of art as a whole supposedly functions as the political speech act, whereas in *Caché*, the power of tales is what is put to the test by the overall economy of the film. That aspect is what I am calling here the ethics of the event of memory. When *Caché* begins, the story that will eventually lead to Majid's death has already been told, and is framed by multiple layers of discourse, generated by many actors, through many different media (including the viewing of video tapes, dream sequences and of course dialogues between characters). If the six-year-old George may have been given the impression that stories (his stories) rendered him omnipotent and that there was a direct link between telling his version of what happened and getting what he wanted, the adult character is forced to admit that no tale is forever written in the stone of *lieux de mémoire*. Therefore, the political power of any narrative is not only uncertain in the present but it can be altered if the narrative is changed, even retrospectively. The performative force of a tale is never a given even if the conditions of its enunciation seem adequately stacked in the narrator's favour: the little boy is the legitimate son and heir whose sense of entitlement is already a language whereas Majid is a stranger and an orphan. The young petit-bourgeois protagonist is aware of the desirable criteria of integration and knows which lies will more effectively activate xenophobic and anti-Arab reflexes (Majid is ill and contagious, Majid is violent).

As an adult, however, he finds that the conditions that made his words powerful have changed. If his tale resonates in the presence of a public that no longer sanctions its effect as truth (and we will see that this is the role given to George's wife in *Caché*) then George is forced to rewrite, revise and reappraise his own position as actor and storyteller. And by showing this process, the film gives us an opportunity to reassess the political effects of a series of what we now know are lies. Perhaps more importantly it calls our attention to what, in the form of certain statements, can be judged not in terms of truth-value but in terms of which narrator they construct. George, as a speaker whose words were meant to exclude, hurt and eliminate, should be recognized as such and what he says should not be verified in terms of truth or lies but in terms of his responsibility, past and present. And of course, this raises very different types of ethical and historical questions.

If the story was only about a six-year-old who lies, ungenerously, to get rid of another child, it would be very difficult to discuss issues of responsibility without bending the narrative to our desire for allegorical readings. What cannot be eliminated from the equation, but what cannot be neatly entered either, is that the story of a lying, selfish child is inseparable from categories that only the adult character (and the spectator) can comprehend. The film both begs readings that raise the question of accountability and makes it difficult to frame them unless we read George and Majid respectively as the allegories of France and Algeria, and Majid's and his parents' disappearance or disappearances (Majid symbolically dies twice) as the allegory of the 17 October 1961 massacre or even as an image of colonial and postcolonial desires to make the Arab vanish. Those spectators who applaud the direct political consequences of a film such as *Indigènes* may well object to *Caché* on the grounds that in the latter, both the past and the present are constructed on the same model: France no longer needs out-of-control security forces to make Algerians disappear, it now reaches the same result, perhaps even goal, by driving them to suicide.

And this is exactly the type of reading that led Paul Gilroy to publish a respectful but harshly critical position paper about Haneke's *Caché* in *Screen*. Like Bernadette Chirac, whose emotions are legitimized as the correct and politically commendable reaction to *Indigènes*, Gilroy does not pretend to provide us with a dispassionate analysis. Instead, he scrutinizes his own response: '... my intense reaction against [t]his film is also worth exploring briefly here. I felt hostile towards what felt like the film's horrible accommodation with many of the things that it appears, at first sight, to be criticizing' (Gilroy, 2007, 233). The narrative is perceived as perpetuating the problem that it pretends to solve. The argument is not that Haneke has betrayed his responsibility as a citizen by making a depoliticized work of art. *Caché*, Gilroy argues, is not a-political but anti-political:

> The film seemed to offer only a shallow, pseudopolitical, or perhaps more accurately an antipolitical, engagement with profound contemporary problems that deserve – or demand – better treatment than an elaborate exercise in mystification can provide ... Many people involved in building a habitable multicultural Europe will feel that there are pressing issues of morality and responsibility involved in raising that history only to reduce it to nothing more than a piece of tragic machinery in the fatal antagonism that undoes *Caché*'s protagonists. (Gilroy, 2007, 233)

What Gilroy finds 'disturbing' about the film can also be theorized as the messy relationship between the revised narrative and what we hope to achieve or to see achieved through the telling and retelling of the improved version. Once the moment of memory creates a public capable of agreeing to the plausibility of a less obviously inaccurate historical version of an event, can we assume that something else will change as a result? Does the new narrative, which we think of as a restored picture of what had been erased, necessarily provoke any kind of political domino effect in the public space? To what extent can we expect social actors who participate in the reiteration of a new version to be themselves changed as social actors in their political or ethical practices?

Ethics as the Politics of Narratology

Caché never tells us what to do, but it suggests that we can at the very least ask of people like George, i.e. like us, that they be accountable, that they give an account of themselves in the past and in a present that does not treat the past and the present, the former 'I' and the current speaker, as irreconcilable entities.

In the film, something or someone makes sure that George must finally provide us with a coherent story of how he behaved as a child. The bourgeois couple starts receiving a whole series of anonymous and incomprehensible messages. Videotapes that show the entrance of their house are pushed through their mailbox. The images that they receive do not tell a story, they only signify some agency's will to let them know that they are being watched. The tapes are waiting for something to happen, for a new event of memory to occur, but at first the characters and the spectators are unaware of the demand (tell your story) and exhaust their energy in a more traditional interpretive act (who sent the tapes and what do they mean?). We will never know who or what this communicative agent is. In other words, a narrative force makes it impossible for George not to implicate himself in a present politicized reading of what he did as an irresponsible child. Neither George nor the other characters nor even the spectator ever identify the source of this memorial trigger. It might be history for all we know. But we are in the presence of what could be called a symptom, a communicative energy that brings the past back as a narrative to be written anew. The unsigned and unnarrativized signal is not perceived as an attempt to start a conversation; it is immediately interpreted as a threat and creates friction between the two characters.

The nature of the threat is imprecise and, perhaps, the feeling of insecurity is a paranoid reading resulting from the impossibility of understanding. The arrival of the first tape marks this moment of discontinuity which destabilizes all the clichés of a so-called normal bourgeois life, whose implicit worship of stasis and appearances is often critiqued in Haneke's films. Just as the director had a serendipitous encounter with the documentary about October 1961, an un-channelled historical energy suddenly forces the characters to take care of history instead of taking the present for granted as a self-contained and coherent reality. Soon, George's fears are caused by the fact that the narrative that he does not want to make is literally forced out of his wilful amnesia.

The moment of memory, during which testimonies proliferate, criss-cross and circulate through various media, functions as a narratological grammar that discredits certain types of stories as illegitimate and implausible. A new norm of storytelling becomes enforceable: when George says 'I do not remember', no one recognizes an effect of truth. The narrator's reluctance is less powerful than the law of the new genre that dictates an imperative to remember.

In the film, the norm is interestingly constructed as a content-free, authorless force that is powerless on its own. An anonymous and relentless will to say manifests itself via the sending of videotapes, drawings and postcards. But its meaning remains opaque unless George agrees to function as a relay device. What the message itself wants or means (wants to say) is and will remain a mystery.

What the videotapes and the drawings mean (the point of their existence) cannot be reduced to what their messages mean (the story that the images tell). Taken separately, the messages mean nothing. We cannot even treat them like the pieces of a puzzle before it is assembled because the rules of the game are not deducible from the form that the messages take. There is no puzzle. Their ambiguity has to do with the fact that *they* do not want to say (something that we do not understand). Instead, they want *George* to say something that he would rather not say. And they want him to start his story with I'. He is forced to give an account of himself that would link the past and the present in a coherent way. The gap between the strong memorial will and the narrative content of that memorial drive is never bridged by the unknown messenger. That entity (we do not even know if there is more than one sender) is not the author of the text that the messages try to elicit. Only George can take responsibility for the narrative if he finally agrees to be accountable or rather to consider that accountability is part of the discussion even if he refuses it.

From a dramatic point of view, the widening gap between George and his wife comes from the fact that he understands very soon, not the meaning of the videos, the messenger's identity, but that there must be a way of making a narrative that explains the seemingly disconnected fragments that he receives. There is a link between what Pierrot, their son, calls 'bizarre' drawings and something that George does not want to talk about. The unknown force coerces him, makes it impossible for him not to tell the tale.

The film will eventually establish a very clear distinction between two historical versions of October 1961: George's tale and something that we could call the canonical version or the narrative sanctioned by the moment of memory, with which George entertains a most ambiguous relationship. He can blame the police for the massacre, but he does not feel responsible for any of what happened: politically, he belongs to his moment of memory and shares the hegemonic narrative. Ethically, however, he has no connection to that story.

The unknown non-author will force him to ethically articulate the relationship between his subjectivity and the politically acceptable narrative, a connection that he has, so far, successfully avoided making. Until then, he had taken one historical script for granted while completely separating it from his own history and memory. The crisis can be described as the fact that George attributes the collective narrative to a 'they' that he never recognizes as 'we' (the French), or to a 'we' from which, paradoxically, he is capable of extracting his 'I'.

At the same time, he cannot connect that script to a narrative that would start with 'I'. And only such a narrative would reveal, not so much the whole truth, but the way in which a traumatized memorial script gets perpetuated. What is hidden by the disarticulation is the invisible gap between 'I' and 'we', and this invisibility is the trace of a melancholic script because what is made invisible is something that can never be mourned.

By erasing the story of how he conspired to prevent his parents from adopting an orphan, he cannot think about, let alone formulate, the different types of responsibility that added up to make the tragedy of Majid's forceful removal from the farm possible. For naturally, George is not the only one to blame and perhaps, as a six-year-old, he is the only one that cannot be blamed. But as an adult, he also refuses to take responsibility for other stories: he does not even entertain the possibility that we should link the results of his action to institutionalized racist stereotypes and to the exacerbated polarization between two people who had been at war for years without admitting it.

Storing Narrative vs. the Reparative in Narratives

George, from a certain point of view, knows exactly what happened on 17 October 1961. The parameters within which he can choose to tell his collective historical script are culturally defined by the moment of history that has multiplied, around him, different versions of the event. The character is able to give a one-sentence account of what happened during the 17 October demonstration. His knowledge of the past is presented as a perfectly understandable reference. He addresses his wife (Juliette Binoche) in a way that shows that he assumes that the historical narrative is perfectly familiar. And this means that the film treats the spectator as though he or she were in the same position. The past is presupposed as known and shared at the level of the nation. His account means that he knows that a quick allusion is enough, that he is not about to start a debate, that the interlocutor will not resist or be shocked into rebelling against his story. At least that is what his performance suggests. Talking about Majid's parents, he says:

> Ses parents travaillaient chez nous, papa les aimaient bien ça devait être de bons ouvriers. En Octobre 61 le FLN a appelé les Algériens à manifester, ils sont allés à Paris. 17 Octobre 61, je te fais pas un dessin, Papon, le massacre policier, ils ont noyé à peu près deux cents arabes dans la Seine. Il semble que les parents de Majid étaient de ceux-là, en tout cas, ils sont jamais revenus. Papa est allé à Paris pour se renseigner et ils lui ont dit qu'il devrait être bien content d'être débarrassé de ses bougnoules.

> [His parents worked for us at the farm. Dad liked them. I suppose they were good workers. In October 1961 the NLF organized a demonstration, they went to Paris. 17 October 1961, no need to draw a picture, Papon, a police massacre, they drowned about two hundred Arabs in the Seine. Apparently, Majid's parents were among them, at any rate they never came back. Dad went to Paris to find out and they told him that he should be glad to be rid of his wogs.]

This paragraph marks the contours of the moment of memory by revealing the limits of what is known, assumed to be known, assumed to be accepted or else controversial in France when Haneke's film was released. And by making the code of non-revelation so obvious, the story also makes it visible. When something goes without saying, the way in which it is said corresponds to a certain discursive practice that *Caché* makes more evident. George's choice of words implicitly requires that the spectator should recognize the story, be familiar with what went on, where and how. The paragraph also anticipates that Anne, George's wife, will not be inclined to propose a counter-narrative or to question his version. In fact, she remains perfectly silent while he tells that part of the story. That version is now to be accepted as the official version, even if we know, as spectators, that for more than forty years a different account prevailed.

The film will focus on the interesting combination of two narratives provided by the same character who is incapable of taking responsibility for his own actions, but quite capable of judging the past of his nation. George relates to both narratives in a way that we might have assumed to be incompatible. He does not mince words. The police are responsible for a 'massacre'. He quotes them in a way that accuses them of racism and cynicism. The word 'bougnoule' is still a perfectly understandable injurious term but it is obsolete or at least historically dated, which reinforces the fact George both attributes the insult to the police officers and distances himself from it.[12] The way in which George puts this story together suggests that we are expected to recognize what he says as uncontroversial facts. And this may not be the case for all spectators, either because they don't know enough and are still in the dark about some aspects of this tragic event or because, on the contrary, they are trained historians who know, for example, that a definitive body count may not have been reached yet. George, remarkably, adopts one of the least conservative versions (that two hundred Algerians were killed was neither improbable nor demonstrated without a shadow of a doubt when Haneke's film came out).[13] He even drops in Papon's name without making any comment, as if we all knew and shared his opinion. His rhetoric blames and judges 'them' and constitutes a community to which he does not want to belong, at least grammatically. And, like his spouse, we are constructed as interlocutors who have neither forgotten nor censured that history.

The film's pessimism or the gap that enables our own critique lies in the coexistence between that assumption and the way in which George treats his historical knowledge. He is not a witness. He recites a history lesson written by others for others. His narrative is the equivalent of a closed case, and instead of restoring, he stores the past in a self-contained compartment.

There is no place for his 'I' in that text. His past is literally disciplined, locked up in an imaginary history book that is severed from the possibility of testifying and reduced to a stereotyped, iterable narrative. Majid's parents are written out of that plot. They have disappeared. And even if George's bitter allusion disapproves of what the police said to his parents ('you should be happy to be rid of them'), his repetition of a stored historical narrative has exactly the same effect of making them disappear between the lines of his own story. From this perspective, Majid's suicide literalizes what George has already accomplished: he has managed to make the whole family vanish from his tale. Gilroy reads Majid's death as a disturbing example of self-destruction that makes Haneke complicitous with the forces that seek to get rid of the colonial subject: 'I was particularly troubled by what could be interpreted as Haneke's collusion with the comforting idea that the colonial native can be made to disappear in an instant through the auto-combustive agency of their own violence' (234).

I wonder, however, if Majid's gesture does not, on the contrary, demonstrate that the consequences of symbolic erasures will not be contained within the realm of the symbolic. The film constructs Majid's death as an answer to George's stories and to his casual acceptance of his disappearance and of his parents' murder. George's narration incriminates him, even if he does not seem aware of it. The narrative force does not let him take what would be the French equivalent of the Fifth Amendment, which allows you not to testify if you are going to incriminate yourself. For the way in which he describes Majid's fate is similar to what he has to say about his parents. From one day to the next, they go missing ('at any rate, they never came back'). In a later version of George's multiple retellings, Majid disappears too and the narrator does not seem struck by the irony of the parallel: '[U]n beau jour il n'était plus là' [One day, he was gone]. He even adds, in an uncanny echo of what the policemen said: 'Et j'étais bien content' [And I was quite happy about it]: *he* was happy to be rid of the 'bougnoule' and why should he ask about what happened anyway? For him, at least in this version of the story, what counts is the result: the parents and the child are no longer there. We can guess what happens to them but George does not put it into words.

But do we really kill someone when we erase them from a story? Many would argue, of course, that even within a fictional space, there could be no direct relationship between discursive and literal death. The film, however, makes us consider the issue from a perspective that also troubles our certainties: we think that we know who killed the parents (the police), that we were eyewitnesses to the fact that Majid killed himself and that neither George nor the spectator can be blamed for any of this. And yet what George does, with words, is to make sure that we cannot find a way to mourn, to grieve for those unjudgeable murders.

As Judith Butler suggests in a chapter entitled 'Violence, Mourning, Politics':

> ... if a life is not grievable, it is not quite a life; it does not qualify
> as a life and is not worth a note. It is already the unburied, if not
> the unburiable. It is not simply, then, that there is a 'discourse' of
> dehumanization that produces these effects, but rather that there is a
> limit to discourse that establishes the limits of human intelligibility.
> It is not just that a death is poorly marked, but that it is unmarkable.
> Such a death vanishes, not into explicit discourse, but in the ellipses
> by which public discourse proceeds. (Butler, 2004a, 35)

George can recite his history lesson without omitting the 'day that went missing' and still turn Majid's parents into unthinkable ghosts. He does not spell out that the parents are dead and they are certainly not grievable because their lives were never recognized to begin with. What Majid felt, what he was told, how he reacted is a non-issue. This type of story makes it impossible for anyone to grieve because even the reality of death is negated. It is not so much that George's words dehumanize Majid's parents (he assumes they were respectable and liked) but that, in his picture, their life and death are interchangeable because they are not envisaged as humans for which anyone should take responsibility. Consequently, his own account-ability is irrelevant; no one is guilty of anything. The parents and the child, from one day to the next, are written out of the story, because it was possible to make their bodies physically disappear, even after history was rewritten.

The film represents George's ability to appropriate the newest historical versions of history and *Caché* shows us how they do not protect the public from testimonies that continue to be 'false'. George is hiding behind history while pretending to invoke it. He does not deliberately lie but his story is a false testimony because its authority comes from the fact that he cleverly uses the truth of one supposedly shocking event to hide what could be shocking about his own lamentable behaviour.

The paragraph that he recites could be mistaken for the pedagogical imperative to which Haneke responded after watching the documentary. By stating what happened on 17 October 1961, George shares his knowledge with a public. Someone, perhaps, will hear about it for the first time. And then I would argue with Gilroy: 'The dead deserve better than that passing acknowledgement' (233). But doesn't the film precisely critique George for radically separating October 1961 from the present (Majid's situation for example) and from his own subjectivity (nothing links this paragraph to his 'I')?

His ability to contain narratives, lives and death is what the film as a whole constantly questions by using narrative and visual techniques that make connections where he would rather build opaque partitions. Events, characters, media, locations are all shown to be interdependent and linked by the secret story that George will not tell. The definition of what it means to witness evolves from the beginning to the end of the film when we discover that George must keep changing his narrative even though he never technically lies about what happened. Anne, George's wife and the interdiegetic recipient of his story, is in the same position as the spectator. She proposes a reading grid of each of George's successive testimonies. Each story makes her react differently and the film explores their narrative negotiation as if the film was a sort of historical, ethical and political laboratory.

When George first recites his paragraph about October 1961, she has no reaction whatsoever. She is silent. No question, no 'and then?' or 'so what?' She has listened to the tirade and shows no pressing desire to edit it. The narrative goes unquestioned and produces no effect. It now passes for a series of facts. The paragraph that so disturbed Gilroy is self-sufficient, it has the last word. But this docile reception of a pre-written paragraph is not the only possibility. The videotapes and drawings that she must insert into her listening experience change the ways in which she interprets what George says. The intrusion of the historical desire for knowledge functions as the beginning of a new moment of memory that modifies her historiographical parameters. She becomes a rebellious auditor. She resists and forces George to revise and revise, and when he finally tells her a story that she is in a position to accept, the distance between this new narrative and the original paragraph about October 1961 is remarkable. It is in that distance that we can measure the film's political accomplishment. Our historical freedom lies in the long, painful, unfinished and ambiguous process of discovery. George is not brought to trial or judged even if the dialogue with his wife acquires the characteristics of an interrogation. It is precisely up to us to decide whether this story wants something from us other than the courage to look at the picture that the film has drawn for us. *Caché*'s unique contribution lies in the way in which its narrativity manages to walk that fine line between accusation and condemnation. And this is mostly achieved through sophisticated techniques that manipulate the audiovisual narrative.

Drawing Pictures and Sending Postcards

One of the phrases that George seems to throw into the conversation as a filler, as if what he is saying is of no importance, finds itself echoed by the visual narrative that forces the spectator to realize that its meaninglessness is only apparent. When he mentions 17 October 1961, he rushes through the historical recitation and says 'Je ne te fais pas un dessin' [No need to draw you a picture]. The claim that there is no need for a picture is always slightly ambiguous: the rhetorical formula suggests that a picture would indeed help but that in this particular case drawing is not really necessary because the statement is not important enough to need substantation or further visual evidence. Words are enough, there is no need for another medium. Yet one of the presuppositions of the film is that pictures, and especially drawings ('dessins'), say different things because they circulate differently. Images are, precisely, what will force George to use words but also what will enable his wife and the spectator to disbelieve him and challenge his narration.

Guy Austin argues that it is important to emphasize the significance of drawings in *Caché* even if it is tempting to focus on the videotapes as most critics have successfully done.[14] He suggests that the drawings,

> visualize the trauma that Georges has denied for his entire adult life, they reawaken a sense of guilt long repressed. It is the drawings rather than the tapes that provoke Georges's nightmarish flashbacks, a mixture of memory and fantasy that returns him to the events of October 1961. (Austin, 2007, 532)

George resists the principle of drawings. But while he is certain that his historical account does not need pictures, the film suggests, on the contrary, that drawings are crucial to the narrative.

Of course, the drawings are not self-explanatory either. They are not the equivalent of a simple illustration whose function would be to confirm the veracity of a given story. Their goal is to literally illustrate, that is to make us visualize, the space of a narrative lack. If we translate the mysterious drawings into words, we can only say that they are incomprehensible and that we cannot find a narrative that would make them logical, understandable and meaningful. But at the same time, they are already more than noise since their presence triggers a will to understand that no one can resist.

The drawings are not signed, they are not addressed to anyone in particular and they are violent (the only trace of colour in the black-and-white space clearly represents blood). Those are three characteristics that they share with the dry historical paragraph told by George. But unlike his recitation, rather than foreclosing other stories they generate the need for other words, other narratives.

Moreover, the drawings seem capable of duplication, of ubiquity and self-multiplication. Several drawings are sent but there are enough similarities between the pictures to give the impression that we have several versions of the same narrative: all the black-and-white stylized silhouettes are marred by a trail of blood. In the first one, a child's head has blood around his mouth, and then we see a decapitated rooster. The handwritten drawings also morph into several visual languages or media. The first instances are on plain paper, but later they circulate as postcards. The pictures may look like drawings made by a child but the postcards indicate that sophisticated media technology had to be used. That connection between childhood and adulthood is precisely what the historical narrative eliminates: this is not a tale told for children. This is history. The drawings, on the contrary, are not as self-contained. A child's drawing is not innocent (in the sense that it knows nothing about the larger picture) if it gets reproduced and sent to different public and private spaces that represent the different facets of George's life: his work, his son's school. The postcard forces him to recognize that he cannot compartmentalize his life, or rather that it is possible to make a drawing that integrates not only all the different spatial locations but also all the temporal moments of his life. The drawings are portraits of George.

They also have the ability to generate other images. While they are still incomprehensible for us, the spectator, they are translated into dream sequences. What the black-and-white silhouettes represent reappears, in the film, as more realistic images (we see a child with blood around his mouth, then the same child who seems to be spitting into a sink, and then a longer and more elaborate narrative sequence in which the child decapitates a rooster with an axe and then threatens the narrator who wakes up in terror). At the same time, this realism is relative since a series of more and more recognizable clues tell us to treat them as nightmarish visions. The way in which Haneke introduces them forces the spectator to vicariously experience the anxiety and terror generated by nightmares because the images suddenly take over the screen and interrupt the course of the already fragmented narrative, just as a dream appears to be coterminous with the dreamer's consciousness. And even those dream sequences do not provide us with a satisfactory narrative. They only explain the main character's increasing discomfort and his fears. As long as George, at the very end of the film, has not taken responsibility for spelling it out (drawing us a picture) as a narrator, as long has he cannot bring himself to recognize that he lied three times and that his lies led to the disappearance of the brother who he did not want, this anxious archive will never make sense but will continue to impose itself. Its lack of meaning is in direct proportion to its anxiogenic qualities. All the characters try in vain to organize it and transform it into a narrative except for George, who spends all his energy on preserving its fragmented, discontinuous appearance because it enables him not to say 'I'.

The revelation of what Stora called 'family secrets' in *La Gangrène et l'oubli* (1992, 13–117) does not take the shape of a documentary written to educate a public. *Caché* does not rely on archival material or on historical coverage of the event. But this film is not only about one individual's traumatic memories. George dreams because he has received pictures; the past has not spontaneously visited him. And his agency consists in processing or rather in refusing to process the material that is obviously turning into an open archive in front of our eyes.

Historians have long deplored the fact that archives were sealed and that they could never have access to police documents to determine what had really happened in 1961. But as House and MacMaster demonstrate, when the French government finally opened the precious doors, no explosion of truth came to replace uncertainties and suspicions. That many people want to know and that archives should be accessible does not guarantee that one narrative will finally emerge as the uncontested version of the event (House and MacMaster, 2006, 9–15). George's negative contribution is to oppose his own determination to thwart another anonymous force's attempt to find or restore an order, a continuity and a meaning that connects all the elements of the mysterious archive. But by doing so, he condemns himself to dealing with a constant series of nightmares: during the day he feels persecuted by the violent presence of the archive, but if he refuses to look at it, his only choice is to literally close his eyes, to sleep, to take tablets to neutralize the images. Except that when he sleeps, he is then visited by nightmares that simply reproduce the visions, in dream language.

For the spectator, what is seen remains a series of shots put next to each other according to a linearity that has no narrative logic. images are accumulated like the documents in a box but they are not articulated. And the film shows that the same thing happens to George's words: when he speaks, he produces sentences that do not add up and never form a story. The film opposes linearity (shot A comes after shot B) to narrative temporality (shot A is linked to shot B as a consequence, or an effect). The spectator is made to yearn for the latter while George's mission is to stop the metamorphosis of the archive into an event of memory, and to avoid becoming the narrating agency at all costs.

The disconnected images are thus not a critique of traditional realistic narratives or even a parody of a world generated by technology, as is sometimes the case in Haneke's films. They are the manifestations of George falsely testifying. The anonymous agency that sends the images and tapes seems to know exactly what happened and could, presumably, tell the tale. But the goal is obviously different: this is about forcing George to take the responsibility for the narrative logic.

Emphasizing the missing or denied link between all the elements is precisely what organizes the quest and the film. Fake thriller, fake detective story, fake whodunnit, *Caché* insists on the absence of a narrative and on the traces and clues that denounce a character's reluctance to testify. The type of cinematographic techniques that defamiliarize the principles of realist cinema (and that spectators familiar with Haneke's other films will recognize)[15] help us redefine truth and lies by disrupting the simple mutual binary pair of which they usually are the two extremes. Haneke often claims and adapts Godard's formula when he states that 'Film is a lie at twenty-four frames per second in the service of truth' (Porton, 2005, 50). In *Caché*, however, we can never be sure we have discovered the truth, but the way in which we are invited to look for it certainly helps us detect lies.

Haneke usually makes sure that the narrative frame warns us that images lie or rather that they can always trick the spectator who trusts the conventions of realism. But when a narrative frame openly declares that it is lying, a new paradoxical situation develops. The first few seconds of *Caché* establish, once and for all, that we will navigate in this sort of paradoxically dishonestly honest universe of signs. Later, when the frame risks disappearing from our view (when for example, the screen coincides with the television set that we watch at the same time as the characters, or when the film does not provide any clue that we are viewing a rewound tape rather than the characters' house), we may remember that we had been warned and that not only this film but cinema as a whole creates the world that it pretends to represent.

Haneke's astute suggestion is that what allows us to recognize dishonesty does not have to do with an unverifiable content but with a formal type of slippage. He does not erase from the screen what is normally cleaned up because it belongs to an undesirable visibility, the proof that there is noise rather than pure communicative energy at work. And this is done both visually and narratologically. For example, there is a narrative echo from the famous beginning of the film. As many reviewers have noticed, when the film begins, we discover, after a few (long) seconds, that the images we are watching are a videotape when George starts rewinding it. We then see the white traces that the fast-forwarding process projects on a screen. Similarly, in certain scenes, dialogues start and then stop functioning adequately. We suddenly hear noise and unassimilable elements that sabotage George's effort at imposing his own (incomplete) story. And what alerts us to his lie is often purely formal. As readers or spectators, we are used to accepting that a story functions as truth if it satisfies the demands of a certain narrative grammar.

In one scene, Anne receives a videotape. She sees George talk to a man whom we know is his non-brother, Majid. George, however, has just called Anne to tell him that no one had answered when he knocked on the door. Anne does not know who Majid is but the tape shows her husband talking to Majid, threatening him, and accusing him of terrorizing their family. The tape proves that her husband's story is incomplete and Anne becomes a resistant reader who demands another narrative, another type of narrative that he will forever try not to tell her.

The two characters have been contaminated by the messages' will to know. He must tell, she must listen. One must ask, the other one must answer, so that their conversations acquire the theatricality of a dialogue between the witness and the prosecutor in a courtroom. Their home becomes the space where they must decide how to deal with history. They can only stop once George has produced at least an acceptable effect of truth.

When Anne asks her husband to tell her what happened, she reacts as a literary critic: she finds George's storytelling techniques unacceptable and his tale, therefore, unconvincing. His way of putting bits and pieces of elements right next to each other without articulating them is now identified as the symptom of a lie of omission. Anne does not have any evidence. But she knows that the story does not work. What George tells her is the opposite of what narratologists call a plot. Anne intuitively relies on the old distinction established in 1927 by E. M. Forster in *Aspects of the Novel* (1956, 86). At the time, Forster opposed 'story' and 'plot', using them to distinguish statements such as 'the king died and then the queen died' (story) from 'the king died and then the queen died of grief' (plot).

Anne can no longer accept George's stories. An uncanny historical presence makes Forster's example particularly relevant to what happens in *Caché*: Majid's parents died and Majid died is George's 'story'. It leaves the dead unmourned, unmournable. Anne knows that it is time to opt for the plot. Haneke's film suggests that writing a history-story is a way of preserving a political secret hidden within the transparency of words. That secret casts a narrative shadow: an aesthetics of guilt that can be recognized even in the absence of a theory of truth (that *Caché* certainly makes no effort to mobilize).

After Majid commits suicide in his presence, and forces him to be and act like a witness, George will try, one last time, to resort to his favourite technique of telling while hiding. Like all the 'stories' that he has told, in which disparate elements prevent us from asking questions of responsibility and accountability, this one exonerates him and shows that he considers that the 'I' is not accountable for the present, the past, or the ethical way in which it can be narrated. 'J'y suis allé, il m'a fait entrer, il s'est tué. Après il y avait beaucoup de sang.' [I went there, he showed me in, he killed himself. Then there was a lot of blood.] Contrary to what happened in Ehni's paramyth, the simplistic and unconnected sentences are not authored by a child. This is an unprocessed series of events narrated in a way that makes us aware of the split between truth and meaningfulness.

But Anne, the resistant reader, identifies and refuses the absence of causal links between the different elements of the story. It is not that she does not understand the logic but that she cannot tolerate the fact that George refuses to be the author of the narrative connections. Her unwillingness to fill in the blanks is an interesting model for the spectator, used to supplying the missing links as part of what we may experience as a normal hermeneutic activity (as we watch the film, we are of course going to suspect that the videos, the drawings, the postcards and the dreamed sequences are only meaningful if they are linked).

When George tells his wife what happened between him and Majid, she starts systematically and patiently highlighting the places where something is missing or hidden. She does not let him treat the past as a meaningless accumulation of archival documents. His responsibility is to insert an organizing principle, his organizing principle that will turn the story into a plot. Her discontent with the formal qualities of the narrative now point to a glaring lack of ethics. The first-person narrator must be the one to supply an answer to her reiterated 'and then?' George is now testifying but only as a witness called to the bar and pestered by the prosecutor or the defence lawyer who cannot be satisfied with what a certain type of historical logic calls 'facts'.

> –Et alors?
> –Eh bien mes parents ont décidé d'adopter l'enfant je sais pas pourquoi ils se sentaient responsables en quelque sorte.
> –Et alors?
> –Ça me dérangeait, j'en voulais pas, il vivait dans notre maison on lui a donné une chambre, il fallait que je partage, tu comprends j'avais six ans.
> –Et qu'est-ce que t'as fait?
> –Rien, je l'ai cafté
> –Tu l'as cafté? … *et c'est tout?*
> –Ben mouais
> –Et c'est pour ça qu'il veut se venger?
> –Apparemment
> …
> –Tu l'as cafté pourquoi?
> –Je sais plus une histoire de gosses qui se caftent les uns les autres, des trucs inventés, des bêtises …
> –Alors?
> –Alors quoi?
> –Mais enfin arrête de jouer au con, si tu l'avais accusé d'avoir fauché ton nounours, il voudrait pas se venger quarante ans après!
> –Je ne m'en souviens plus!

–Tu peux pas m'en parler c'est ça?

–Mais nom de Dieu qu'est-ce que tu veux de plus, j'en ai aucune idée, je ne me souviens plus, tu te rappelles des bêtises que tu as faites à six ans toi?

–Qu'est-ce qui lui est arrivé?

–On l'a envoyé ailleurs il était malade, dans un hôpital ou un home d'enfant, j'en sais rien. *Un beau jour* il était plus là et j'étais bien content, et j'ai oublié tout ça, c'est normal non?

[–And then?

–Then my parents decided to adopt the child, I don't know why, they felt responsible in a sense.

–And then?

–It bothered me. He lived in our house, we gave him a room, I had to share, you know, I was six.

–And what did you do?

–Nothing, I snitched on him.

–You snitched on him? ... *and that's all?*

–Yeah right.

–And that is why he wants to get even?

–Apparently.

...

–You snitched on him for what?

–I can't remember, kids' stuff, kids who snitch on each other, made up stuff, nonsense ...

–So?

–So what?

–But will you stop playing dumb? If you had accused him of having nicked your teddy bear, he would not want to get even forty years later.

–I can't remember.

–You can't talk to me about it, right?

–But for God's sake, what more do you want, I have no idea, I can't remember, do you remember the stupid things you did when you were six?

–What happened to him?

–He was sent elsewhere, he was sick, to a hospital or a children's home, I don't know. One day, he was gone and I was quite happy about it and I forgot all about it, it's normal isn't it?]

Whereas the paragraph that summarized the events that took place on 17 October 1961 was concise and to the point, the answers that require George to start with 'I' are evasive and narratively weak. So what?', 'I can't remember', 'I have no idea', 'What more do you want?' suggests that the listener's demands are illegitimate. George's strategy is to continue to contain the past by trying to build symbolic walls around this childhood.[16] He first refuses to translate the child's words as if another had said them (just as he repeated the police's racist formulas without implicating himself but without denouncing them either). His story is caught up in the past where he used to say 'cafter' [snitch] and when the children were not legally responsible, which makes them interchangeable: the story he is telling is about 'kids who snitch on each other' [une histoire de gosses qui se caftent les uns les autres]. And even when his wife asks the right question and understands that something happened to the Algerian child (What happened to him?), George makes sure that his sentence does not incriminate himself. He had no agency, he cannot be linked to what was done to Majid: he was sent somewhere else ('on l'a envoyé ailleurs'). He disappeared and what really happened to him now appears as the sinister truth missing from this tale. George 'snitched on him'. Majid was sent elsewhere. According to George, the two elements are self-contained and self-sufficient. But Anne craves articulations because she knows that it is their absence that betrays George's guilt (not what he did then but his refusal to recognize the death of a grievable life).

There remains, however, one articulation that even Anne will not make him formulate, and it is that George has killed his brother. The innumerable references to blood will eventually be linked and will make the point that blood was spilt because George was never able to recognize that the blood that ran in the little Algerian's veins was the same as his: not diseased, and not dangerous, certainly not more diseased and dangerous than his own. To make those two points, which will remain at the symbolic level, the film resorts to other visual techniques. The first example that I wish to examine occurs just after Majid's death, in a scene that seems to constitute an interruption or at least a digression in the sequence of events but which draws the spectator's attention to the unrecognized brotherly bond between George and Majid. Reinforcing this allusion to a broken kinship, all the dream sequences that regularly trouble George's sleep have to do with blood, and more specifically with the ways in which George interpreted its presence.

The scene that shows Majid committing suicide is remarkably static and is constructed like a painting. Majid's body is in the centre of the screen and becomes the camera's point of reference. When

George moves, the camera does not follow him. He even disappears on the right and the camera allows him to go out of the frame, or get away, without reacting. He says nothing, just emits a sort of animal grunt. And all of sudden, without any narrative transition, the next shot shows him coming out of a movie theatre that Parisians will recognize as one of the Odeon cinemas. Above his head, clearly visible, appears the poster for Jean-Jacques Arnaud's 2004 *Les deux frères*.

Two Brothers

Like the very last scene of the film, this shot contains visual elements that some spectators will overlook and others will struggle to make sense of.[17] It may be a detail or a coincidence that the film in question should be about two brothers.[18] On the other hand, *Caché* is a film about how George deals with, interprets and processes images. What he sees gradually becomes his own portrait for the spectator. When we put together all the videos and all the drawings, the image of a couple of brothers slowly comes into focus, which makes the reference to Arnaud's film much more relevant than it may appear at first. Majid is both the enemy and the brother, a quasi-allegorical combination that continues to saturate the historical imagination of the France–Algeria axis. Majid and George conjure up the ghosts of decades of French-Algerian figures such as Germaine Tillion's 'ennemis complémentaires' [complementary enemies] (Tillion, 1960) or Patrick Rotman's 'Ennemi Intime' [Intimate Enemy] (2002).

For once, George has deliberately chosen the images that he watches (instead of playing the role of reluctant viewer that the tapes and postcards demand of him). He is not at home and he is away from the giant TV screen that relays the news or the messages that have been sent to him. His decision to consume fiction immediately after Majid's death partakes of his systematic process of reception. As long as he can, he refuses to interpret, refuses to put into words, and when that is no longer possible, he flees and retreats into a dark place, and various forms of sleep. But even the fictional sleeping aid that George chooses in this scene ironically mirrors his own predicament. The spectator may well notice that the desire to dull the pain caused by the story of fraternal hatred and violence is ironically doubled by an optimistic counter-tale about two brothers whose tragic fate is to be separated but whose success is to be able to find each other again and to create an alliance against those who would want them to fight against each other.

The motif of the enemy brothers is also what links the dream sequences and the drawings. A biblical topos doubles George's trajectory and enables us to read Majid as the unrecognized brother. When his wife angrily questions his description of the past as a self-contained 'episode' [an intermède], he both proposes and rejects the word 'tragedy'. This is not a mythic murder and George will not be his brother's 'guardian' (Genesis 4.1–16): 'Bon qu'est-ce que tu veux que je te dise? Une tragédie, peut-être que c'était une tragédie, je n'en sais rien mais je m'en sens pas responsable, c'est normal non?' [Look, what do you want me to say? A tragedy? Maybe it was a tragedy, I don't know, but I do not feel responsible, surely that's normal?]. One of the dream sequences even includes a sacrifice that will, of course, not be accepted because it is the result of a lie: George has told Majid that his father had sentenced the rooster to death. Majid, assuming that he is following the father's order, sacrifices the animal in vain. He does not know that he is figuratively cutting his own throat, a plot that he will be able to reveal graphically when he forces George to witness the literal equivalent of this suicide.

The videos that show us three different types of housing (George's town house, Majid's shabby flat and also the huge country house where the two children grew up) recognize, retrospectively, that the parents' farm could have been the two brothers' home. The three different spaces are the three facets of what could have been two trajectories, united, rather than separated, by the disappearance of Majid's parents.

The blood that makes them brothers is not biological but symbolic. In *Caché*, blood is invoked as a figure of filiation, or more exactly as a counter-figure. When blood appears on the screen, one of the two brothers is violently refusing to recognize the other as family but contrary to what happened in the past, a memory event is framing this rejection as a violent spectacle. Majid as child, whose presence is inserted into the film in a series of dream sequences, is constantly linked to different types of blood, which all point in the same direction: George would rather kill him than share his house with him. Haneke's fascinating construction of Majid as dangerous relies on the principle of the scapegoat. Because George, as a child, is incapable of hospitality, all the myths and stereotypes of the Arab are mobilized to exclude him. George may not be racist but he manipulates images and symbols in a way that will be superimposed over larger national myths and will result in the fabrication of a threatening outsider.

In *Caché*, blood is visible and frightening. It is not the symbolic link that runs in the family and becomes the symbol of social legitimacy; it is the blood that is shed, a symbol of disease, death and violence. It is not the blood that you claim but the blood that covers the culprit's hands. In the first two dream sequences, the child has blood around his mouth. He seems to be spitting blood into the sink. In the third dream sequence, he is holding a bloody axe and his clothes and face are covered in blood. The drawings and postcards are simultaneous versions of both scenes. The picture is black and white and the only other colour is red, drawn across the rooster's neck or coming out of a humanoid shape. When Majid commits suicide, a long red trail writes itself on the wall as if he had finally decided to be the one who writes the story and signs with his own blood.

When Majid sheds blood, it is his own; he is in danger, he is dying. When George links blood to the young Arab, the family is at risk, they are threatened. He insinuates, for example, that the child has tuberculosis. His blood is tainted and he is contagious. The imperfect stranger will make everybody else sick and the only relationship between the two brothers, or what they represent, is the risk of contamination. But when a doctor examines Majid, the boy's individual health contradicts the potentially stereotypical narrative. In other words, George is able to mobilize a set of pre-existing images but he is not always able to make them appear true. But stereotypes derive their power from their inherent iterability and George is not restricted to the contaminated blood image. In the next dream sequence, Majid kills a rooster with an axe. Blood splatters on his face and clothes as the body of the decapitated animal dances its dance of death. In that sequence, Majid raises his axe and apparently threatens the dreamer who wakes up, terrified. Majid is a potential murderer, the child will argue when he tells his parents that his brother killed the rooster to terrorize him.

Max Silverman is right to point out that

> a set of assumptions about the behaviour of Algerians similar to those of the French psychiatrists described by Fanon rises to the surface. In *The Wretched of the Earth*, Fanon says the following of the western imago of the Algerian: 'Every colony tends to turn into a huge

farmyard, where the only law is that of the knife'; 'The Algerian kills savagely ... The Algerian, you are told, needs to feel warm blood, and to bathe in the blood of his victim. (Silverman, 2007, 245)

But he also suggests that the film is not complicit in the reiteration of such images. Instead, *Caché* 'operates, loosely, in a way similar to Fanon in that it reverses the gaze of the western colonizer and exposes the hidden fears and fantasies still at play today in a postcolonial re-run of the colonial encounter' (245). Haneke's narrative relies on different tactics to identify George's adult fears as 'fantasies' and to discredit them. Not only are the dream sequences presented as the dark secrets of a troubled narrator who is systematically denounced as unreliable, but even the way in which those supposedly damning memories are represented in the dreams ironically contradicts George's manipulation of a stereotype.

The scene that shows Majid holding an axe does not correspond to the perfect stereotype of a dangerous Arab whose knife is an immediate threat. The only knife in this story is the pocket-knife that Majid, as a grown-up, pulls out of his pocket to commit suicide. The blood is his and if the stereotype is lethal, George is not its victim. As for the Gallic rooster who is conveniently destroyed by the Arab child during the war of independence, it is not stabbed but decapitated, like the *moudjahidin* guillotined in the courtyards of French prisons. The film treats Majid's gesture as part of George's nightmare, suggesting that the French's fears that Algerian 'terrorists' had invaded Paris were nightmares too.

Conclusion

To get closer to an unverifiable historical truth, the film trusts neither individual testimonies nor historical discourse. George is not one of the silenced witnesses to whom we are finally able to listen. As in Ehni's novel, the narrator is not one of the victims even if he is not as clearly identified as one of the perpetrators. But he does not even wish to testify. He is a hostile witness who incriminates himself and will only talk when he is forced to do so. As for history, it manifests itself as ready-made paragraphs that do not require us to 'draw a picture' and by-pass the tragedy that it pretends to reveal. The film never ventures into the territory where repentance is discussed and the 'war of memories' does not take place between identifiable communities but between two adults who, as children, lived under the same roof. That Majid and George should be brothers is the thesis that the film presents as both obvious and invisible to the narrator, whose narrative adamantly refuses any responsibility. *Caché* explores the way in which such a narrative encodes itself as acceptable and plausible or, on the contrary, as inadequate and incomplete. The law of that historical genre signals the existence of a moment of memory that sets the limits of what we can repeat, accept or refute. By staging the birth of a narrative that emerges in spite of the narrator's will, *Caché* reverses the principle of detective stories that makes us hope that the truth will finally be discovered and that the discovery will, in itself, constitute a solution. In typical thrillers, the character who looks for the solution of the enigma must obtain enough elements to put the narrative together. In *Caché*, the mystery of who sends the tapes and drawings will never be lifted but that narrative energy shares, with George, a story that it cannot or will not tell. The messages sent to the couple are like *Caché* itself: they do not tell us what to do, they do not tell us what they mean, they must be translated by a voice that agrees to take responsibility and declare him or herself accountable. And even once the story is told, it is not clear at all that we can exclaim: 'Il faut faire quelque chose!' [We must do something!] and it is even less obvious what that something should be.

When the story is over, however, what has changed is that Majid's and his parent's death can be counted as the loss of grievable lives to which no monument has been erected in spite of recent historical rewritings. At the end of the film, in a poignantly open-ended scene, Majid's son faces George and quietly tells him that he wanted to see what a man who has someone else's death on his conscience looks like. Majid has thus been able to make his death audible and visible. Paradoxically, the very act that should make it impossible for him to ever testify puts an end to the cynical confusion between death and disappearance that George has conveniently entertained to avoid having to answer the question of who must grieve. That Majid and his parents both disappeared from one day to the next now appears as a cynical euphemism. It sounds as if the disappearance was a natural catastrophe, maybe an act of God instead of an act of war or a murder. It takes the whole duration of the film for the grown-up, confronted by a mysterious narrative force, to finally recognize that he can no longer construct a story that justifies his refusal to take responsibility. His 'je ne me sens pas responsable, c'est normal non?' [I do not feel responsible, it's normal isn't it?] is no longer a rhetorical question but a radically infelicitous attempt at defining the norm. By hiding the absence of the link between 'I' and the type of history that 'gets rid' of Majid's parents, he has so far managed to foreclose the beginning of a discourse of mourning, of responsibility and perhaps of forgiveness. The film does not even suggest that we could witness the end of that inchoate attempt, an implicit answer to those who claim that we should 'be done with it'. *Caché* witnesses the extreme difficulty with which this process starts and does not seem optimistic about our chances to be 'done with it' any time soon.[19]

Compared to *Indigènes*, the film complicates the opposition between denunciation and praise or between representation and critique, and provides a cautious starting point for a reflection about what constitutes ethical or political historical rewriting. *Caché* invites us to make a difference between what, in history, allows us to state, clearly but provisionally and incompletely what constitutes an improvement, and what, in history always depends on the possibility that each historical moment forces us to rethink our ethical position, namely the way in which we read the relationship between a historical moment and the values that we seek to defend in the name of history, for history.

The tension between what we achieve politically and ethically may well account for what, in Haneke's film, looks like a contradiction or at least a tension between two possible readings of the film: *Caché* is the history of the West's inability to change history, or *Caché* is about how to use history ethically to focus on the illusions of using history as a political force.

CHAPTER FOUR

Gisèle Halimi's Autobiographical and Legal Narratives

Doing to Trees what They Did to Me

Halimi grew up in the 1930s in Tunisia, in the midst of a Jewish community that she describes as poor, in a family whose members were not particularly receptive to her ambitions and feminist sense of justice. She spent her formative years in a country marked by colonialism, at a time when the party of future president Habib Bourguiba was beginning to organize against the French protectorate (Perkins, 2004, 95–105). The Second World War was about to engulf Europe and France's North African colonial territories would be involved as a reservoir of military forces, as the theatre of operations and also as an area where anti-Semitism could be exported and locally practised.[1] In her autobiographies, Halimi describes this period as a moment when the little girl was made acutely aware of the sometimes improbable and contradictory alliances generated by the constant violence of colonialism. The German occupation of Tunisia in 1942 is a period that already 'troubles' (Halimi, 1988, 73) Gisèle's political and historical consciousness. On the one hand, she hears her father worry that Tunisian Jews are about to suffer the same fate as European Jews: 'Ils vont nous mettre dans des camps de concentration, et nous porterons l'étoile jaune' [They will put us in concentration camps and we will wear a yellow star] (1988, 7). But Gisèle also witnesses the reaction of Tunisian Arabs who greet the Germans as heroes capable of giving them back 'une parcelle de dignité tunisienne' [a fraction of Tunisian dignity] (1988, 73) after defeating the colonial power. Already developing (with the help of her 'uncle Jacques' and against her own parents' views) a strong anti-colonial position, the child recognizes the complexity of the situation: 'Cette histoire me troublait. Comment des victimes du racisme parvenaient-elles à s'allier à Hitler et à *Mein Kampf*, dont l'oncle Jacques m'avait vaguement parlé?' [It troubled me. How could victims of racism ally themselves with Hitler and with *Mein Kampf*, which Uncle Jacques had vaguely mentioned?] (1988, 73–74).

The difficulty of articulating the connection between different forms of resistance against different forms of violence is already present at that early stage. Gisèle acknowledges the ambiguity of the situation: 'Le racisme colonial, à son tour, écrasé par plus raciste que lui!' [Colonial racism now crushed by an even more racist system!] (1988, 73), and she remembers that, for Tunisia, no clear victory is possible because both sides (Europe as France and Europe as Germany) constitute a different threat.

For Europeans and Westerners in general, the end of the Second World War may have inaugurated an era of reconstruction, but for North Africans one tragedy led to another and it was impossible to look away. No sooner had the Germans capitulated than a new conflict, or perhaps a new version of the old conflict, broke out, even closer to home, between France and Algeria. On the day when the metropole celebrated the Armistice, 8 May 1945, anti-colonial protests started in Setif and Guelma (Algeria), leading to the death of one hundred Europeans and thousands of Muslims (Mekhaled, 1995; Planche, 2006). The war of independence had started, unofficially, unnoticed by most.

Halimi noticed. After the war of independence broke out, when silence soon became the norm and the default position in France, she was one of the few public figures who spoke up against what many French people would be able to ignore until the beginning of the 1990s. For intellectuals such as Halimi, who intervened in the 1960s, the idea that France has recently rediscovered its colonial past and finally agreed to deal with its consequences must sound like a rather ironic refrain. Films such as *Caché* or *Indigènes* resonate very differently and perhaps produce different cultural effects if we watch them in the context of Halimi's work. By the beginning of the war of independence, Halimi had become a lawyer and had made it her responsibility to say loudly and publicly what most would rather keep quiet. And it was not enough to speak up. Halimi had to make sure that what she had to say, often on behalf of powerless clients, would be heard.

Cultural analysts are fully aware of the risks and limits that such a position of appropriation entailed, which is why it is well worth analysing not only Halimi's political activism in general but also the unique characteristics of her voice. The set of principles that guided the lawyer's choice of struggles also shaped the speeches that she delivered and the stories that she published. In other words, this chapter is about the multifaceted aspects of colonial violence, its most public and most intimate forms, its institutional and domestic guises but also more specifically about the solutions that Halimi found to address, simultaneously, different facets of specific tragedies without ever giving up on the hope of imagining a solution to predicaments that were hers and others'.

I propose to focus on two idiosyncratic and remarkably effective features of Halimi's interventions: first, the ways in which she uses words and narrative techniques against silence, and not so much against silence in general but against different types of silence that she identifies, analyses and critiques. Secondly, this chapter studies how she refuses to let her words and ideas be limited by the borders of propriety, class or gender. This freedom of movement proves especially useful when those categories create disempowering tautological systems (what is private must not be talked about in public because that is forbidden and only what is public can be addressed because it is already seen as legal). What is remarkable about Halimi's work, compared to the type of cultural productions that are analysed in the other chapters, is that she stretches the reader between the realm of the most intimate (so-called 'domestic' violence) and the most public (institutionalized colonialism), the most professional and the most personal, the most subjective and the most factual (while questioning the value that we ascribe to the terms of the binary opposition). A lawyer and an autobiographer, she is both a writer of autofiction and a historian, a woman involved in theatrical (legal) performances and the author of a most individual memoir.

The texts that Halimi has been writing since the first third of the twentieth century have contributed to what has become known as the contemporary debate on 'repentance'. Her work suggests ways of looking back at potentially traumatic events without letting a traumatized story reproduce or perpetuate the violence that it denounces. Working with and through the past, it considers how each historical period struggled against its own norms and constraints, and at the ways in which individual and collective energy sometimes joined forces and sometimes opposed each other.

Legal Autobiographical Narratives

Like doctors or psychoanalysts, lawyers deal with acute cases, with pain and injustice. Halimi's job was to face the types of situations that would seem to encourage, even to demand, paranoid readings. After all, it is presumably out of a strong conviction that something is deeply wrong, that something must be repaired, that the lawyer agrees to lend her words to a cause and to translate, for her client, the story of a wrong.

One of the most salient characteristics of Halimi's work is that many published volumes document her trials, taking the debate out of the courtroom and into public space. Without the publication of *Djamila Boupacha*, would the black book of colonialism (Ferro 2003) not be missing crucial pages on the relationship between gender and torture during the war of independence? While it would take decades for historians to make the French officially acknowledge that their nation had been at war in Algeria, let alone that the use of torture had been frequent, Halimi was not only defending men and women accused of terrorism but also denouncing unspeakable practices and trying to bring the perpetrators to trial. In 1960 a young Algerian woman confessed to having planted a bomb in Algiers. In all likelihood, she would have been tried, found guilty and disappeared from history as so many of the anonymous terrorists that the French military insisted had to be eliminated at all costs (via the sort of tautological logic previously mentioned). But when Halimi took the case, silence, shame, guilt and the definition of 'confession' had to be re-distributed along categories that her arguments forced her audience to include in the list of acceptable statements. One of the unspeakable words was, of course, torture, so that one of the most visible effects of Halimi's intervention is that the name of Djamila Boupacha went down in history as the tragic protagonist of a story of victimization. The book that Gisèle Halimi published in 1962 bears her name. It was co-authored and prefaced by Simone de Beauvoir.[2] The book brings together three women, Beauvoir, Boupacha and Halimi, three religions, three native lands, three different trajectories and as many opportunities to see the world differently.[3]

In 1972, years after the Djamila Boupacha affair, the Bobigny trial drew the nation's attention to the issue of abortion. And once again it is fair to ask to what extent it would have been possible to make abortion a political issue rather than an 'affaire de femmes' [woman's thing] if Halimi had not insisted on making the trial public. She retranscribed, and illegally published, the narratives that were supposed to be protected by the walls of the courtroom.[4]

In the 1960s, speaking up against the OAS, the so-called 'secret army' that continued to fight for 'Algérie-Française' to the bitter end, required great courage and determination. Its members had not hesitated to target President Charles de Gaulle, and many of the public figures who spoke in favour of an independent Algeria were the victims of violent attacks.[5] Ten years later the situation had obviously changed and the risks that Halimi took when she chose to fight for the legalization of abortion were of a different order. They were, however, just as real, and the struggle to legalize abortion was not a peaceful journey either. If defying the OAS was clearly a matter of life and death in the 1960s, survival was also an issue for women who sought to have an abortion before the 1970s. Not only was the procedure potentially life-threatening but in the 1960s the famous or anonymous women who co-signed the 'Manifeste des 343' probably remembered that the last female to be guillotined in France was sentenced to death for her involvement in illegal abortions. At the beginning of the 1970s it was still a crime for a woman to 'confess' that she had undergone an abortion, and a public confession could therefore also be used as a political tool. On 5 April 1971, one year before the Bobigny trial, *Le Nouvel Observateur* had published the famous 'Manifeste des 343', sometimes known as the 'Manifeste des 343 salopes' [The manifesto of the 343 sluts], a short but explosive text signed by hundreds of women, including Halimi and Beauvoir. They were eager to denounce the fact that, each year, millions of women aborted illegally in precarious and sometimes life-endangering conditions. Demanding that contraceptives as well as safe abortions be legalized, each claimed, or confessed, that they had personally broken the law: 'On fait le silence sur ces millions de femmes. Je déclare que je suis l'une d'elles. Je déclare avoir avorté.' [These millions of women are silenced. I declare that I am one of them. I declare that I had an abortion.]

Claiming to be one of the millions of women whose names would not be remembered was part of the answer to a related problem that Halimi considered to be urgent and partly beyond the scope of legal changes. In her book, *La Cause des femmes*,

Halimi makes it clear that gender was only one of the factors to be taken into account. Class, she argues, was just as significant, which explains why legalizing abortion would only constitute an imperfect solution. Halimi was keen on developing a whole new culture; she wanted to promote access to contraceptives and family planning centres. The anti-abortion laws discriminated most against lower-class women, and Halimi suspected that the new legislation would perpetuate the same social injustices. In *La Cause des femmes*, she points out that the women who had trouble with the law were rarely from the middle- or upper-middle class: 'Avortement: justice de classe s'il en est!' [Abortion: a typically classist justice!] (1973b, 93). She insisted that legalization would not put an end to what she called the 'véritable clivage ... l'aiguille à tricoter pour les pauvres, les cliniques de Neuilly pour les riches' [the real disparity ... knitting needles for the poor and clinics in Neuilly for the rich] (1973b, 99).

Many of Halimi's texts thus historicize famous trials and the defence lawyer's involvement in high-profile cases. We know that Halimi defended well-known political figures whose memory is adequately preserved. Yet, for the purpose of this chapter, it is even more important that her narratives often made her clients 'political' in the sense that her interventions successfully reconfigured the borders between who could be heard and dismissed (as making incomprehensible quasi-animal noise) and who could be heard as speaking a rational language (Rancière, 1995, 51). Halimi's stories function as retrospective evidence: the individuals that she defended, successfully or not, became political subjects as a result of the lawyer's ability to use words to make their causes heard as political. Reading these books today helps us reconfirm that it is always possible for some wrong never to be put into words, at least not words that count as words.

Consequently, what I am archeologizing here, as the contemporary effect of Halimi's legal interventions throughout the century, is not the fact that her words were public rather than inserted in fictional narratives. Unlike the authors considered in the previous chapters, Halimi is not a novelist or a filmmaker. She is not an artist. Yet what she does have in common with Fellag, Haneke or Ehni is that stories are an indispensable part of her trade. Her profession demands that she use words in a context that is neither literary nor academic, for when she appears in court, her goal is to fight injustices, to make sure that whatever wrong was inflicted is recognized as such and possibly repaired.

It is undeniable that Halimi's words were once heard in a courtroom rather than being printed on the pages of a novel but that is not sufficient to account for what I view as being reparative and memorially constructive about her work. Nor do I mean to equate her effectiveness as a professional (she won many cases) with the specific type of felicitously performative reparative energy that I have been looking for in certain types of narratives. That outcome cannot be assumed to coincide with a verdict or be deduced from whether or not a trial was won, whether or not a victim left with a sense of justice and whether or not the lawyer has successfully played her role.

If a legal tale succeeds in being recognized by the system that laid down the rule of what is legal and what is not, some form of reparative work will have been achieved, but such victories may be pyrrhic because they leave the system itself unchanged and foreclose the critique of its norms. Some elements, in Halimi's discursive tactics and in her storytelling practices, constitute an even more productive way of working through and with traumatic issues, and especially those against which the legal system, at a given historical juncture, offers 'us' no protection. The 'we', thus identified, is what Halimi's stories will allow us to imagine and interrogate at the same time as her books subjectify the fragile and unprotected 'us' that she creates when she defends some of her clients. There is no such thing as a predictable or archetypal reparative legal narrative, but the belief that such narratives can make a difference allows readers to approach them as a complex and perhaps unique type of experimentation.

Moreover, Halimi's legal writings represent only a fraction of her work. Many of her books clearly belong to the genre of autobiography. Often published at the occasion of life-altering events or personal turning points, the texts that I refer to in this chapter have accompanied the woman's life and the lawyer's career. The first part of this multi-volume autobiography is *La Cause des femmes*, co-authored by Gisèle Halimi and Marie Cardinal, who played the role of the interviewer or confidante.[6] *Le Lait de l'oranger* appeared in 1988, after Halimi's father's death, while *Fritna* came out in 1999 after her mother's funeral. *Une embellie perdue*, written between 1991 and 1994, focuses on Halimi's political role after François

Mitterrand's election in 1981,[7] and the 2001 *Avocate irrespectueuse* is a history of Halimi's career as a lawyer. And even if the last two books seem, at first glance, less personal, even if they belong more clearly to a cultural history of legal or political practices than to the genre of autofiction, Halimi's personal life is never irrelevant. She always paints the picture of a woman whose activity as a defence lawyer is only one aspect of her involvement as a public intellectual, but also as a mother, daughter or friend. And at the same time, passages that we could call 'legal fictions' are constantly interspersed in the narration so that even the most intimate self-portraits are also public statements about the law.

Collectively the books form a complex textual network, a historical and autobiographical hypertext in which the same characters keep reappearing in different contexts and in which the same episodes are re-examined from different angles. That narrative technique enables Halimi to avoid distinguishing too neatly between her heroes and her minor characters, the historical figures whose names are, by now, familiar, and the anonymous friends whose role was, at times, crucial to the outcome of a trial. Halimi's community is not defined by nationalities, or biological gender, or ethnicity but by encounters whose meaningfulness has to do with tactical alliances and ethical compatibility across distance and across time.[8]

From Silenced Un-birth to (un)Born Lawyer

One thread, however, runs through all of her narratives: in all of her texts, Halimi finds a new way of confronting the issue of silence. She faces different types of silence, silences that theoreticians have analysed in different disciplines and in different contexts. Some of Halimi's clients experience what Jean-François Lyotard called 'différend', cases in which the 'plaintiff is divested of the means to argue and becomes for that reason a victim' (Lyotard, 1988, 9). Others demonstrate the force of what Rancière describes as moments of 'mésentente' during which the issue of whom the law recognizes as members of the community is under dispute (Rancière, 1995). In most cases, Halimi shows that a discrepancy exists between what someone seeks to say and what the Law welcomes or tolerates within the realm of what can be articulated and heard as parts of the legal discourse.

What I mean by the 'Law', in these cases, is larger than the collection of texts or decrees that make up a given legal (national or international) code. It exceeds the purely legal and includes the normal: the law imposes a norm (the lawfulness of the law) whose values are seldom re-assessed or even appreciated as historical constructs. Whenever a reader opens Halimi's books today, a performative scene opens up that gives men and women a story. The narrative recognizes that it was at the very least legitimate to ask whether they were suffering (rather than or as well as exercising violence) or whether we should grieve for their loss and see it as ours. It is claimed that they suffered a wrong even if the establishment could not, at the time, articulate what the lawyer argued in terms of truth or rights.

Halimi, then, always works against and with silences. But the challenge is that silence is not the opposite of words. Each silence has a reason, an agenda, a specific way of imposing its norms. And Halimi's texts are not only replacing silence with a narrative. She must adapt her response to each context; her stories must be capable of recognizing what is similar between silences and of distinguishing between different types of harmful or beneficial silences.

One of the very first encounters with the meaning of silence is narrativized and re-interpreted, long after the event, by an adult narrator who had discovered that her own birth (a little girl's birth) had been experienced as a traumatic non-event by a father who wanted a boy. Years later the adult tells the tale in a story that both turns the non-event into an event and also elucidates the type of subjectivity produced by such a non-narrative of origin. Edouard's reaction will shape Halimi's subjectivity in such a profound way that it can be seen as the interpretive key that gives meaning to her specific type of storytelling. The formative aspect of the encounter with someone's refusal to welcome her gender is both crippling and enabling because it defines the narrator's appreciation of what is supposed to matter or even to exist. What counts as suffering and the way in which a narrative can attempt to negotiate forms of being in the world that go beyond biological survival can all be compared to that point of non-origin. The arrival of a girl, the second child in a family that already has one boy, is perceived as a calamity. The father's reaction is extreme and becomes a powerful scenario through which all the other members of the tribe will have to interpret the event.

The type of sexism that makes us (or them) perceive the birth of a little girl as infinitely less desirable than that of a boy is often read as a sign of cultural backwardness. The phenomenon is familiar, almost a cliché. It is thus tempting to dismiss Halimi's father as the typical representative of his 'culture' or even of his 'time'. But the danger with such a reading (and Halimi's intervention highlights this aspect of such interpretations) is that the generic cultural explanation is a narrative that both exonerates the father (he could not help it) but also deprives him of his agency (there was nothing he could have done or could do). It also protects the reader from the responsibility of judging or at least assessing the damage done by his sexism. One traditional reading of the episode is that the father had a typically negative reaction. He resented the fact that he did not have a male heir.

Yet such a summary is deaf to the specificity of Halimi's narrative, the one she chooses to write, precisely to avoid such ultimately fatalistic and predictable accounts. Her story provides us with the means of hearing another point of view, that of the little girl whose individual destiny threatens to be swallowed by this so-called cultural script. What matters in Halimi's text is how she describes the details of how the father reacted. Told here in what is called a historic present, they are collected and organized, turned into a dossier that can be used as evidence against whoever acts like Edouard:

> Pendant une quinzaine de jours, chaque fois qu'on lui demandera si sa femme a accouché, Edouard, mon père, répondra sans sourciller: 'Pas encore ... C'est pour bientôt ... Mais pas encore ...' Quinze jours pour se faire à l'idée qu'il a cette malchance: une fille ... Alors, il *avouera* enfin. (1973b, 9; my emphasis)

> [For about two weeks, when asked if his wife has had the baby, Edouard, my father, brazenly answers: 'Not yet ... Soon ... but not yet ...' Two weeks to get used to the idea that he has the misfortune of having a daughter ... Only then will he finally *confess*.]

This inaugural scene is a particularly violent example of what Butler calls 'girling' in *Bodies that Matter* (Butler, 1993, 7). The denial itself is a form of engendering, the girl is girled by being refused the right to have been already born and the process of subjectivation functions as an Althusserian *non*-interpellation. In Butler's text, the exemplary moment of gendering is explained as the passage from one non-gender-specific pronoun to the 'he' or 'she' that starts the process of iterable girling:

> Consider the medical interpellation which (the recent emergence of the sonogram notwithstanding) shifts an infant from an 'it' to a 'she' or a 'he', and in that naming, the girl is 'girled', brought into the domain of language and kinship through the interpellation of gender. But that 'girling' of the girl does not end there; on the contrary, that founding interpellation is reiterated by various authorities and throughout various intervals of time to reinforce or contest this naturalized effect. The naming is at once the setting of a boundary, and also the repeated inculcation of a norm. (Butler, 1993, 7)

Halimi's story describes the girling process as the (theoretically indefinite) delaying of the passage from 'it' to a gendered identity. And whatever is later constantly reiterated but also resisted is the construction of the little girl as unborn. The narrative treats the knowledge of those missing two weeks as a moment of origin that will allow every fight, every attempt at dis-identification with gender norms. Paradoxically, the force that tries to annihilate femaleness founds femaleness as resistant to such attempts. *As a woman*, Halimi was not born, for two weeks. The mother delivered a baby but the father negated her existence. During those two weeks he stopped the child from being born many times, every time he was asked, a process of repetition that symbolizes the endless struggle against what Halimi describes as a constantly reiterated attempt to erase women's bodies. For two weeks the child was and yet she was not. The father's words symbolically aborted her, 'brazenly', 'each time' he had the opportunity to do so.

Halimi's rendering of the episode, however, is more than merely a good example of what Butler analyses, and her text is not invoked here as an illustration of the philosopher's theory. The specific contribution of this story is that it invites us to ask and then answer two related questions. First of all, how does Halimi succeed in portraying this incident as some inaugural subjectivation scene (how is the reader persuaded that those two weeks are fundamentally formative and not a detail of her family history)? And then, if we are persuaded of the traumatizing effect of the father's denial, to what extent does the narrative manage to restore, repair the damaged subject, or at least to resist not so much that norm (since it appears either obsolete or culturally foreign) but the effects it produced.

After so many years one might wonder, is this not much ado about nothing? The father's reaction was childish, he was in denial and naively tried to prevent what he could not avoid. The child had indeed been born and she was his daughter. There was not much he could do about it. But the words that Halimi carefully chooses symbolically denounce, fight but also recover from what was done to her. The telling of her erasure risks reinforcing the process of erasure. Instead, the tale re-empowers the little girl by turning her into a judge, capable of assessing the father's role. For in the end, he 'confessed', like a criminal and the writer makes us witness his confession.

The paragraph has told us enough to make the word ambiguous: he confesses because he finally admits that his daughter exists. But he also confesses that he has erased her because he feels like apologizing for her existence. Halimi was interpellated as an embarrassment, but she reconstructs the moment of her non-interpellation as a public confession. The father is now in the position of the accused who must 'confess' something. The narrative retrospectively re-assigns blame but without revisionism: it recognizes the father's point of view but also distances itself from it. Edouard does not regret at that point. What he thinks he must confess is that the child is a woman, not that he has acted cruelly. From his perspective, the child's gender requires an apology. On the other hand, the narrative has, by now, given a voice to the subject who can testify and accuse the father of symbolically killing her. Her story forces him to 'confess' the attempted murder.

The writing subject, constructed by this two-week delay, is the lawyer who sees herself as having been sentenced to death for two weeks. And she now uses, to describe the consequences of this supposedly long-forgotten injustice, the same images and words that will help her defend her clients. The two-week period is written as one of the founding myths of the child's subjectivation in which life and death are inextricably linked: 'J'étais toute gosse quand on m'a raconté l'histoire de ma naissance' [I was still a kid when I was told the story of my birth] (1973b, 10). The moment when the father traditionally 'recognizes' the child is replaced by a story about her own symbolic death. Halimi invites the reader to share her experience of being murdered by equating each retelling of the episode with a public announcement of her disappearance: she writes that she 'hears' the story 'résonner comme un glas' [echo like a tolling bell] (1973b, 10).

She recognizes her premature death retrospectively. Her birth is not the event that coincides with the beginning of her new life but a tale of denial and delay. Here, the particular type of 'girling' has to do with the erasure of the possibility of being born a woman.[9] t is not even a question of 'becoming' a woman, it is a question of reappropriating two missing weeks during which, as a daughter, she did not exist because of the father's words.

This sort of non-interpellation is even more destructive than the type of encounters described by Fanon in *Black Skin, White Masks* (Fanon, 1991). Fanon has taught us to recognize the moment when a subject is forced to construct him or herself as a racialized body. n one of the most famous scenes of a book which was published when Halimi was in her 20s, a clear moment of (mis)recognition is identified. The black man is brutally confronted by the meaningfulness of his physical appearance when he realizes that his skin colour frightens a young child: 'Maman, regarde le nègre, j'ai peur!' [Mama, see the Negro! I'm frightened!'] (Fanon, 1991, 112). The encounter is obviously traumatic and as Gwen Bergner puts it, '[t]his racial mirror phase precipitates the formation of racial identity by forcing a "recognition" of lack' (Bergner, 1995, 78). Still, the narrator's existence is not radically negated and Bergner can talk of a moment of 'racial birth' (78). In Halimi's case, even the regime of visibility that might lead to violent or at least stereotypical forms of identification is radically denied.

And yet, as is always the case in Halimi's narratives, this non-birth, this social death before birth, is not written as an experience of utterly disempowering victimization. Edouard's gesture is carefully reinserted into a complex narrative and historicized vis-à-vis the child's individual trajectory. The moment when the narrator learns that her own father socially killed her for two weeks appears in a sentence that links death and rebellion. The child's imagination and the narrator's words make us hear a tolling bell and they are also capable of reassigning the meaning of that sound. The metaphorical bell tolls but also calls the woman to action: 'Comme un glas, et en même temps comme un appel' [like a tolling bell but also like a call, an appeal] (1973b, 10). In the original, the word 'appel' has interesting resonances since the bell both 'calls' her, as in a call to arms, but also 'appeals', as in the use of the juridical system to question the outcome of a trial that has already taken place. By making us hear both types of bells/appeals, the text thus transforms the wrong that was done to the female child into something that can be argued against, refuted in legal terms. While the account of her birth leaves no doubt as to the violence that was perpetrated, it is not too late to recapture what was stolen. Finding out about the father's behaviour leaves the little girl shocked but not crushed. The grown-up's autobiography writes this tension with words that enable the reader to go back in time and address a wrong. We are invited to listen to an 'appeal' and to reconsider the case.

The autobiography writes Edouard's denial as a story of attempted murder but the violence that he inflicted is what triggers a desire to resist. The bell does not only announce death, it signals the beginning of a process during which the consciousness of a wrong emerges and transforms itself into rebellion. The text does not emanate from the perspective of a non-subject who was not allowed to be born. The 'I' is a child who finds energy in her refusal to accept 'la malédiction d'être née femme' [the curse of being born a woman]: 'Je crois que la révolte s'est levée très tôt en moi. Très dure, très violente.' [I believe that revolt rose in me very early. Ruthlessly. Violently.] (1973b, 10).

Revolt thus 'rises' in the little girl as a sort of leavening agent, in the absence of a historical or theoretical model. It does not have to be learned. The narrative describes its emergence as a sort of chemical reaction, and the reader is invited to accept the consequences of the metaphor: the child's revolt 'rises' as if the father's violence had acted as a catalyst and not only as a destructive force. The image becomes a founding myth for the little girl who refuses, as soon as she is old enough to hear stories, to adopt the role of the suspect whose guilt brings shame to the whole family.

The next logical step in this gradual reclaiming of the story is to recognize this principle of silencing even when it does not directly affect the little girl. The father's denial of her birth is one of the most obvious instances that force the narrator to narrativize an attempt to impose non-existence and non-subjectivation, but a few years later a domestic tragedy raises, once again, the issue of how the family deals with what Halimi chooses to put into words. Her brother dies in a domestic incident, burned alive under her sister's eye. The autobiographical narratives often come back to the brother's story as if Halimi was constantly visiting a textual grave and regularly paying her respects. Her story obviously cannot change the child's fate and cannot make it more acceptable. But Halimi must rewrite something about the past: she deplores the way in which the tragedy was turned into a non-event by the parents' reaction in refusing ever to talk about their loss.

The brother disappeared twice because his memory was erased. Halimi's story proposes to put an end to the unhealthy silence that followed the accident and poisoned the grieving process. Both the child's life and his death are obliterated by the relentless absence of stories that the parents deliberately impose. Just as the father stopped her from being born, the refusal to talk about André's death retrospectively denies that he ever lived. Even his name is taboo: 'André a-t-il existé seulement? Rien, aucune trace de sa courte vie … J'ai tenté d'en parler, une fois ou deux, on me fit taire. Plus jamais ce nom-là.' [Did André even exist? Nothing, no trace of his short life … I tried to talk about him, once or twice, I was silenced. Never mention than name again.] (1999a, 43).

In *Fritna*, the source of the prohibition is not specified: the imperative 'never to mention the name' is not attributed to any character in particular. But in *Le Lait de l'oranger*, Gisèle's mother is clearly responsible for the injunction. Her presence is enough to enforce the law of silence and to prevent words from doing whatever work they might be able to do. The ability to narrativize André's death would constitute a limited and insufficient representation of his loss but Halimi points out that the prohibition treats André as a culprit who is banned even from a linguistic universe, the only community that he could inhabit and share with others. 'Ma mère présente, interdiction de prononcer le nom de mon jeune frère' In the presence of my mother, it is forbidden to mention my little brother's name] (1999a, 39). In the context of a national debate about the value of looking back at a violent past, Halimi's suggestion that victims are turned into culprits by those who wish not to talk goes well beyond the borders of her family history.

In this particular example, the reason for the parents' silence is relatively clear. Halimi disagrees with their decision that transforms the difficult mourning process into an ambiguous theatre of implied accusations (against the son and against the little girl who witnessed his death). In other contexts, however, the status of silence is much more ambiguous and the autobiographical text struggles to make sense of what the absence of words mean.

For Halimi, one of the great ambiguities of how to treat silence has to do with the fact that a decision must be made about whether to consider it as absence and lack (nothing is said because there is nothing to say, there is nothing) or as censored or repressed words (what is not said exists in some imagined pre-elocutionary state that would turn into speech if resistance disappeared). As usual, this theoretical difference has a domestic and a legal side, and different though similar consequences for the little girl who remembers her childhood and the clients whom the lawyer defends.

When Halimi's autobiography focuses on her mother's death, the book is a desperate attempt to interpret Fritna's silences. The printed words do not replace what the mother cannot or will not utter but weave a narrative to frame her silence and make it tolerable. The project does not mean to speak for the mother or put words into her mouth, but rather to interrogate the violence of a silence that forever managed to keep its meaning a secret. The text, in a sense, theorizes silence and asks difficult questions about the status of the mother's absence of speech.

> Force principale, le non-dit. Les mots ne devaient pas le dire. C'eût été transgresser la pudeur, la tradition, frapper leur histoire de vulnéra-bilité, de précarité. (1999a, 157).

> [Their [my parents'] main strength, silence. Words were not supposed to tell. They would have broken the law of shame, of tradition. They would have made their history vulnerable and precarious.]

To the extent that the book only appears after her death, Fritna's silence is final and the story does not and cannot repair. Halimi's decision to write coincides with the moment when her mother's body and her coffin forever disappear from the world of the living. Fritna, whose whole life was dominated by silence, can now be transformed into a text that will not replace her participation in a dialogue but will at least problematize her relentless refusal to answer the daughter's questions. Just as the father does not get away with denying the girl's existence because his reaction is supposed to correspond to a cultural norm, the parents' definition of 'shame' is both explained and questioned.

It is during the funeral, the narrator remembers, that she first considers writing about her mother's life. But what is even more important is that the 'I' makes a very specific decision about the type of storytelling and the poetics that she will have to use in order to write the book whose title is the mother's name. One ultimate form of silence is ironically replaced by words that will scrutinize and try to come to terms with other forms of narrativized silences.

At the end of *Fritna*, the narrator gives us the interpretive grid of the book that we have already read: she explains that on the day when the mother was buried, she made a decision: 'J'écrirai un livre sur Fritna, entre confession et plainte. Il faut que je m'ordonne au plus profond de moi.' [I shall write a book on Fritna, between confession and complaint. I must put myself, my innermost self in order.] (1999a, 211). The narrator describes the project at a meta-level, telling us what her words will do. In French, the word 'plainte' suggests a complaint but it is also the legal term used in the expression 'porter plainte' [to press charges]. The grown-up child wishes to complain but she also intends to press charges, as a victim. And the word confession (once again) nuances the statement and seems in contradiction with the intention to press charges. Here, the word also places her book in a long tradition of autobiographical narratives in which the 'I' expresses his or her desire to make a clean breast about less palatable aspects of his or her (public) life. But is it possible to both accuse and confess? Is the child a victim or a culprit of the same act? What type of subject is created here or what sites of enunciation are we expected to recognize or imagine? The narrator does not even claim both territories but rather what is in 'between' (complaint and confession), a grey area that may be even more mysterious to the reader.

The autobiography inspired by Fritna's life and made possible by her death thus allows the narrator to carve out and occupy the in-between place between two roles that are normally occupied by two different characters in the theatre of justice. In traditional legal scenes, one actor seeks reparation, the other deserves punishment. nstead, the grown-up lawyer's discourse seems to believe in a different type of 'order' which she is willing to accept as her own organizing principle. She will re-order herself, at the deepest level.

Once again, the narrative re-arranges, redistributes the players and the rules of the game so that *Fritna* (the story) re-inscribes Fritna, the character, in order to be able to reorganize the parts of the community but also the parts of a self who must re-arrange the disorder left by the violence of silence. The iconoclastic legal narrative intervention does not respect the boundaries of genres (this is a complaint *and* a confession) and resists assigning positions to individual actors (accused and accuser are one and the same person). And that apparent disorder in a legal theatre is what creates the possibility of a new 'ordering' of the self. Once again the polysemy of the French word is remarkable: 'ordonner' means to tidy up, to give an order but also to ordain. Fritna's daughter validates her own position through a mixture of performativity and voluntarism that can only be legitimized from within the narrative. Only the narrative repairs the silence, but on the other hand it is too late to press charges against a dead Fritna and the self-ordering produces no verifiable effect even within the text. Halimi is a lawyer, a priest who has ordained him/her/self.

After the funeral, Fritna is both spared from an accusation that would force her to appear in court but also denied the right to defend herself. As a fictional character, she is recast in a role that she would not but also could not have played. Only then can the autobiographical process start. And the book both attacks and defends her, presents her as the victim and the guilty party at the same time.

The charges against Fritna have to do with something that the beginning of the book has spelled out, in a brutal manner, which this specific passage is precisely re-interpreting. In order to understand the seriousness of the charges brought against Fritna, we must remember what was said earlier: 'On l'a compris, ma mère ne m'aimait pas. Ne m'avait jamais aimée, me disais-je certains jours.' [You will have understood, my mother did not love me. Sometimes, I thought she had never loved me.] (1999a, 15). Understanding Fritna's silences, then, has to do with whether or not she ever loved Gisèle. And in order to indict and defend, in order to write the confession-complaint, the text presents a character whose behaviour is not yet decipherable. The fact is that Fritna's silences hurt because they may mean that there is nothing to say, no love to express. But the absence of recognizable signs of love may be read in at least two ways:

> Amour ou pas, une femme comme Fortunée ne s'exprime pas ... N'est-il pas 'honteux', ahchouma, de dévoiler ses sentiments ... On peut dire sa colère, sa joie, les petites choses de la vie, mais jamais l'amour, la tendresse. C'est trop fort, trop dangereux, les mots dans ce cas peuvent vous entraîner Dieu sait où ... (136)

> [Love or not, a woman such as Fortunée does not express her feelings ... What a shame, ahchouma, to reveal one's feelings ... Anger, joy, the little things of life, yes but never love or tenderness. It would be too strong too dangerous, God only knows where words would lead you ...]

It is almost impossible to spell out the grievance as such. The reader must decide, as a judge or a jury would, to what extent Fritna is guilty of not having loved her daughter, and to what extent she was a victim who was always prevented from expressing her love for her child. Fritna was not able to 're-order' herself. She did not write the story that would have enabled her to resist the forces that demanded silence. Here, the defence lawyer ironically cites her client and gently mocks her fear of feelings but, at the same time, she also accuses her of having hidden behind the interdiction. It may be the case that Fritna did not express love because she had no love to express. And Gisèle herself admits that she has been guilty of lying to protect her mother: 'J'ai construit l'alibi de Fritna' [I constructed Fritna's alibi] (137) she writes.

The specificity of the narrative position adopted here is highlighted by the difference between this passage and another episode in the same book where the potential force of such re-ordering is absent. When the story is not told from the point of view of the lawyer, Fritna becomes a quasi-omnipotent figure, as a distraught little (grown-up) girl agrees to formulate a much more bitter version of the story. It was at that point that she had written: 'On l'a compris, ma mère ne m'aimait pas. Ne m'avait jamais aimée, me disais-je certains jours.' [You will have understood, my mother did no love me. Sometimes, I thought she had never loved me.] (15). Here, the narrative voice recruits the reader. The 'on l'a compris' [you will have understood] rhetorically enforces the idea that the truth was obvious, and that Fritna's absence of love had to be acknowledged (rather than discussed and debated, even in the equivalent of a court of law). The text, this time, leaves the reader no space: we are told what we have already 'understood'. Whatever the story has not told yet promises to be a repetition of what has already been made obvious. All the new evidence presented by the narration, after this point, can only serve as a confirmation.

In the other passage, the narrative tactic is both more ambiguous and less authoritarian. As long as the narrator maintains the difficult balance between confession and complaint, the story can suggest that words of endearment and love were not said but they can at least be written and therefore shared as a horizon of possibility. Of course, the tragedy of Fritna's ambiguous silence is not abolished by the account. It is impossible to prove, beyond reasonable doubt, either that Fritna did not love her daughter, or that she did love her but was incapable of expressing her feelings.

This relationship to silence and to a form of silence that must be translated becomes one of the lawyer's preferred narrative techniques. Unlike her parents, she chooses words and it is her mission to speak publicly of what no one wants to talk about, because it is banned, but also because revelations are so painful (if silence turns out to hide nothing worse than the silence itself). The long 'plainte-confession' [confession-complaint] that unfolds from book to book is framed as a specific genre, the very same genre that the lawyer adopts when she defends her clients. Whatever boundary we may presuppose between a personal autobiographical account and a supposedly more professional and historical report on Halimi's trials is systematically denied by her narrative performances. Both supposedly pre-existing narrative realms are altered, trials are personal and the personal is a trial. Even more importantly, two processes coexist in this attempt: adopting one unique narrative system instead of different genres contributes to the celebration of a value system that neither autobiography nor legal memoirs could, in and of themselves, uphold and promote.

Tortured Bodies and Tortured Boundaries

At times the blurring of the boundary between two traditionally separate discursive realms is decidedly disturbing. For example, even when Halimi talks about torture, she talks about her own body, a rhetorical choice that may well be disconcerting. The word 'torture' can be used, metaphorically, to describe an extremely painful mental state but readers may wonder about the ethical implications of comparisons made between experiences that we may think of as incommensurable. For example, is it possible to equate what Halimi went through as the result of an illegal abortion procedure and what Djamila Boupacha suffered at the hands of paratroopers? What is the value or the effect of such narratives, what type of knowledge can such a story impart?

Halimi decided to have an abortion at a time when the procedure was illegal but she is telling the story decades after its legalization, which means that some readers may reasonably be expected to take for granted the fact that women have a right to terminate a pregnancy in a safe medical and social environment. Now that abortion is legal, Halimi's story does not constitute a 'confession' but makes us aware that the very same narrative, told at a different moment, could have been perceived as such. The assumptions that we make about what must or even can be 'confessed' are reconfigured as problematically linked to a questionable norm. That we cannot, today, receive this story as a 'confession' means that we are not expected to judge, let alone to forgive, and becoming aware that we may have felt entitled to do so sheds light on the past but also on what we perceive, today, as a 'confession' that requires our benevolence or tact.

Even if 'confessing' no longer has any legal value in this case, Halimi's story invites us into one of the most intimate aspects of her personal life before talking about torture, an issue that is frequently discussed in abstract and philosophical terms. The link between Halimi's abortions and Boupacha's case highlights what universal discourses about torture sometimes miss: the significance of the specific type of torture that Algerian women endured.

Halimi remembers how a sadistic doctor deliberately failed to anaesthetize her before going into her uterus to repair the damage caused by a botched abortion. The pain causes, at first, an experience of bodily and mental disintegration and, later, an 'assimilation' of the fact that torture exists and that it must be acknowledged as part of the woman's reality.

> J'entends encore la voix mauvaise du jeune médecin: 'Comme ça, tu ne recommenceras plus'. (Ce en quoi il se trompait d'ailleurs.) J'en suis restée pantelante, brisée. Plus tard, j'ai assimilé cela à la torture. Un tortionnaire de sang-froid, volontairement, décide de me faire souffrir de me désintégrer. (1973b, 31)
>
> [I can still hear the young doctor's vicious voice: 'That way, you won't do it again' (and naturally he was wrong about that). He left me gasping, disintegrated. Later, I made the connection with torture, I assimilated torture. A cold-blooded torturer deliberately decides to inflict pain, to break me.]

The pain that Halimi describes has to do with the discovery of what it means to be tortured. Confronted with the evidence that torture exists, she is othered by the experience. The process of 'assimilation' that she talks about is a form of knowledge that is both irreducibly personal and immediately generalizable. Halimi's body becomes the mediator of the very idea of torture. She writes that she was 'anéantie par la douleur mais aussi par cette découverte de la torture, de son existence' [annihilated by the pain but also by the discovery of torture, of its existence] (1973b, 31). It enables her to state what it means to be destroyed twice, first by the physical pain and then by the reality of torture. 'Assimilate' does not imply that she retrospectively equates what the doctor did to her with any experience of torture or that she knows what Djamila Boupacha went through. The verb suggests that something in her has integrated the knowledge and been changed by it. The process of 'assimilation', which we normally associate with the assimilation of knowledge, of culture or of a foreign tongue, changes the way in which she recognizes other forms of torture, the way in which she deals with, relates to, and then writes about them, even if everyone, including the victim or the victim's friends, relatives or community wish that she would not frame the narrative in a certain way.

The difficulty of the enterprise highlights Halimi's narrative decisions. When she gives an account of her relationship with Djamila Boupacha, she does not, and ultimately cannot, separate the way in which she can speak about her from her own gender-specific and embodied experience. What happened once to Halimi's body, long before she met Djamila Boupacha, constitutes the elements of a narrative grammar that the lawyer-narrator can now utilize. As a result, Halimi's narrative of what happened to her client goes well beyond a humanistic and universalist denunciation of torture. She is capable of taking into account the specifically gendered aspects of Djamila's ordeal. To do so, without ever suggesting that the two women's experiences are similar, she shares, with the reader, the story of two abortions.

What makes her different, as a lawyer-woman who met the vicious young doctor, is that she is able to recognize and spell out that there is something specific about the type of violence that the soldiers inflicted on their victim. Consequently, she turns the account of what happened to her into a narrative that becomes an interpretive starting point, an intertextual echo that enables the lawyer to go beyond a familiar and, for her, incomplete, denunciation of torture as an intolerable, non-gender-specific practice. What her encounter with the young sadistic doctor has taught her is that the paratroopers meant to destroy Djamila as a human but also and specifically as a woman and as a Muslim woman. It was not irrelevant that her body was constructed as female and tortured as such.

To make sure that Djamila Boupacha was heard in court as a victim of torture was not enough. To reveal, publicly, that she had been tortured by the soldiers of the Republic was only one part of the mission. To bring together the bottle used to rape the prisoner and the instrument that the doctor forces into the lawyer's uterus is the difficult objective that the narrative sets for itself: the comparison between the two situations cannot afford to trivialize any element of either event, but that textual territory is a conceptual minefield. Accustomed to national histories that commemorate heroic deeds and fallen martyrs, to paintings and sculptures that represent soldiers in arms or bare-breasted allegories, we may not be ready to accept the parallel between torture and any type of surgery. Even if the doctor's behaviour was insensitive and if he deliberately hurt his patient, we may be shocked by Halimi's rapprochement between that episode and the barbaric raping of a woman by paratroopers. But the question that the text forces us to consider is why it seems nobler or more politically strategic to denounce torture from a more universal standpoint. In which way would it diminish the harm done to Djamila to point out that the sadism that she encounters was gender-specific?

There is no direct answer to the question except Halimi's text, which takes the risk of bringing together two very dissimilar experiences. It is her way of denouncing both torture in general and Djamila Boupacha's unique plight. To treat the rape as an epiphenomenon would exacerbate the violence done by the paratroopers. Everything conspires to silence the description that the lawyer wishes to make when she insists that her client's body suffers from a particular type of disintegration. The rape is both not important enough and too important to be talked about: not important compared to torture in general, and too important because potentially damaging for Djamila herself and so many other members of the community. The woman's shame, her family's tarnished honour, the grand narrative of heroic liberation that needs 'sisters' rather than raped *moudjahidate*, everything makes the story of the rape undesirable and implicitly recommends some form of silence. And by deliberately choosing to talk about herself as a woman, and of Djamila Boupacha as a woman who could also be herself, Halimi crosses the border between different types of silence, between different female bodies.

In her own story, the invasive medical procedure that follows her abortion was made worse by the fact that she could not talk to anyone, least of all to her parents, when she discovered that she was pregnant. The structure that could have functioned as a shelter increased the pain. The absence of a narrative was the implicit norm that the current story must transgress to frame the reality of past silences. The violence caused by silence is revealed and explained as the consequence of the father's normative refusal to allow her daughter to exist as a future mother, i.e. as a vulnerable body in need of protection:

> Pas question d'en dire un mot chez moi. Mon père m'aurait tuée, ou se serait tué, ou aurait fait les deux, ou je ne sais quoi encore ... Sa fille enceinte et célibataire, c'était pour lui impossible. Et puisqu'il ne l'imaginait pas, ça n'existait pas. Ça ne pouvait pas exister. (1973b, 30)

> [It was out of the question to breathe one word of this at home. My father would have killed me, or killed himself, or both, who knows what else ... That his daughter should be pregnant and unmarried, that, to him, was impossible. And since he could not imagine it, it did not exist. It could not exist.]

Silence is not the absence of a story but a story itself or rather the active and deliberate construction of a story. The father's lack of imagination rules an event out of existence. The narrative of Halimi's pregnancy is more scandalous than the pregnancy, than the (unimagined and therefore unexisting) pregnancy. By revealing what happened, the story cannot undo the cruelty of what happened. It makes us understand, however, that the father's silence had already symbolically aborted the possibility of that life and that the young doctor's ferocious words are a translation of the no longer internalized silencing norm.

Discovering such patterns in a most private and intimate context, the lawyer's argument seeks to change the way in which we can talk about torture. She finds ways of making us see the absence of evidence as evidence, to change the parameters of what is relevant, what allows us to include or exclude certain elements of the story. The text shows how the system relentlessly seeks to deny, to erase and to silence Djamila Boupacha's testimony and how silence responds to her desire to be heard. Even her tortured body is read as if it could not speak.

Djamila Boupacha's recovering body must endure the indignity of countless medical examinations which conclude that nothing ever happened because no visible trace of the rape can be identified. The lawyer's narrative must then write invisibility into the story, as a concept that can be captured by words and can resist the doctor's evaluation: 'Une bouteille qui emporte l'hymen – les gynécologues le disent – laisse peu de traces ...' [When a bottle goes through the hymen – gynaecologists agree – it leaves hardly any trace] (Beauvoir and Halimi, 1962, 137). The destroyed hymen is the opposite of a trace. No visible scar turns the body into an allegorical witness, it cannot speak. The lawyer's task is to plead in the presence of something that is not being said, something that is not seen, and that still must be acknowledged and remembered.

The missing hymen and the missing stories are similarly instrumentalized by the system that wishes to deny the use of torture. The doctors find no trace of what is no longer there and the ambiguity of the absent evidence cannot be turned into a story. The forces of death are never acknowledged, and no counter-interpretation can transform them into a call for help or a call for justice. Djamila was tortured but the event leaves no archive except a broken hymen read as an absence that separates before and after. No one can be a witness to a before that supposedly no longer exists. It is part of the specificity of the torture to destroy the trace that could have been used as evidence in a codified, legitimate, medical narrative. Halimi's story does not serve as evidence, only as evidence that evidence was erased. The doctors choose to state that they cannot state, a paradoxical position in itself since they claim that they cannot know. In other words, they should not even be capable of making the non-statement that they deliver. Yet it is the lawyer and the narrator's job to highlight, for the reader, the difference between silence and a non-statement. Like the little brother whose death is constantly re-enacted every time a story is silenced, Djamila is forever vulnerable to the reiteration of the violence that was done to her, not because she is constantly visited by nightmares but because the possibility of telling the tale is repeatedly denied to her, to her lawyer, to those who wish to testify.

Halimi's response to the original non-interpellation is to carve a space, within language and within society, which does not exist yet. When the autobiographies come out, she has 'become a woman' in the most literal sense of the word, but she has also redefined the gender codes that constituted the norm. Very early on, she explained, she had made herself a promise: 'Je serai avocate et rien d'autre' [I shall be a female lawyer and nothing else] (1973b, 23). Translating the French as 'I shall be a lawyer' accounts for the quasi-performative power of the declaration but it misses the significance of the feminine ending. Halimi uses 'avocate' instead of 'avocat' at a time when feminizing the name of professions and titles was not standard practice. Even if it is no longer revolutionary to let grammatical gender reflect social gender, the fact that the -e ending should be almost invisible today is the paradoxical evidence of a hard-won victory. The discretion of the final 'e' hides the formidable obstacles that had to be surmounted for Halimi to become, not simply a woman, but the type of woman that she indeed always was.

The 'I shall be' proclaims the narrator's desire to re-subjectify herself through language, in a gesture that echoes and cancels the father's fatalistic position. Faced with one interpretation of femininity: the 'malédiction d'être née femme' [the curse of being born a woman] (1973b, 10), she edits what, to Edouard, is a 'mektoub' (what is already written). To that type of 'writing', Halimi opposes another use of her logos, the lawyer's argument, her ability to plead a case, to propose an alternative narrative genre. Her rebellion pre-exists her discovery of the political and theoretical tools that will help her articulate her refusal to believe in a curse. 'Je serai avocate et rien d'autre' [I shall be a woman lawyer and nothing else] is a decision and the rewriting of a destiny. It is not a constraint ('I' is the subject of the verb) but it is not a choice either to the extent that no other possibility is ever envisaged. The 'nothing else' changes the project into a sort of *amor fati*: the subject embraces her destiny. The two-week delay makes it impossible for her not to become the female lawyer, that is, a subject position that already exists but that is negated by the father. In order to be recognized at all, to be recognized as the 'avocate' that she is, she must force the father to 'confess' that he knew that she existed. She must demonstrate that she who does not exist exists. That is the definition of her legal work and narratives.

The link between denied existences and being an 'avocate' is spelled out when Halimi specifies which meaning she gives to the word: 'Et être avocate, pour moi c'était, tout simplement, défendre' [and to be a female lawyer meant, very simply put, to defend] (1973b, 23). The 'very simply' hardly hides the semantic richness but also the ambiguity of Halimi's conception of her job. Halimi is and has always been a defence lawyer, because her very existence depends on her winning a trial against those who force others (herself included) into non-existence. She explains: 'plaider une cause était toujours, serait toujours, est toujours défendre donc se défendre. Plaider la cause (des femmes), c'est toujours plaider celle de la Femme en elle, ou bien plaider sa propre cause en tant que Femme défendue collectivement.' [To plead someone's case was always, would always be, is always to defend and therefore to defend oneself. To plead (women's) cases, always means to take the defence of the woman in oneself, or to plead one's own case as Woman, collectively represented.] The distinction between the universal and the particular which can always manifest itself as a potential conflict of interest between Woman and a historically and cultural embodied 'I' is here re-articulated as a felicitous identification practice. I am (female) because I plead (women's case[s]).

While the 'I' who identifies with the victim runs the risk of erasing the specificity of her plight, the 'avocate' brings together her identity as a woman and her practice as a defence lawyer who speaks for others as soon as she speaks for herself and vice-versa. She was born a female lawyer because, or more exactly at the very moment when, she was not allowed to be born a female child. Paradoxically, this is the opposite of essentialism because being a woman was, at some point, an impossible narrative, a story that must be imposed to resist the misogyny of supposedly universal natural laws.

The grown-up's autobiographies are thus understood as the text that rewrites a myth of origin in which the beginning of life coincides with the emergence of (her own) revolt. One birth was denied, the moment when a social subjectivity could have been acknowledged was erased. The new birth occurs when the little girl claims her autonomous resistance. She declares the father guilty of having symbolically kidnapped his daughter's body for two whole weeks. The child's rebellion is always political no matter what she rebels against, and even before she is able to formulate the links between the wrong she suffered and the violence inflicted upon those that she will eventually 'defend'.

Domestic Politics:
The Milk from the Orange-Tree

When the narrator documents the tension between the child and her parents, she rewrites the family romance in political terms, but she also describes her rebelliousness as something that precedes the emergence of her political consciousness. Revolt has always already been there and it is close to revulsion. Often it has something to do with food and ingestion, as is made obvious in *Le Lait de l'oranger*, in which revolt is described as a bodily reaction.

The father's myth of her non-birth and the mother's food can be equally dangerous if they wish to nurture the same stereotypical construction of femininity. The little girl literally rejects, expulses what constructs her body as undesirable and victimizable. Written after Halimi's father's death, *Le Lait de l'oranger* politicizes the little girl's resistance to her parent's authority. At ten years of age, she opposes her elders not as a capricious child but as a militant already committed to a cause:

> Très tôt mes parents comprirent qu'ils ne pourraient pas me contraindre. Mise en quarantaine, enfermée dans mon silence, isolée par celui des autres, je n'hésitai pas, à dix ans, à me lancer dans une grève de la faim illimitée. (1988, 15)

> [My parents understood very early on that they could not use coercion. Quarantined, confined in my own silence, isolated by the silence of others, I did not hesitate, at ten years of age, to start an unlimited hunger strike.]

The narrator does not portray the little girl as a child who sometimes refuses to eat her food out of spite or because she is angry. She does not suggest, for example, that she had anorectic tendencies, although this may well have been the case. The relationship between food and rebellion is a familiar topos in novels that portray the difficulties experienced by adolescent girls or young women.[10] In Halimi's case, the refusal to eat could, in retrospect, have been interpreted as a type of self-destructive defence mechanism. Anorectic symptoms could have been diagnosed as an attempt to mimic the father's demand that Gisèle should not exist as a daughter. Such re-inscriptions of the little girl's decision to deprive her body of nourishment would not have been implausible and they would have been compatible with a type of master narrative about anorexia that theoretical literature has popularized in the 1980s and 1990s (Orbach, 2001; Bordo, 1993).

I am arguing that it may well have been the case that the child had anorectic tendencies, or more accurately that her attitude would, nowadays, have been diagnosed as an eating disorder. But the autobiography does not authorize that type of interpretation because the vocabulary used to describe the child's behaviour makes a point: the narrator claims that the little girl had engaged in a recognizable political act of rebellion. A hunger strike is a concerted and reasoned strategy, a deliberate staging of one's extreme will to sacrifice one's life if demands are not met. It is a heroic form of struggle that is spectacularly life-threatening. It historically links the little girl to the British suffragettes who continued their fight for equality by starving themselves in prison.[11]

The narrative deliberately politicizes her refusal to eat. Consequently, the little girl does not emerge as a stubborn child who tests the limits of authority, let alone as a patient who needs medical help, but as one of the dissidents who will eventually become the lawyer's clients and whose decision to stop eating will be read as a manifestation of heroic resistance. Halimi's words legitimize the child's attitude and enable her body to talk in spite of the wall of silence that the parents had erected. The words 'hunger strike' are the answer to their weapon: the absence of words.

Consider, for example, the title of the passage that gives its name to *Le Lait de l'oranger*. The strange and poetic image is particularly arresting. It is hard to understand and even harder to translate. The unexpected 'de' that links milk with the orange tree makes no sense at first: should this be translated as 'the milk *from* the orange tree'? And what would the phrase mean? Orange trees bear oranges, they obviously cannot be milked. Perhaps the image is meant to evoke the way in which some trees are harvested? But the parallel between, say, rubber trees and orange trees sounds far-fetched. In the absence of any plausible explanation, the reader is forced to wait, to assume that the title is meant to be opaque and that the book will clarify the striking but bizarre image of a milk-producing orange tree. The desire to understand the title does two things: it puts emphasis on the exact nature of the link between the two parts of the title and requires that we accept a delay.

The narrator will, eventually, provide us with a perfectly logical explanation, but the process of decoding will have given the reader the opportunity to test the ways in which relationality, agency and powerlessness are expressed and put at the service of different agendas. After reading the story of the orange tree, we understand that it is crucial to decide whether the 'de' indicates origin, possession or destination, whether it refers to the milk's intended or hidden purpose. By then, it becomes impossible to separate the episode from a much larger personal and political context. At the end of the tale, the phrase is less surprising, less poetic and more plausible. It can be more adequately translated, more accurately talked about because the text has taught us something.

Understanding the exact nature of the relationship between the orange tree and the milk enables us to reinterpret what it means to feed and to be fed in a colonial context. The story makes the point that the conflicts waged within the nuclear family must be read in the context of colonial relationships between countries and between people. The milk of the orange tree is a little personal fable that enables Halimi to articulate complex and far-reaching arguments about colonial kinship and (post)colonial autobiography. What happens between the tree and milk is a mirror image of the way in which the author succeeds in giving an account of herself in a narrative that proceeds by successive jumps forwards and backwards and constant re-articulation of the narrator's position or level of awareness. The way in which Halimi will construct herself as an 'I' in the presence of a tree and milk constitutes another moment of textual re-ordering, a narrative technique that the reader can appreciate and practise. Halimi positions a subject in a way that was not predicted by the context in which she grew up.

The reader discovers the meaning of the title approximately one hundred pages into the book. Out of the blue it seems, the writer explains that she hated milk. Every morning she adamantly refused to drink the bowl of milk that her mother prepared for breakfast. Her stubbornness was a source of serious frictions between the child and her parents who threatened and cajoled, in vain. The little girl would simply not drink milk. And since none of the characters involved in that daily struggle was willing to change their mind, life was transformed into permanent guerrilla warfare.

Inserted in the middle of a book devoted to the lawyer's famous trials, this short episode reads, at first, as a digression. The three pages are devoted to a childhood memory, a most intimate, personal, domestic and apparently apolitical scene. The first sentence of the passage is in the present tense and sounds like a general remark about the author's likes and dislikes. Politics seems to have receded into the background: 'Je n'aime pas le lait. Le beurre m'écœure et les odeurs de fromage me font presque vomir.' [I don't like milk. I find butter disgusting and the smell of cheese nauseating.] (Halimi, 1988, 93). Gisèle's remarks about the foods she likes and does not like sounds rather anodyne and the reader may wonder what the point is. Yet the series of verbs marks a clear progression and the narrator's reactions are described in more and more violent physical terms. Psychoanalysis but also ethnography and anthropology have taught us not to dismiss our unexplained gut responses to food especially if disgust is involved. In this passage, the reference to milk is not coded as a religious interdiction and the narrator does not allude to the impurity of certain food combinations. Milk is not forbidden or taboo, it is rejected by the little girl's body.

And it is hard not to notice that only milk and its by-products are objectionable, and that, at least according to one possible narrative, the girl dislikes what the mother provides as first nourishment. Julia Kristeva's text on abjection and horror explicitly formulates the link between the reluctance to absorb milk and a problematic subjectivation scene. In this passage, the mother, rather than the father, is presented as the origin of the refused interpellation. The subject refuses what, in oneself, is other, or rather the self that one refuses to become:

> Food loathing is perhaps the most elementary and most archaic form of abjection. When the eyes see or the lips touch that skin on the surface of milk – harmless, thin as a sheet of cigarette paper, pitiful as a nail paring – I experience a gagging sensation and, still farther down, spasms in the stomach, the belly; and all the organs shrivel up the body, provoke tears and bile, increase heartbeat, cause forehead and hands to perspire. Along with sight-clouding dizziness, nausea makes me balk at that milk cream, separates me from the mother and father who proffer it. 'I' want none of that element, sign of their desire; 'I' do not want to listen, 'I' do not assimilate it, 'I' expel it. But since the food is not an 'other' for 'me', who am only in their desire, I expel myself, I spit myself out, I abject myself within the same motion through which 'I' claim to establish myself. That detail, perhaps an insignificant one, but one that they ferret out, emphasize, evaluate, that trifle turns me inside out, guts sprawling; it is thus that they see that 'I' am in the process of becoming an other at the expense of my own death. During that course in which 'I' become, I

give birth to myself amid the violence of sobs, of vomit. Mute protest of the symptom, shattering violence of a convulsion that, to be sure, is inscribed in a symbolic system, but in which, without either wanting or being able to become integrated in order to answer to it, it reacts, it abreacts. It abjects. (Kristeva, 1984, 4)

Kristeva distinguishes between the extreme reactions caused by a certain type of food and the food itself. The subject knows that the object of his or her distaste is 'harmless' (4). The refusal cannot be rationally explained. The source of horror is nothing but the 'skin on the surface of milk – harmless, thin as a sheet of cigarette paper, pitiful as a nail paring' (4). And yet the child's revolt against this 'harmless', 'thin', 'pitiful' substance is immense and produces a reiteration of an independent, rebellious 'I': '"I" do not want to listen, "I" do not assimilate it, "I" expel it' (4).

As was the case with Butler's analysis of 'girling', the goal is not to apply Kristeva's theory of abjection to Halimi's passage. We may otherwise be tempted to read the episode as a typically domestic incident that can be universalized and read as an example of what is, in essence, an eternally perpetuated conflict between mother and daughter, or child and parents. Although Kristeva is not specific about why the 'father' intervenes as the provider of milk, the first-person narrator in her story is non-gender-specific and stands for any subject, male or female, who finds milk repulsive. In Halimi's case, this narrative of repulsion is also a story of revolt and political rebellion. The mother is the subject's other but she is also the political enemy.

In other words, we risk simplifying Halimi's text if we stick to the letter of the psychoanalytically derived explanation; for what is both unique and differently generalizable about this story is that the author reorients our possible interpretation of a domestic scene by linking it to a larger historical dimension. As a child, she was not able to put the context into words but as a storyteller, she can alter the course of her story and repair the omission. After mentioning her gut reaction to milk products, the narrator immediately complicates her statement by describing the specific geographical and historical context in which the episode takes place. The little girl and the orange tree will not disappear as objects of the narration but will give meaning to the opposition between the child and her parents.

Let us go back to the first sentence: 'Je n'aime pas le lait. Le beurre m'écœure et les odeurs de fromage me font presque vomir.' [I don't like milk. I find butter disgusting and the smell of cheese nauseating.] (Halimi, 1988, 93). It reads as a general statement, enunciated in the present by a narrator who does not dissociate herself from the content of her claim. The very next sentence situates the narrator in time and space. Both are specified in a way that will prove essential for the comprehension of the passage: 'En Tunisie, le bol de café au lait matinal – du lait à peine teinté – était considéré comme l'arme absolue contre toutes les maladies' [In Tunisia, the morning bowl of café au lait – barely coloured milk – was considered as the ultimate weapon against any disease] (93).

While the first statement invites us to invoke some universal motif (milk is milk), the second makes us revise our interpretation. This may have nothing to do with milk in general. The 'bol de café au lait matinal' is encoded as specifically Tunisian. The narrator plays the role of a native informant and does not wholeheartedly adhere to what she describes as a cultural norm. The passive voice (milk *was* considered) implicitly questions the myth of milk as a prophylactic weapon. That is a story, a story that cannot be separated from Tunisia and from the fact that the parents are Tunisians.[12] The bowl of milk is not inserted into a discourse of (local) medical truth but recontextualized as the source of what an amused, grown-up narrator treats as superstition. When she writes that her morning café-au-lait was supposed to be a magic potion 'cet élixir miraculeux qui, seul fait grandir' [the only miraculous liquor that could make us grow] (93), the reader is obviously recruited as a non-believer. In other words, if Halimi functions, here, as a native informant, she is a de-mystifying bearer of cultural 'truths': when she explains the composition of the mixture ('du lait à peine teinté'), she claims a type of knowledge that is due to her insider's status and rejects the authority that such a position could give her by disqualifying her science as popular superstitions.

I hesitate to read too much into the 'coloured' milk, but for some, the reference to a 'café-au-lait' redefined as a culturally specific type of mixture, namely as a bowl of milk barely altered by a small quantity of coffee, may function as a metaphorical allusion. Should we decode a reference to ethnicity, and is Halimi's text talking about a specifically Tunisian hybridity, or about her own mixed family, or even about her own position?[13] What is clear, on the other hand, is that the narrator knows that her community has associated milk with therapeutic and mythic connotations. The bowl of café-au-lait is not only maternal but also national or pre-national. It is Tunisian. It functions as a 'weapon'. A community is imagined here, a community that shares a belief in the power of its traditional breakfast. But this is also a community from which the narrator excludes herself when she describes the milk's alleged power in slightly hyperbolic terms.

The subject's reaction to milk products is not only that of a child who violently opposes a generic set of biological parents. Conventional Oedipal narratives, which we sometimes naturalize and often simplify when we use them as interpretive grids, will not account for what is going on in this passage. The little girl is already constituted as a political subject reacting against a certain canon, the Tunisian folklore. This is no longer or not exclusively 'abjection', this is dissidence. Not only is the milk off-white but it is also presented as non-French and historically situated at a time when Tunisia was a French protectorate, and would remain under French rule for another ten years. The morning café-au-lait is different from the béret-baguette imagery that colonization could have imported.

The Tunisian café-au-lait is opposed to 'soup', which the native informant associates with the metropole, with France. 'Nous savions, depuis toujours, que la soupe ne profite qu'aux Français, comme d'ailleurs la légende de nos ancêtres – les Gaulois' [We had always known that soup is good only for the French, just as the legend about our ancestors – the Gauls] (93). The narrator is both an insider and outsider. On the one hand, she constructs a 'we' to which she belongs, a community united against the 'Gauls' who are suddenly relegated to the realm of the legendary (and not of history). 'We' have a different type of knowledge. But although the 'I' chooses to participate in that 'we', she also takes her distance, underlining that the Tunisian 'legends' are just as legendary as the Gauls, and that 'our' beliefs about the virtue of café-au-lait are not to be taken at face value. In other words, 'my' culture, even if it is colonized, is no guarantee of truth.

The grown-up's retrospective irony refutes both mythologies and the text as a whole takes advantage of the comment to point out that the episode cannot be dissociated from a Franco-Tunisian dialogue (café-au-lait vs. soup) and also that there is no unanimous Tunisian camp. The story is constructed to make us question the boundaries between or within communities and the effectiveness of forms of resistance that would fall into the trap of unifying oppositional practices.

Here, the fact that the parents so adamantly insist that the little girl should drink her milk and the determination with which she just as adamantly refuses is described as an open conflict. The author meticulously documents the serious consequences of her refusal, the attempts at negotiating, the quickly broken deals, the short-lived truces: she alludes to 'engueulades' [screaming matches], to 'gifles' [slaps] but also to a 'vil marché' [ignoble deal]: 'Si tu bois ton lait, tu auras deux francs par semaine' [If you drink your milk you will get two francs per week] (93).

The potentially amusing details of this domestic guerrilla warfare acquire a more sombre resonance given that *Le Lait de l'oranger* is dominated by the spectrum of the war between France and Algeria. The description of this spectacular war over café-au-lait creates implicit parallels between Halimi's personal history and the history of a (divided) people fighting against a still triumphant colonial ideology.[14]

But suddenly the tone seems to change. The long list of violent events is interrupted by one quick, almost brutal announcement: 'Un jour béni, je trouvai la solution' [One blessed day, I found the solution] (93). The sentence signals a 'Eureka' type of event, a quasi-scientific discovery. The narrator gives us the impression that the child is about to take credit for a simple and perfect transformation. She has single-handedly managed to put an end to a long and painful conflict.

As we are about to see, however, the so-called solution is nothing but a substitution, or rather a displacement of the problem. The child decides to treat the milk that she hates, that her body systematically rejects, as something that she will impose on the powerless object of her affection. The orange-tree will receive the poisoned gift. The day that the grown-up remembers as 'blessed' is the day when the child, a clever tactician, puts an end to the fight with her parents by exporting the problem. Every morning, she empties out her bowl in the middle of the courtyard, at the foot of the orange tree that used to 'grow' there, or rather 'not grow' as the narrative voice immediately adds: 'Ou plus exactement il ne poussait pas' [or to be accurate, it did not grow] (93).

This three-page fable thus introduces a new figure, almost a character. The sickly tree is a mirror image of the already divided colonial 'Tunisian' community. Gisèle's orange tree does not grow. t can no more 'profit from', or be nurtured by, the soil of the native land than the inhabitants of La Goulette can benefit from the legends about the Gauls. The tree does not get any bigger, it bears no fruit, and, in the text, it loses all dignity: 'Il présentait toujours cette forme ridicule d'arbre avorté' [it always had the ridiculous shape of an aborted tree] (94). Like the famous 'Negro' whom the narrator of Césaire's *Cahier d'un retour au pays natal* compares to a pathetic baudelairian albatross lost in the racist city, the orange tree is a pathetic and undignified victim. It is 'ridicule' (Césaire, 1983, 40–41), it is 'comique et laid' [comical and ugly] (41). The tree is 'Petit, trapu, feuillu, sans grâce ... et sans fruits' [Small, thick, graceless, bearing leaves but not fruit] (Halimi, 1988, 94).[15] Moreover, the allusion to a symbolic abortion further complicates the description by reminding the reader of the little girl's problematic birth and of her involvement in the political and legal aspect of the issue.

The bowl of milk becomes the orange tree's daily meal. And at first the strategy seems to work wonders since the parents do not notice anything except that the milk disappears. For a while, peace is restored. The girl had apparently come up with an elegant solution.

> Opération cent pour cent réussie, cent pour cent à profit. Je ne bois pas ce lait qui me soulève le cœur, j'en transmets les vertus à mon oranger qui va (enfin) grandir, et je m'enrichis toutes les semaines. (94)

> [The operation is a hundred per cent successful, one hundred per cent profit. I do not drink the milk that nauseates me. I transmit its values to my orange tree that will (finally) grow and every week, I get richer.]

The word 'profit', which has already been used to explain the difference between soup-eaters and milk-drinkers, between Tunisians and French people, reappears as the keyword in this exchange. The twice-repeated 'one hundred per cent' emphasizes the (excessive) feeling of victory. Not only does peace finally reign in the family but the little girl, as well as the orange tree (or so she thinks), benefit from the truce [profiter]. The spectre of bad faith casts a strange shadow over the episode and functions as textual dramatic irony since a number of clues invite us not to be duped. The unilaterally negotiated *pax romana* depends on the parents' ignorance and on the powerlessness of the anthropomorphized orange tree. After all, the narrator is right to call this an 'operation', a word that sounds dangerously familiar in this context. 'Opération' is the euphemism used by the French government to deny the existence of a war in Algeria. The grown-up author implicitly suggests that this 'operation' was part of an armed conflict even if she mistook it for the beginning of a peaceful period.

And not only does this spurious peace only temporarily mask the tensions within the family but it also exports and reproduces the problem. The logic that enables the little girl to get rid of the milk while preserving her good conscience depends on the construction of the orange tree as the autochthonous, deaf and dumb victim. It is loved but only as a powerless object of compassion and the source of condescending pity. The orange tree is colonized.

The literary critic does not need much imagination or interpretive flair to come to this conclusion since the last sentences of the episode provide us with a quasi-explicit comparison. Like a philosophical tale, the passage closes with a moral, an openly didactic statement that severely condemns the little girl's behaviour and her bad faith. Like ancient or seventeenth-century fables, the text opens up at the end and zooms out from the particular to the general, to the whole of humankind.

First of all the story debunks the reassuring myth: 'Le lait de l'oranger ne produisit pas de miracle. Parce que les orangers n'aiment pas le lait.' [The milk of the orange tree worked no miracles. Because orange trees do not like milk.] (95). Then, the narrator immediately moves on to a more general statement: 'Les hommes sont comme les orangers. Il leur faut choisir ce qui les aide à vivre, ce qui les épanouit.' [Men are like orange trees. They must choose what helps them live and what makes them thrive.] (95).

The orange tree is a speechless non-agent who needs a translator. The narrator notes that the tree, which is in no position to display happiness or reluctance, does not really 'profit' from the operation: 'Mon oranger bien-aimé ne prit pas un millimètre' [My beloved orange tree did not grow one millimetre] (94). Irony of ironies, it will finally be destroyed by another great Liberator figure whose bombs are meant to free Tunisia from a supposedly common enemy: 'Il mourut sous le bombardement des forteresses volantes américaines en 1943' [It died in 1943 under the bombs of US flying fortresses] (94).

The private and supposedly self-contained domestic scene exceeds its limits. It refuses to function as a detail, a localized and processed memory. The fact that the episode gives the book its title suggests that we can read it as a political and narratological scene of origin. This is a matrix that we must recognize as such. Otherwise, the whole book might remain as enigmatic as the poetic expression 'the milk of the orange tree'. The episode allows us to share a story of origin that is unique and individual but also mythical.

The grown-up's interpretation of what could have remained a detail constitutes her intervention. Good and evil are now seen from the point of view of the allegorical orange tree. The narrator, who made the typical mistake of trying to speak for the orange tree as a little girl, is now capable of seeing through her own contradictions: 'La vie entre les gens, l'histoire entre les peuples sont faites de ces contradictions. Se font à travers ces contradictions.' [The lives of people and history of nations are made of such contradictions. They construct themselves through such contradictions.] (95). What matters here is not only what the little girl has done but the way in which the grown-up's narrative takes responsibility for it.

Halimi's narrative provides us with a reparative vision of memorial issues because she refuses two traditional ways of returning to the past. She takes responsibility, as a grown-up, for what she did as a little girl. She does not absolve herself on the grounds that, as a child, she did not know any better. That is the tactic adopted by the narrator of *Caché* who, as we have seen, both forgets the past and, when it becomes impossible to do so, constructs the present as a completely separate sphere.

But neither does Halimi indulge in a sort of melancholic posture that would consist of forever blaming herself for having been a historical accessory to colonization. What matters here is not so much what the child did but what the adult identifies and acknowledges as a wrong that she inflicted. The story allows two seemingly incompatible positions to co-exist: giving the milk to the orange tree was both deliberate but also conceptualized as a good deed. The adult narrator reinserts her literal innocence in an overall structure that accepts her part of the collective guilt.

For after all, from a purely biological point of view, the glass of milk offered to the orange tree was surely meaningless. The contemporary reader might well resist the narrator's cataclysmic interpretation as paranoid. I doubt that even a daily cup of coffee-tainted milk poured at the base of a tree would have enough power to stunt its growth. Of course, the narrator is right to point out that orange trees do not need milk, but she is already anthropomorphizing when she uses the verb 'like' as if trees had feelings and conscious preferences. There is no strong reason to argue against the statement that they '... aiment la terre tendre, l'eau pure et le soleil' [like soft soil, pure water and sun] (94), but when the 'I' adds: 'Et surtout, ne développent de solides racines et ne se chargent de fruits que nourris de leur vérité' [And most of all, they only grow strong roots and only bear fruit if they are nurtured by their truth] (94), we have clearly moved from gardening to a political metaphor. The rhetorical gesture is similar to the vegetal figures that we are used to finding under the pens of philosophers and poets such as Gilles Deleuze, Edoudard Glissant or Aimé Césaire.[16] The allusion to 'truth' and its influence on the strength of roots reveals that the narrator exaggerates or at least over-interprets the power that the little girl had over her 'beloved' tree.

The text, which puts so much emphasis on the deleterious consequence of the daily, selfish, cynical and hypocritical glass of milk, chooses to forget, at that particular juncture, that even when the child was taking care of the tree in a more altruistic and perhaps more traditional manner, she was not such a successful gardener either. Before that episode, the little girl did not appear to be making any obvious mistake, and still the orange tree

> ... ne poussait pas. Malgré tous nos efforts et tous mes soins. Je l'arrosais, creusais la terre avec ma petite pelle de plage pour y mettre de la cendre, lustrais ses feuilles avec un chiffon humide pour qu'elles emmagasinent l'oxygène ... Rien n'y faisait. Je me morfondais à son pied, lui murmurais mon inquiétude, le suppliait de prendre quelques centimètres, un ou deux pas plus. (94)

> [... did not grow. In spite of all my care and all our efforts. I would water it, dig up the soil with my little toy spade to add ashes, clean its leaves with a damp cloth so that they would store oxygen ... All in vain. I stood at its feet, worried sick, I whispered my concern, begged it to grow a few centimetres, one or two, not more.]

The grown-up narrator who proposes a pessimistic interpretation of the damage caused by the bowl of milk is no more realistic than the little girl's triumphant vision. The orange tree does not 'profit' from the operation but was never in good shape to begin with. Granted, orange trees in general do not care for milk, but this particular plant did not seem to respond to a biologically correct treatment. Probably because a symbolic tree is no more interested in water than it is in milk. When a tree represents a colonized people, it will probably be receptive to abstract types of nourishment, be it its freedom or, as the narrator puts it, more than thirty years after the end of the French protectorate, its 'truth'.

The little girl's talent as a gardener matters less than the fact that the grown-up recognizes, retrospectively, that she is capable of violence, and that she directs her violence against this other-same, the other that is both so familiar and so unknown, the 'beloved' tree ['si cher'] (95) that she cannot nurture. Ultimately, the milk matters less than the position it occupies in a chain of power relationships within which the little girl has not been able to carve her place yet. The future lawyer, who speaks for those who cannot be heard, those that the system tortures and guillotines, is a curious sort of bully. She exports her problem with a good conscience and a massive dose of bad faith. But only the grown-up narrator is capable of making us see a little girl who both inflicted pain and still congratulated herself on the effectiveness of her trafficking.

And she is able to rename that pain, inflicted on the other, to identify the problem much more accurately. For the bowl of milk, in the end, stood for 'constraint' (95). After suggesting a relatively traditional linkage between dairy products and the figure of the mother, the story leads us in a different direction. The little girl did not reject the milk itself but the accompanying therapeutic discourse, a form of indoctrination that her parents seek to transmit through it.

For just as the narrator implicitly establishes that the orange tree was sick long before the milk was administered, she also demonstrates that the little girl does not hate the beverage itself but the fact that she was forced to drink it. When her little trick is discovered, the consequences that she must suffer are relatively negligible when compared to the violence that the symbolic tree continues to endure. Once the indulgent father's fit of anger has subsided, the only punishment that he can think of is to supervise the little girl's breakfast. Every morning, the parents will make sure that a responsible adult watches as she finishes off her bowl.

The daily bowl of milk was apparently no more and no less effective than any other form of fertilizers that the tree received. When given to humans, its alleged miraculous powers are irrelevant compared to the fact that its absorption by the little girl is linked to the exercise of a form of power that she adamantly refuses. Her parents have the power to impose their will, their truth.

Whether the milk is indeed drunk or not, its virtues are unverifiable and the narrator makes a point of mocking her parents' belief: when she gives the milk to the orange tree, 'mes parents me fichaient la paix et s'extasiaient sur ma bonne mine: "Le lait ... rien de tel" répétait Edouart avec satisfaction' [my parents left me alone and marvelled at how healthy I looked: "Milk ... there is nothing like it" Edouard would repeat] (94).

But conversely, when it becomes impossible to get rid of the bowl of milk, the child is quite capable of adapting to the new situation. She simply changes tactics: under her mother's watchful gaze, 'Je ne bus le lait qu'à doses homéopathiques' [I drank the milk, but only homeopathic doses of it] (95). The therapeutic virtue of the milk is now seen as part of a different system, a different discipline: we move from allopathy to homeopathy, a less conventional and more controversial form of medicine. The little girl also stages her reluctance via a performance that the grown-up clearly identifies as an act: 'je me livrai, avec ce talent de l'enfance, à la comédie des nausées, des hoquets, des malaises' [With a child's talent, I indulged in a little comic act, feigning nausea, hiccups, malaises] (94).

At the end of the passage, the narrator is finally capable of naming the form of violence that she both endured and had wished to inflict on her beloved orange tree. The bowl of milk was ultimately a symbol: 'Je n'aimais pas le lait et je détestais la contrainte' [I did not like milk and I hated constraint] (95). Constraint (i.e. the parents' power over her) is more unbearable than the milk itself which, after all, is but a politicized metaphor.

Le Lait de l'oranger is the volume of autobiography that is devoted to the beloved father's death. The next book was written after the mother's death and is entitled *Fritna*. It is not insignificant that the text devoted to the mother should have been given her name whereas 'Edouard' does not appear in the title of his own story. His proper name is replaced by the orange tree as if the fable has taken the place of the father's name. It tells us about a child growing up in a colonized land and enables the narrator to write a form of memorial narrative that implicitly anticipates some of the issues debated at the beginning of the third millennium. Halimi acknowledges that her position has changed and shows us how she gradually discovered, without a teacher, and without necessarily articulating it, that cohabitation, in a colonial context, is founded on institutional violence. The story also demonstrates that the structure of colonial violence was reproduced within the domestic sphere so that the parents' power becomes an allegory. The narrative implicitly accuses the colonial regime of infantilizing the Tunisian people but also shows that children do not have a monopoly on innocence. Memories about a lawyer's childhood or private life may seem irrelevant to how Halimi chose to defend Algerians accused of terrorism or accused the military of torture. In a France that kept rediscovering the war against the former colony, it would not have been inconceivable for her to yield to the temptation of self-righteousness. She could have retrospectively vindicated her position and pointed out that she was right all along. Instead, she chooses to highlight her own zones of ethical ambiguity and uses, as a sort of ideological flag and alert indicator, this enigmatic and poetic phrase that forever unites the best and the worst, the beloved tree of her political ambitions and the detested milk of coercion, her good intention and her bad judgement.

The narrative makes us realize that the lawyer who always spoke in the name of those who could not speak for themselves was aware of what we could call the orange tree syndrome. Halimi, who always defended those whom the colonial structure had constructed as the others of Europe, of Reason and of civilization, gently refuses the role of the heroine who has always been on the right side of history. Like those who refused to tell the truth or censored unspeakable stories, she knew about family secrets and unhealthy silences.

Conclusion

Halimi's multifaceted career enables us to consider all the different types of narratives that she has written as an ensemble. The reparative function of her work occurs gradually, little by little, from book to book, and remains an unfinished process. While a novel such as Nicolas Ehni's *Algérie roman* provides the reader with a self-contained account that forever resubjectifies the author of the tale, in Halimi's work the process of reparative mourning and sustaining narration continues from personal and public testimony and across genres. The critical decision not to separate her autobiographies from the legal accounts mirrors Halimi's practice. She constantly crosses generic borders, treating confessions as legal texts and her own closing arguments as moments of autobiography. She constantly disassembles and reassembles categories (gender, class, nationality, ethnicity, religion) which she refuses to isolate, but which she cannot dismiss either because they produce powerful cultural effects against which she must fight. Halimi is definitely not a born postmodern nor did she become a deconstructionist, and her work is less a hybrid and multifaceted performance celebrating multiplicity and pluralism than a coherent and legible series of books written as an insider capable of radically but slowly and painfully transforming the shape of that inside.

What enables the reader to imagine a reparative version of the events described in the books has nothing to do with Halimi's particularly arresting style or narratological idiosyncrasies. Professional lawyers might be frustrated by her writings because Halimi's attempts to make us aware of constraining discursive norms cannot be explained in purely legal terms. And literary critics looking for the perfect disciplinary object might hesitate to classify her texts as 'literature'. Her deceptively simple and linear stories are miles apart from surrealist automatic writing or *nouveau roman* experiments, but she shares with the former a belief in the revolutionary power of words. Besides, a Sartrean engagement and a sense of her responsibility as a writer permeate her work as a public speaker and published author. Language names and brings the world into existence. Her description of how words function turns them into 'miraculous weapons' as Aimé Césaire famously put it in 1946.[17] The books are written by someone who always had to treat words as the tools of her trade and who must believe that they have an effect. In *Avocate irrespectueuse*, she writes:

> Les mots. Les mots, seule arme, mais arme absolue. Pour qu'ils expliquent, frappent, emportent, ou, à défaut sauvent la liberté ou l'honneur de l'accusé, les mot doivent dire, se mouvoir, se nouer, courir, s'appesantir, s'arrêter, se répéter. Le tout dans la plus absolue liberté. (2001, 131)

> [Words. Words as the unique but ultimate weapon. In order to explain, strike, carry away or, at the very least, save the accused's freedom or honour, words must tell, move, tie themselves up, run, weigh down, stop, repeat. And this, in the most absolute freedom.]

Words do things, they are almost anthropomorphized or at least animated. The string of verbs suggests that their power of movement is almost unlimited, but Halimi's conceptualization of the lawyer's speech is not a form of performative language. There is no pre-established protocol that ensures that when she has uttered a sentence, the community will agree that an event has occurred. Words, in Halimi's vision, have a seemingly boundless energy but the freedom she talks about means that their power is far from absolute and far from predictable. The work remains to be done.

Halimi knows that the courthouse is supposed to be a theatre where only certain types of words count, can be heard. The lawyer must speak in the presence of a judge and a jury for example. Only if the proper ritual is preserved will certain statements acquire the force of law. But words, according to Halimi, need freedom from such constraints. If speech act theory invites us to treat the conditions of elocution as almost as important as what is said, Halimi's position, instead, grants every word the ability to move about freely. Her words are free, must free themselves from the theatrical protocol that restricts legal speech acts from the generic constraints that establish distinctions between autobiography and a closing argument.

The words that the lawyer uses in court and those that she uses to tell the story of what happened in court (in a book or in the privacy of her own home) are not qualitatively or theoretically different. In an institutional setting that carefully identifies the genre of everyone's language and the position of those who are allowed to speak and the conditions of the address, the idea that only certain words count would appear to be self-evident. Instead, Halimi suggests that the power of words to 'save' someone depends on their quasi-literal freedom of movement.

The lack of emphasis on a potential distance between language in general and the lawyer's performative (and therefore perhaps formulaic) pronouncements may seem to disempower the professional speaker, but instead the gesture re-empowers the lawyer as woman and storyteller. There is no such thing as 'in other words': the autobiographies, the personal and intimate stories and the court cases are different examples of words in motion.

If Halimi is likely to help us find examples of non-paranoid critique that succeed in troubling clearly identified norms but also the usually invisible and hard-to-contest regime that Rancière would call the 'distribution of the sensible' (Rancière, 2004; 2007), it is not, or at least not only, because she has won many cases and makes us hope that we will find relief in the ritual retelling of success stories.

t may be the case that her work has created an archive that we will wish to invoke, optimistically, as evidence that the legal system, at times, works. But theoretically speaking, the hypothesis is slippery: in order to be convinced that justice was indeed served when Halimi won a case, we must already be on 'her' side, which means that the story has already done her cultural work (what of men and women who, today, are not convinced by her pro-choice discourse: must they be assumed to be hopelessly obsolete, not yet or perhaps no longer enlightened, as if history had by passed them?). Perhaps more dangerously, if we only look at Halimi's cases in terms of legal decisions, we must agree not to ever revisit the judgment in question and treat the verdicts as new quasi-sacred texts, decrees that, as readers, we simply must abide by. Halimi's usefulness is her ability to make us doubt that such final and definitive narratives exist.

While solidly grounded within what the system calls the real, Halimi never assumed that she had to abide by whatever borders the norm dictated. And this is one of the things that makes her work so relevant to the purpose of this study. Halimi shares, with authors who use imagination and fiction to transgress and critique the norm, a desire to fight injustice even if the fundamental injustice is perpetrated by the legal system itself. The issue of whether or not the Bobigny trial was a success is less relevant than the way in which Marie-Claire Chevalier's mother frames her response to the legal system that accuses her of helping her daughter to have an abortion. Halimi quotes her as she addresses the judge, objecting, in simple and still powerful words, to the definition of guilt and rights. She does not recuse the judge himself as if she thought of herself as above the law or as if she did not see herself as a member of the community that recognizes his authority. She questions the article of law that he proposes to uphold: 'Mais, Monsieur le Juge, je ne suis pas coupable! C'est *votre* loi qui est coupable!' [But your honour, I am not guilty! *Your* law is guilty! (my emphasis)] (1973b, 78).

Note that she does not say that 'the' law is wrong but that the judge's law is guilty. The formulation displaces the notion of accountability away from the supposedly always powerless human being, whose innocence or guilt is relative, to the law itself, which no longer appears as an absolute point of ethical reference. The sentence suggests that every law is always someone's law, which elegantly and concisely questions the supposedly non-gendered and classless legal system. Chevalier reminds us that we are not only accountable to the law but also responsible for, owners of, authors of the law that we abide by.

In 2008 Chevalier's statement would not even exist because the law has changed. She would simply not have the opportunity to address the judge from within a court of law that accuses her of something that is no longer a crime. But the reason why this whole conversation is not merely a historical piece of evidence, the trace of how things were, is that Chevalier's tactic, as relayed by Halimi, documents the precise cultural and narrative moves that were necessary at the time. We may have forgotten about them when we say, much later, that mentalities *have* changed, as if something had just happened. Halimi did not only speak up in favour of the legalization of abortion, she not only acted on behalf of an adolescent who would be powerless in the face of the juridical system, but she wrote a text that testifies to exactly how a radical reformulation of what is legal and what is not takes place.

To the extent that the power of the law is also what puts a border around what we imagine to be feasible, even if we opt to transgress, what the narrative performs has to do with a redeployment of our imaginary space. As readers of Halimi's books, articles and interviews, we can now state, confidently, that her accomplishment as a lawyer is not to have convinced a judge to opt for leniency or to pardon a culprit. Now that the law has changed, a new frontier is in place. Only in retrospect can we perceive the mother's intervention as a performative moment during which the role prescribed to each participant was exceeded and finally re-distributed. That the law, any law, might need to be further challenged is already present in Halimi's account.

Written before critical legal studies became a well-recognized discipline, Halimi's texts tested the borders between storytelling and legal discourse, between autobiography and legal testimonies. She stretched the limits of the sometimes unconsciously theatrical or performative normativity of the court of law. Halimi's autobiographies resemble the type of autobiographical-legal social critique and meditations that Patricia Williams started publishing in the 1990s,[18] emphasizing, like her, the difficulties of constantly walking the line between a disembodied universalism (that would refuse the historical contingencies of certain definitions of subjectivities)[19] and an under-theorized identity politics that risks forcing the militant to opt for gender against class, for example.[20]

CONCLUSION

Repentance and Detective Fiction:

Legal Powerlessness and the Power of Narratives

n January 2008, after the evening national news, France 2 network showed an episode of the popular *P.J. Saint Martin* detective series called 'Erreurs de jeunesse' [Mistakes of Youth].[1] I remember following the plot with a growing sense of astonishment as it slowly became apparent that the puzzle the investigators were slowly putting back together was telling a story about France's colonial past or more importantly about its impact on the immediate present. The episode made three assumptions that I thought were remarkably revealing about the recent thematic and generic norms that govern memorial narratives (even if they remain invisible). First, the story expected the audience to be familiar with the history of the war between France and Algeria. Secondly, *P.J. Saint Martin* gambled that a story about the rape of an Algerian woman by a French soldier would not systematically alienate prime-time viewers. Finally, it was also assumed that we would be interested in discovering how the past affected the lives of two characters who had previously been on each side of the national and ethnic line and were now living in the same French neighbourhood.

Contemporary Frenchness is here defined as the complicated weave of memorial threads that cannot or can no longer be reduced to a mosaic of narratives that each emanate, supposedly monolith-ically, from a given community (the [sons and daughters of] the former *moudhahid*, harki or French soldier, the colonizing or colonized civilian, the former 'pied-noir' or 'pathos').[2] The Algerian war is neither relegated to an irrelevant past nor the topic of the episode. The emphasis is not on the repressed memory of a given community[3] but on the national social fabric as that is made up of what appear, in other narratives, as distinct memorial threads.

This work of fiction thus performs the kind of practice that Stora recommends: in the introduction, we saw that he wished to encourage 'une réflexion sur les *rapports* entre groupes porteurs de "la mémoire algérienne" ...' [a reflection on the *relationship* between communities who are the guardians of 'Algerian memory'] (Harbi and Stora, 2004, 13, my emphasis). The episode is neither 'ce savoir immense mais cloisonné et éparpillé' [immense but compartmentalized and fragmented body of knowledge] (Harbi and Stora, 2004, 11) nor simply 'mémoire retrouvée' [recovered memory][4] but a look at the kind of memorial trace that must construct itself, in the present, when several memorial threads are forced to come into contact.

In this episode, an elderly woman (she looks about sixty) is arrested for assaulting an older man. The man is a stereotypical white bourgeois while the woman is encoded as Arab. She was screaming something in Arabic, something that street-vendors all heard (the scene takes place on a busy Parisian boulevard on a market day) but her victim either did not hear or did not understand what she said (or does not care to repeat it even if he does). At first this is all we know, this is all the detectives know. She was caught red-handed, and it is apparently clear who the victim is and how his grievance can be put into words: he was assaulted by a woman whom he does not know. He is calm and composed, she is wild, violent and irrational. Both are too old to fit a 'crime of passion' scenario. Nothing makes sense at first.

Still, the hermeneutic gesture that can be generalized from this episode and that we can extrapolate as a relevantly historical interpretive technique is that when such an apparent gap opens up, it may be worth relying on one experiment: could it be that the scene can only be properly read if we go beyond the limits of the immediate present and turn our attention towards the colonial past?

Before analysing the episode in detail, it is worth replacing it within the context of the series and examining the place that *P.J. Saint Martin* occupies in what the French call the audiovisual landscape. Since 1997 the series has matured into a complex media phenomenon.[5] Its success as a cultural project that needs to be constantly sold and bought can only be guaranteed by its ability to reach (or create) an interested audience, and the long life-span of *P.J. Saint Martin* suggests that it addresses issues that are always legible, or at least understandable, as a relevant representation of contemporary France. When the characters of *P.J. Saint Martin* address issues of multiculturalism and racism, of institutional and symbolic power, when they represent undocumented immigrants or religious and ethnic minorities, they provide us with a snapshot of what the French view as culturally and political relevant. Clearly, in January 2008, the time had come to talk about the memory of the Algerian war and not only about what happened to the so-called 'second or third generation'.

At the same time, the series plays on the margins of the debate and does not shy away from potentially controversial topics. It is one thing to look back towards the colonial past, it is quite another to choose prime-time television to focus on those French citizens, residents or immigrants whose fathers were soldiers and rapists and whose mothers were or are Algerians and rape victims. I am not suggesting that the issue of rape is the next frontier in some journey towards historical progress. The figure of the Algerian woman as rape victim was discussed by Fanon in 'L'Algérie se dévoile' as early as 1959 in *L'An V de la Révolution algérienne* (Fanon, 1968);[6] it plays a crucial role in Ehni's book and we have seen how important it was for lawyers such as Halimi to emphasize the gendered aspect of torture. Yet it is rare to come across a story that fictionalizes the embodied legacy of such violent encounters (the child) to ask questions about the link between kinship and Frenchness. More generally, what makes *P.J. Saint Martin* such a remarkable object of study is that the series always addresses issues that are just beginning to be considered a legitimate object of public discussion in contemporary France. It is a good indicator of what constitutes the progressive edges of this conversation.

The detective team itself always included what the French were beginning to call 'visible minorities' in the 2000s[7] and the plot makes room for enough discussion of the detectives' private lives to give the viewers information about their origin or milieu. In other words, it exposes the range of categories that are defined as private or public, but also thought to be relevant as private within the public sphere. Depending on which season we watch, we know that Alain Porret's family (Thierry Descroses) is from Guadeloupe and that he grew up in Gergy Pontoise; that Agathe (Emmanuelle Bach) is Jewish; that Karim, the receptionist (El Driss), and lieutenant Rayann Bakir, one of the star officers (Jalil Naciri), are Arabs; and that Nadine (Valérie

Bagnou-Beido) has a lesbian relationship with her black colleague, Tina (Nadege Beausson Diagne). The plot of each of the episodes, but also the identity of the individual actors who have been chosen to play each of the detectives' roles, draw our attention to issues of multiculturalism, racism, gender and history. The series reflects the evolution of social paradigms (the writers providing a sense of continuity by building upon previous seasons). At the same time, the script takes great trouble to invent situations that demonstrate that it would be absurd to assume that the character's ethnic identity, cultural, religious or regional background function as a social matrix and explain in any way their reactions or political opinions.

Of course, *P.J. Saint Martin* belongs to the realm of fiction and is framed by the conventions of prime-time television and the constraints of the genre. I am therefore not suggesting that the episodes should be studied as though these characters were French subjects analysed from an ethnographic or sociological perspective. At the same time, it may be even more important to notice the narratological grammar capable of constructing characters whose coherence then allows viewers to organize their perception of the social spectrum in a different manner.

A number of episodes about undocumented immigrants involved Eastern European characters, white women or children involved in prostitution or portrayed as the victims of human trafficking. However stereotypical the images may be, they represent a moment of change in the way in which the relationship between Frenchness, whiteness, ethnicity and the past are articulated. In the early 1990s most media and especially television taught us to expect that undocumented migrants would look like Arabs or black men or women (bodies whom we then assume that we know to be *from* the Maghreb or Sub-Saharan Africa, that is, from previously colonized lands). The obvious other of Frenchness was non-European, ethnicized and postcolonialized. But perhaps we only realize that such a narrative was a simplistic though powerfully implicit code when it is destabilized by new fictional figures that alert us to the existence of a grammar of representation. In *P.J. Saint Martin*, black bodies are statistically more likely to occupy the role of police officers and the undocumented immigrant is often (Eastern)-European, the alien from within, the insider-other.

P.J. Saint Martin is neither angelic nor widely optimistic and the genre justifies that the focus should be on the presentation of conflicts. Disenfranchised housing projects are sometimes the backdrop of criminal activities. When such neighbourhoods are filmed, viewers are presented with forms of social and ethnic segregation and the investigation leads to aggressive confrontations between perpetrators and victims. Yet it is the main protagonists' job and narrative challenge to expose the relatively unpredictable nature of the link between what we see and what we imagine to have happened. The purely scientific aspects of the collection and interpretation of evidence is not emphasized as much as the detectives' ability to interpret human behaviour. What is extremely sophisticated are their fine hermeneutic cultural skills rather than the experiments carried out in their laboratory.[8] The best case-solver is the best cultural analyst, capable of closely reading the text that the case constitutes from an interdisciplinary and imaginative perspective. Social categories are essential units of knowledge. Each new problem gives the detectives an opportunity to test our their assumptions about which categories should be mobilized to explain what happened (young or old, male or female, white, beur or black, gay or straight, rich or poor, citizen or alien). It is never denied that such taxonomies exist. *P.J. Saint Martin* is decidedly turning its back on what was long assumed to be the French universalist knee-jerk reaction. But it is always implied that we should know better than to predict the ways in which such categories work. They function both between the detectives and the public (many versions of the 'ethnic minority criminal vs. white cop' binary are tested and rejected) but also within the team (which is ethnically heterogeneous, clearly gendered and also sexualized, and does not represent a unique political front) or within the victim–aggressor dyad (that provides unexpected reversals or complications).

For example, we cannot assume that the series will adopt a unified discourse about the *definition* of ethnicity, skin colour, origin, identity and the ways in which these markers interact. The principle of the token black officer has obviously become too obvious a gimmick and other implicit theories of how people represent themselves are constantly mobilized. In one episode, a black officer is written into the scenario as the character who will adamantly refuse any type of ethnic identification while his 'client' will act as an African man who blames his 'brother' for betraying his ancestors or his land of origin. The 'colonial fracture' (Bancel *et al.*, 2005) is played out in nuanced and multi-layered ways as each of the characters has an opportunity to test his or her reflexes when confronted with cases that activate different aspects of their ethnic or sexual identity, religious or political convictions.

On the other hand, the team of detectives is not idealized either. For example, previous episodes have taught us to expect Chloe Mathieu (Raphaëlle Lubansu), one of the inspectors, to react in ways that her colleagues identify (and condemn) as racist. She first appears in 1999.[9] She is said to be from Cannes, and straight out of the police academy. In those early episodes, the character is pictured as the new kid on the block, a newcomer whose position within the team is going to be complicated by her cultural or political secret. Her relatives (including her father whose visit to his daughter runs the risk of importing a rather stereotypical Southern France into the supposedly more representative French capital) have National Front sympathies. But a few years after President Chirac's (in)famous second round against Jean-Marie Le Pen more or less put an end to the leader of the National Front's political career (2002), the contours of Chloe's character have changed. She may still be inclined to gut reactions that signal her distrust of what she perceives as otherness but she is extremely aware of her tendency to do so and acts accordingly.

In 'Erreurs de jeunesse' individual and collective colonial memories are deliberately written into the plot as a problem: the 'memories' in question are sometimes traces, sometimes an unformulated desire to know more, that are interpreted as someone's intuition (not evidence). Something needs to be noticed, investigated and interpreted by the representatives of the state who stand for a certain sense of justice. But the detectives, including Chloe, don't know what the something is and it is not neatly superimposed over the crimes that they are familiar with.

Chloe has already arrested her suspect and there is no doubt that the woman is responsible for destroying precious vases in a man's house and then attacking him. The legal system should be satisfied. Her guilt is incontestable (and she does not deny anything), evidence and witnesses confirm that the old man was assaulted. The reason why the episode does not stop right away has to do with Chloe's interpretation of her own shortcomings. What the scenario suggests is that it is possible to identify moments of misunderstanding even before being able to turn them into coherent narratives. Chloe knows that her explanation is not adequate and the episode's conclusion suggests that this type of knowledge is a form of haunting or resistance to particular stories that is slowly becoming easier to recognize. Chloe allows for the possibility that something, in her own logic, is being challenged by a past that she is willing to examine even if it destabilizes the identity markers that enable her to do her job of interpreting the real.

The man claims, for example, that the woman was supposed to clean his house and had no reason to behave the way she did. At first the account is set resolutely in the present and forces the protagonists into stereotypical ethnic, gender and class roles: the ethnic minority female cleaner is employed by the white bourgeois male who is also a womanizer (he is obviously eager to get rid of the detectives who ask him questions due to the imminent arrival of a young mistress).

Interestingly, more than one of the elements of the narratological grammar are questioned and successively experimented with: first, the issue of gender and, then, the issue of temporality that cannot be separated from the characters' ethnicity. Chloe recognizes, in herself, two areas of possible incompetence. Like a reader aware of his or her own blind spots, she focuses on what she may not be seeing in order to go further. At first she admits that she is not very sensitive to gender issues and seeks help, asking Agathe to ascertain whether she is right to assume that there is more to the story that the woman will admit. Perhaps the woman refuses to speak to Chloe, perhaps *she* is not the right conduit for the woman's grievance. Chloe suspects that the assaulter was in fact raped by her male victim and that silence is a form of shame. In other words, she interprets the suspect's story as a screen, as a problematic text that she may not be able to decode and that other members of the team could read. I am suggesting that this type of self-awareness is to be added to hermeneutic grids: the decision not to confuse (disguised) silences with the absence of a (different) story is a certain type of historical intervention made possible by previous encounters with difficult categories. Being conscious that gender, ethnicity and past traumas play a role is what enables Chloe to concentrate on transforming the story that silence tells into a narrative. Assuming that she may be in the presence of a 'différend' à la Lyotard enables her to treat the woman in a different way (Lyotard, 1988).

The second attempt at reconstructing the story involves languages and, implicitly, the relationship between the truth, national identity and linguistic norms. In this episode, we discover, for example, that Chloe has been learning Arabic. No naive assumption is made about the inherently pacific intentions of any type of language learning. But while the episode makes it clear that even such supposedly commendable attempts at developing linguistic skills are not neutral (after all, the attempt to understand is unavoidably linked to a desire to police more effectively), her investigation continues because she realizes that a woman was screaming something that she could still not understand in a language that she is trying to learn. She knew, however, or suspected, that she must understand in order to decode the story. She is able to make it her business to decode the information that comes to her in Arabic in a public space. Far from the debate about whether or not 'banlieue cultures' and that specific type of language should be encouraged or denounced, this story suggests the possibility of a multilingual France, going beyond the idea of accented cultures, books or films (Naficy, 2001).

Chloe is the same character who, in a previous episode, had reacted with hostility to the fact that the teenager that she was interrogating had turned to his father and said something in Arabic. In that episode, her request that he speak French meant that she felt threatened in her ability to police by the presence of a language that she could not understand. She assumed that Arabic protected the youth from the authority of the (French and Francophone) police officer. Here, the situation is reversed. Something was said, in the public space, that cannot be understood by the police and Chloe is willing to test the hypothesis that what they cannot understand is worth listening to as a claim, as a rational accusation, a legitimate appeal to the legal system. The language of the accused is not dismissed even though it is not the national language. It is not just the noise of pain as in the Rancierian models, neither is it something that the colonizing army will always suspect of being a threatening call to arms.

Chloe keeps trying to look for witnesses who were there at the open market that day and would be willing to translate for her. But her desire to understand does not mean that anyone is willing to speak to her or to put their bilingualism at her disposal. Only when she catches a pickpocket red-handed is she able to negotiate. The young thief exchanges a translation for a reduced sentence, a scene that adds languages to the list of things that an informer can use as leverage. Yet the informer is not a traitor or a Malincha.[10] He does not translate in order to enable the powerful to subdue, feminize and dominate the sexualized other. In fact, his translation is meant to protect the Algerian woman from being reduced to that role.

But the problem is that even with the translation, the story makes no sense. As Chloe suspected, but had no way of proving, the woman was indeed accusing the man of rape, an accusation that radically redefines the position of aggressor and victim. If the man raped her, she was acting in self-defence and not only should she not be arrested but she should press charges against him and not the other way around.

And if there is an element of disingenuous narrative seduction in this episode, it is in the way in which the audience is led to want to believe that we are closer to the resolution now that a violence-against-women narrative comes to replace a random-violence scenario. If the woman was raped, the man is guilty. What is still missing, however, is the way in which gender issues interact with postcolonial and historical issues. What is reparative about this narrative is that it finds a way to connect all three issues.

In retrospect, it will become obvious, however, that such a gender-specific reading fails to take into account the woman's ethnicity and her past. For now that the seemingly obvious narrative (she was raped) has replaced the original man-attacked-by-woman scenario, something, in the story, continues to resist. And the dimension that no one, at first, is capable of taking into account is the importance of the past, of history. The originality of this episode is that we will later remember that what we were refusing or forgetting was not the colonial past, but an intuition that seemingly inexplicable violence in the present had to do with violence committed in the past. In an interesting critique of our tendency for presentism, the episode shows that the woman's accusation 'he raped me' is immediately interpreted by all as an immediate past: the victim is sent to the nearest hospital in the hope that doctors will collect evidence that will incriminate the rapist in the absence of his confession (physical traces will perhaps compensate for an inadequate story). The scientific aspect of the truth-seeking activity seems to be taking over, as if narratively, the episode had reached a dead-end. Except that when the results of the doctor's examination are known, Chloe's fiction turns out to be unverifiable. The woman shows no signs of having been raped, at least no sign that a hospital collection-kit could turn into solid evidence acceptable at a trial.[11]

The story is thus impossible to verify and it takes the opening up of a new space of listening for the woman to add to the story the one element that has so far been ignored: the fact that her grievance is forty years old. Only once the woman is ready to talk to a female officer does she finally reveal that she recognized a man that she had not seen for decades. The old respectable bourgeois man was once in Algeria, during the war. He raped her. She was sixteen.

What could be the end of the secret, however, is only the beginning of legal problems for the detectives and an opportunity for the episode to bring up an issue that is rarely discussed in popular culture: that of the law of amnesty adopted after the war. When the man refuses to take responsibility, like George in *Caché*, the detectives turn to their superior to see what the law authorizes them to do. And in a scene designed to make his colleagues' frustration palpable if not contagious, he explains why it is absolutely out of the question to bring up the issue of the rape. Not because there is no evidence, but because the culprit is protected by the law of amnesty. The law, adopted on 31 July 1968 (# 68–697), stipulates that 'sont amnistiées de plein droit toutes infractions commises en relation avec les événements d'Algérie' [all crimes committed in connection with the Algerian events are fully amnestied] and this includes 'toutes infractions commises par des militaires servant en Algérie' [any crime committed by soldiers serving in Algeria].[12] The episode does not go into depth but the officer's allusion to the law is sufficiently clear for viewers to understand what is at stake. Even if they are not familiar with the details of the legal saga that developed after the war, they will now be in a position to read the title of the episode very differently. 'Erreurs de jeunesse' will, in retrospect sound bitter and cynically ironic given that the 'mistake' in question would be a crime were it not for the law that protects the culprit. The fact that the description of the act now sounds horribly euphemistic reflects and critiques the way in which crimes committed during the Algerian war were historically dealt with. Even revelations are useless. The inspectors are powerless and so is the rape victim. The culprit can get away with the exonerating narrative alibi: war did it. Just as problematically perhaps, he (and others) are offered no alternative story should he choose to accept responsibility.

If nothing more happened in that episode, however, the viewer might wonder if *P.J. Saint Martin* is arguing that scrutinizing the colonial past is dangerous: it does not repair any harm and only contributes to unnecessary flare-ups of violence. Far from contributing to a peaceful conflict resolution, the detectives have disclosed the truth only to reveal how powerless they are to offer any kind of compensation, legal or symbolic reparation, to the victim. The past is not repaired. But the way in which the story ends does propose a resolution of sorts. It both takes into account the absence of any possible reparation and suggests that some forms of disclosure have a different kind of reparative power. They may not help the individuals who suffered from institutionalized injustice but they affect the fabric of the nation and the definition of Frenchness. To those who argue that an emphasis on past conflicts can only make social divisions more acute, the episode suggests that there is a difference between what reparation means for one woman or for the nation as a whole.

The last scene of the episode can be analysed as a second narrative closure provided to counteract, yet not cancel out, the consequences of the law of amnesty. If the history of the legal system prevents the detectives from articulating a script that places the woman in the position of the raped victim and the man in that of the accused, fiction authorizes the multiplication of possible endings that exist on different paradigmatic levels. The second ending has to do with the power of visual signals, which will supplement the story of powerless knowledge told by the detective.

Towards the end of the episode, the man and the woman are still at the police station, together, in separate rooms. They will be released almost at the same time, and therefore forced to share the same public space once again, at least for a little while. They are both sent home and, for the viewers, it is now clear that this 'home' must include both of them even if their physical and emotional proximity has nothing to do with a harmonious relationship. That they share, knowingly, the same (national) space is something that forever separates them. They will never be the individualized allegory of the Franco-Algerian couple: the violence of what went on between them foreclosed what we may first interpret as sexual intimacy. The rape put cruelty and humiliation in the place of any (symbolic or real) sex. But it matters that they are portrayed as characters who know that it is the case and that we are in the position of witnesses who do not misinterpret the women's screams as noise or incomprehensible anger.

We also witness, at that particular moment, the difference between the ways in which both characters will inhabit the space that they must share. This departure from the space of the police station functions as a sort of counter-destiny. A colonial war had put these two individuals in the same narrative, another plausible scenario had separated them via markers of class and social status: she was the cleaner, he was the owner of a house. As viewers, we understand why they had never met again, even if they apparently lived in the same area. But the episode stretches that horizon of verisimilitude by suggesting that their common past has, in a sense, caught up with them, with us. Without explaining why it happens at this particular historical juncture, the episode reflects on the current moment of memory that makes it possible to study the consequences of colonial history when talking about the here and now.

A new element is now introduced into the story. We discover that the woman has a son and the way in which this new figure is inserted into the narrative is worth a detailed analysis. Visually and symbolically, the fact that the father (who did not know he was a father), the woman and their son are all united and then immediately separated is a striking statement that forces us to think about issues of gender, generations, genealogy and memorial narratives. The man leaves alone, protected by the law, but followed by the detectives' obvious disapproval and contempt. The legal code, it is suggested, has become, if not obsolete, at least contestable. A wedge has been inserted between our sense of justice and what now appears to be the specific historical legacy of the mentality that prevailed during the war. Socially, the man has been changed; he was stripped of his supposedly obvious respectability and innocence. The white bourgeois womanizer was not only an old Don Juan whose mistresses come and go. We discover, in this last scene, that he was a biological father, he has a son, whose existence refutes any claim that the national ethnos is monolithic.

The woman, on the other hand, does not leave the police station alone. Someone picks her up, her son, a grown man who has come to help. The spectator immediately knows that the new character is her son but also the rapist's because he is encoded as having inherited a visible trace of his father's genome: in case any doubt remained in any of the protagonists' minds (including ours), the camera forces us to notice that the son's face bears the same remarkable birth mark as Lionel Dumont, the rapist. What seemed to be an irrelevant detail of the older actor's face is now reinterpreted as a constructed sign, which functions within the diegesis. Both actors were made up to have a similar red patch on their faces. The woman, when questioned, had made an allusion to the large red patch on the man she had attacked, claiming that she had recognized that distinctive sign. But when the son appears, the type of 'recognition' that she mentions opens up a whole array of theoretical issues that the programme can smuggle in through the effect of surprise. The woman recognized a man who did not recognize his son in the symbolic order. The type of 'physical resemblance' that the episode constructs is both biological (it is inscribed on the body) and symbolic: it is such a rare and unique mark that it functions like the signature of kinship, although the traditional definition of kinship is of course problematized.

Here, what matters is that the son is not ethnicized: the issue is not to insist on a new hyphenated or hybrid generation (a 'Beur' look). Paradoxically, his physical appearance emphasizes the biological heritage (the birth mark) but not the type of markers that are sometimes expressed in terms of phenotype or ethnic bodily features.[13] The issue of 'passing', which involves performing so as not to correspond to the racist's stereotype, a process often thematized in Beur literature, is completely absent here: the son is not being denied entry by a racist discotheque bouncer, he is not dyeing his hair like the heroes of Begag's novels or of *Michou d'Auber*.[14]

We know that whoever comes to pick up this woman at the station will probably be a close relative, and given the man's age and demeanour we simply assume that this is about filial love. What is never assumed is that the process of recognition will have to involve more than the mother and her child. The distinctive patch of colour, which symbolically functions as a stain, or even a scar, forever keeps the trace of what happened but also slightly changes the ways in which we can interpret what happened. On the more gruesome side, the presence of the son makes it undeniable that the act of violence did take place, and that it was sexual, as was often the case during the war of Algeria, and as is often the case during wars in general. The spectre of Djamila Boupacha looms large here. Furthermore, the presence of the marked son makes it impossible to entertain the illusion that the rape happened in the past and can be contained there, as if it were a choice to look back, to actively resurrect something that is dead or to exhume something that was buried. The presence of the child deconstructs the opposition between living in the present and looking at the past. Relegating the past to 'another country' is impossible and the present is not safely cordoned off.

Looking at the child means looking at the future and the past at the very same moment. The metaphor of the archaeologist who digs up old sedimentary layers so that new discoveries may help us deal with a reconfigured surface is not appropriate here. Nor does the episode implicitly define fiction as the equivalent of burial rites and healing commemoration. An interesting intertextual dialogue thus develops between this type of story and Assia Djebar, whose novels are based on a theoretical and fictional reflection of such a paradigm. In *La Femme sans sépulture*, the raped woman is a *moudjahida* who dies at the hand of paratroopers and her daughter's life is destroyed by an endless search for the missing grave. Here, the woman did not die. The issue is not whether it is counterintuitively less respectful to give her a proper burial place or let the tortured body rot in the sun and tell its poetic tale of grief (the dead woman speaks about 'des heures ensoleillées qui m'avaient rendue bourdonnante et fertile' [the hours of sunshine which made me buzz with fertility] (Djebar, 2002, 207)). In *P.J. Saint Martin*, the woman's body becomes 'fertile' in a different, perhaps more traditional way. She bears a child. But the son and therefore the rape can never be separated from any of the aspects of her present and daily life. The son's face is the face of the violence done to her. Yet, if his physical appearance is constructed to make him a walking piece of evidence, his attitude reassures us that the rape victim has become a loving mother whose child is here to support if not protect her.

From the point of view of his father, the issue of recognition functions in a different way. It has been established that he could not be legally punished and he is still capable of dismissing his act as something that was normal within the parameters of the war. In other words, as long as he can contain the rape within the borders of a certain temporal and physical territory (back then, over there), he does not have to address the issue. But the physical presence of his son, and the fact that he recognizes him as such because of what they share, makes a number of points that no character needs to talk about. No dialogue accompanies the scene. It is for us and them to draw a conclusion about the long delay and about the present. The man and spectator discover that a sort of symbolic investment was growing, without him knowing about it. Symbolically, national memory has come of age, marked, identifiable as the son. He is suddenly confronted not by something that happened to them in the past and that can now, once again, be put in perspective, but by the fact that his present is forever habited by a witness, a human who is the embodiment of his crime. There is no over there or back then.

The borders between the past and the present and between Europe and its others have been upset. What Arjun Appadurai calls 'the fundamental, and dangerous, idea behind the very idea of the modern nation-state, the idea of a national ethnos' (2006, 3) is rewritten by the fact that the woman has been raising this son on French soil. Nothing allows us to determine whether the characters are citizens or not (the film does not ask for their passports), but the narrative does treat them as perfect insiders of a lively neighbourhood.

The deciphering codes that allowed us to deal with the episode have thus been changed. The efforts that the detectives deployed in order to to understand were a first indication that parameters were different. It has been made clear that disclosing does not repair past traumas: when one looks back, one can bang one's head against the wall of how history was constructed to protect, legally, the dominant. Even if they can be proven to be guilty, they are untouchable, which seems like a most pessimistic conclusion, one that will perhaps comfort those who claim to be against 'repentance'. Even from the victim's point of view, what is the point of remembering a past that can only reactivate pain and suffering? In a sense, the woman is raped a second time around, taken to hospital, where she undergoes another ordeal. The denunciation is illegal and all she does is create a situation where people are going to suspect and hate each other. On the other hand, the son's strong physical presence and its visually obvious yet unnarrativized effects on the father re-establish a number of parameters that are far from fatalistic. The presence of the child shows that social order was disturbed much more seriously than by two individuals who had a fight, and the episode manages to historicize and de-individualize the issue without resorting to simple identity politics. The officers' investigation creates a narrative whose reparative function is that it bursts the temporal and spatial bubble that the man counted on. The *lieu de mémoire*, or perhaps more accurately the moment of memory, is reinterpreted: we do not have to either include or exclude the past because the social fabric has already been 'fractured' so that our present is already hybridized by the violence of the colonial past. But even if this hybridity is the opposite of some multicultural utopia, it does not amount to social disintegration.

The son, who survived, who picks up his mother, contains both histories. He is obviously not the only human to occupy this position and the terrible possibility that he may be paradigmatic rather than exceptional of any supposedly 'national ethnic' character is part of what the episode proposes as reparative critique, in spite of its own inability to fantasize about a better distribution of justice.

The episode functions as a representative fictional microcosm of the ongoing debate about the direct role that national memory plays in the evolving definitions of Frenchness, in the norms of daily conduct that govern French society, and in the policies that the government can or must implement to take into account the dominant narrative that each moment of memory imposes as the norm. The past is a story that we weave with the type of material that contemporary norms authorize us to use. The episode that focuses on the unresolved issues of situations that no longer need to be disclosed reveals the limits and borders of that moment of memory. The contours of what France is today are enabled and limited by the possible pasts that are recognizable and addressed. The complex mechanism that brings the colonial past to the fore is not a simple linear and temporal process that replaces one layer of memory with a more recent one. Several pasts are now entangled.

Silence is not the default position any more; in fact, silence may be taboo today. And even the voices that resist what could be called the postcolonialization of French society suggest that the paradigm is no longer emergent.[15] It has emerged. Postcolonial narratives, however, do not constitute a monolithic block that could easily be turned into a new national myth, as the episode about two individuals caught up in an inseparable present-past demonstrates. In the episode, something remains to be done. Nothing is solved and an element of irreparability resists any attempt at fictionalization.

This episode both exemplifies and recaps a conversation that reveals what is at stake when public voices either welcome or reject the seemingly unstoppable flow of testimonies and images about how the Algerian war and France's colonial past echo in the present. The instrumentalization of history and the evolution of national identity are linked. This episode confirms that history is always at least partially instrumentalized, if by that we mean that contemporary memorial narratives have different logics and different agendas. They both reflect and construct the way in which France gives an account of what it is necessary to remember, and in doing so they also establish the current borders around, or characteristics of, Frenchness itself.

Yet a number of new phenomena seem to have provided the French with a historical New Deal. At the beginning of the twenty-first century, the legacies of the Second World War and of the colonial past have become intertwined, whether one period is used to talk about the other or even sometimes to avoid talking about the other.[16] Regardless of individual trajectories, one specific aspect creates a strong connection between the memory of the Second World War and of the wars of decolonization. The point is not that both periods are comparable (talking about the Holocaust would lead precisely to questions about incommensurability). But contemporary critics do not even have to compare the two periods to notice the ways in which the nation has dealt with memory and commemorations. In both cases, post-war reconstructions evolved radically. A long period of silence was followed by a proliferation of narratives, of historical interventions whose effects on the national community are perceived as either beneficent (trauma is being worked through) or dangerously divisive (the truth turns the community into hostile descendants of victims or perpetrators). There is a direct relationship between the way in which history is told and the way in which the nation sees itself, in terms of who belongs and who does not but, perhaps even more accurately, of who is a victim and who is not, and of whom.

In the decades that followed the Second World War, France had slowly and painfully to learn to deal with the different stages of a process of collective and individual memorization. The most traumatic aspects of the conflict would remain shrouded in traumatized silence for many more years to come, and different, quasi-mythic narratives were successfully constructed and rejected. Historians have since then meticulously analysed how the heroic or demonized figures were used to build a coherent narrative whose collective meaning changed depending on whether resistance or collaboration were highlighted or downplayed. Both the *résistant* and the *collaborateur* were insiders who could not be put at a distance. The nation's core had to grapple with the narrative. The figure of the veteran, who comes back from afar and has to be re-integrated as if he or she had become a stranger to the nation that was at war raises very different issues, and in the case of Algeria it was possible to see the war as what was happening to other (different types of French) people on the other side of the Mediterranean. But as soon as the nation finds it impossible to police the border that it has erected between the former enemies (the feared fellagha but also the victim of torture), the national and the stranger, the conscripts and the civilian, the nation finds itself, once again, confronted by narratives that link the construction of the past with the construction of Frenchness.

When narratives compete about the colonial past, and especially about the ways in which the memory of past conflicts influences the present, they serve different, sometimes unformulated, agendas: the story about the past does something to the nation if the nation reads such accounts as something that promotes national reconciliation or conversely that has a divisive influence. What this study on the 'reparative' has sought to demonstrate is that this opposition leads to sterile debates and that there is a way out of such binaries.

Some stories are productive and fruitful in their way of posing the problem. They provide us with a different type of historical vantage point. When the reparative energy succeeds, it is capable of turning the silent victim into an agent. Here, the woman (who should be the quintessential Spivakian subaltern) is a witness who cannot be heard in a court of law. The reparative aspect is not so much the moment when we (perhaps condescendingly) choose to listen to her because we suspect that she is actually speaking, making a claim that some level of translation could turn into a rational sentence. It is rather the moment when the citizen who is in control of the language and of the legal discourse starts realizing that his or her position is what constructs the other as someone who, no matter what, can only hope to be translated into my own set of codes and laws, brought over into my way of understanding the world.

Notes

Introduction

1 In 2000, Jay Winter was talking about a 'memory boom' (Winter, 2000). See Andreas Huyssen's analysis of the acceleration of this tendency after the 1980s in Europe and the United States. According to Huyssen, 'one of the most surprising cultural and political phenomena of recent years has been the emergence of memory as a key concern in Western Society, a turning toward the past that stands in stark contrast to the privileging of the future so characteristic of earlier decades of twentieth-century modernity' (2000, 21).

2 Sometimes the choice of seemingly transparent language embeds a text in a layer of historical sediment. In retrospect, the difference between 'les événements en Algérie' [events in Algeria] and 'la guerre d'Algérie' [the Algerian war] is obvious – the latter is officialized at the very end of the twentieth century. But we may not be so sensitive to the difference between 'the Algerian war' (seen from a French perspective) and 'the war of independence' (seen from an Algerian perspective). Moreover, as long as no alternative formulation presents itself, we may remain blind to the ideological implications of the currently acceptable formulation.

3 See the identificatory power of 'nostalgérie' for the community of repatriated European settlers who form the 'pied-noir' community in France. For a study of the link between 'nostalgeria' and the type of collective mourning that develops in pied-noir associations or informal gatherings, see Jordi, 2002, 21–22.

4 See, for example, Michael Ann Holly's intriguing analysis of why, 'in general, the discipline of art history is eternally fated to be a melancholic one' (Holly, 2003, 177).

5 See Terdiman's illuminating analysis of how a nineteenth-century journal (*Le Charivari*) responded to censorship: when a caricature attacking the new law on censorship was banned from publication, *Le Charivari* published a blank page bordered by a funereal frame and described, elsewhere, in a textual space, what the forbidden drawing represented. While many of the books and films analysed here make use of similar tactics of displacement, they are not necessarily opposing one dominant

paradigm, here the state's definition of what can be said (Terdiman, 1985, especially Chapter 3: 'Counter-images: Daumier and *le Charivari*', 149–197). In the context of memory, counter-discourses sometimes take the place of discourse and the contested space does not boil down to a binary tension between powerful and minority positions of enunciation.

6 'Repentance' emphasizes the always unfinished process of repenting. In a deconstructive perspective on forgiveness, that impossibility of ever putting an end to the process would probably be the ethical moment par excellence, but this is obviously a problem for any political leader.

7 Nicolas Bancel and Pascal Blanchard suggest that this manifesto demonstrates that 'Pour lui, il est évident que l'*histoire* doit fortifier la *mémoire* de la Nation – ou l'inverse on ne sait plus très bien – et fabriquer du mythe républicain. L'histoire a une fonction instrumentale, qui ne saurait être remise en question par des problématiques par trop déstabilisantes ou périphériques, facteurs de "communautarismes". Or, à ses yeux, l'histoire coloniale pose problème, car elle est "à risque". Il voit donc dans les recherches sur les "violences coloniales", ou celles articulant périodes coloniales et postcoloniales, un danger imminent: que "la France s'agenouille". Or, si "nous" acceptons de "nous" culpabiliser, précise-t-il, nous serons livrés "aux bandes communautaires"' (Bancel and Blanchard, 2007, 132). [It is clear to him that history must strengthen the nation's history – or maybe is it the other way around – and construct the Republican myth. History has an instrumental function that should not be put in question by destabilizing or marginal problematics, which cause 'communitarism'. He views colonial history as 'high risk'. And research on 'colonial violence' or on the articulation between colonial and postcolonial eras pose an imminent threat: France will be 'on its knees'. And if 'we' accept guilt, then we will be at the mercy of communitarian groups] (Bancel and Blanchard, 2007, 44–45).

8 The goal is not to salvage 'repentance' by using it in the same manner as Negritude poets have re-appropriated 'nègre' or GLTB critics the word 'queer'.

9 It was President Chirac who adopted the phrase 'la fracture sociale' during an electoral campaign and the formula later evolved, becoming the 'colonial fracture' when Nicolas Bancel, Pascal Blanchard and Sandrine Lemaire published their book in 2005.

10 *La Guerre des mémoires* [a memorial war] is the title of one of Benjamin Stora's books (Stora and Leclere, 2007).

11 Bracher refers to a round table entitled 'La France malade de son passé colonial' [France affected by colonial-past disease] organized on 17 October 2005 in the context of 'Les Rendez-vous de l'histoire' [Encounters with history] in Blois. The panel was led by Antoine de Baecque, a journalist for the Parisian newspaper *Libération*, and featured journalists

Philippe Cohen and Hervé Nathan, along with professors Pap Ndiaye from the EHESS (École des Hautes Études en Sciences Sociales) and Françoise Vergès from the University of London. See Bracher, 2007, 69 <http://www. clionautes.org/spip.php?article879> (accessed 30 May 2008).

12 For a series of articles whose authors meticulously counter this postcolonial phobia, see the special issue of the journal *Mouvements*, entitled *Qui a peur du postcolonial* and more specifically the editors' introduction (Cohen et al., 2007).

13 And yet melancholia and its role in postcolonial societies has been carefully and productively documented by scholars such as Gilroy (2004) and Cheng (2000), works that the debate organized around the word 'repentance' does not seem able to take into account.

14 As usual, many intellectuals reacted to Sarkozy's declarations or perhaps to their theatricality. One of the first public figures to respond negatively was Simone Weil (she called the proposal 'unimaginable, unbearable and unfair' [Cédelle, 2008]), and when her opinion was relayed, newspapers such as *Le Monde* made sure to emphasize her previous experience as a deportee and the fact that she is the honorary Director of the Foundation for the Memory of the Shoah (Cédelle, 2008).

15 One of the first memorial laws was passed on 30 June 1990. Dubbed the 'loi Gayssot', it makes it a crime to deny the existence of crimes against humanity (and it is used against negationists). Immediately historians objected, claiming that the government should stay out of their field and refrain from policing history. Pierre Vidal-Naquet, who spent his life fighting against *Les Assassins de la mémoire*, declared, in an interview granted to *Libération*: 'Je vomis les négationnistes. Mais j'ai toujours été contre la loi Gayssot. Ce n'est pas à l'Etat de dire comment on enseigne l'histoire.' [Negationists make me throw up. But I have always been against the Gayssot Law. The state should not tell us how to teach history.] (Vidal-Naquet, 2005).

16 Law # 99–882 (18 October 1999). <http://www.legifrance.gouv. fr/affichTexte.do;jsessionid=1954713AE2098D75CD172F61DFFBCC68. tpdjo07v_2?cidTexte=LEGITEXT000005628635&dateTexte=> (accessed 5 May 2008).

17 'Liberté pour l'histoire' [freedom for history], petition signed by Jean-Pierre Azéma, Elisabeth Badinter, Jean-Jacques Becker, Françoise Chandernagor, Alain Decaux, Marc Ferro, Jacques Julliard, Jean Leclant, Pierre Milza, Pierre Nora, Mona Ozouf, Jean-Claude Perrot, Antoine Prost, René Rémond, Maurice Vaïsse, Jean-Pierre Vernant, Paul Veyne, Pierre Vidal-Naquet and Michel Winock, published in *Libération* 13 December 2005 <http://www.liberation.fr> (accessed 25 May 2008).

18 'Loi 2005–158 du 23 février 2005 portant reconnaissance de la Nation et contribution nationale en faveur des Français rapatriés' [Law

2005–158, 23 February 2005, recognizing the nation's gratitude and national contribution in favour of French repatriates]. <http://www.legifrance.gouv. fr/html/actualite/actualite_legislative/decrets_application/2005-158.htm> (accessed 30 May 2008).

19 Another title by Rousso, *La Hantise du passé*, lets us imagine reverse case scenarios in which the French title contains a reparative impulse that a non-literal translation might counteract. Like 'working through', the French word *hantise* pulls in two directions and a translator may wish to highlight, in a footnote, the lack of a perfect overlap between the French word 'hantise' and the English word 'haunting'. If 'hantise' does evoke a potentially poetic and uncontrollable haunting, a sort of Derridean hauntology that will generate narratives and perhaps promote reparative energy, the word also means something else in a more colloquial register. A 'hantise' when applied to going to the dentist, to losing your keys, involves relatively strong anticipatory anxiety, a type of worrying or obsessive fear that has nothing to do with ghosts or with the kind of traumatic events that Rousso writes about in his book. Those who object to a certain type of political instrumentalization of the past might choose to translate Rousso's title as 'Obsessed with repentance'. They would privilege, in *hantise*, the idea that someone is taking too seriously an undesirable and irrational fear. Compare the effect thus produced to Ralph Schoolcraft's decision to render *La Hantise du passé* as *The Haunting Past* which, admittedly, cannot accommodate the first connotation but proposes to name the relationship between the past and the present, recognizing that the past does something to the present to render it haunted.

20 For reflections on the way in which reparation can be productively defined in the case of the Holocaust and of descendants of slaves, see Brooks, 1999 and 2004. See also Antoine Garapon's plea in favour of a supranational (European) paradigm and his discussion of mutual 'désend-ettement' [de-owing] through politics (Garapon, 2008).

21 Anne Rigney observes (and critiques) the power of what she calls the '"original plenitude and subsequent loss" model. This involves looking at memory as something that is fully formed in the past (it was once "all there" in the plenitude of experience, as it were) and as something that is subsequently a matter of preserving and keeping alive' (Rigney, 2005, 12). She favours instead a 'social constructivist model that takes as its starting point the idea that memories of a shared past are collectively constructed and reconstructed in the present rather than resurrected from the past' (14).

22 After all, the past may well be beyond reparation and the relationship between the reparative and the irreparable may resemble the link that Jacques Derrida makes between forgiveness and the unforgivable: '... it is necessary, it seems to me, to begin from the fact that yes, there is the

unforgivable. Is this not, in truth, the only thing to forgive?' (Derrida, 2001, 40).

23 Even though some of the narrators were witnesses of the events they remember, Marianne Hirsch's analyses of 'postmemory' are relevant here (1997).

Chapter One

1 In his 2007 novel, *L'Allumeur de rêves berbères*, the narrator is a writer whose manuscript radically changes after he and his friend receive death threats in the mail. Like Boudjedra's *La Vie à l'endroit*, Fellag documents the destructuring effects that the letters have on his characters' lives and on their ability to tell a story. The tale of unspeakable violence is told ahead of time, imagined by a protagonist whose time is literally out of joint. Unlike Boudjedra's text, however, Fellag's fragmented novel is not a tragedy and its heroes are portrayed with the same tender humour as those of the stage performances. The writer's perception is affected by alcohol abuse and nightmares, but both are interpreted as antidotes to madness and not as its unavoidable effects. As in Ehni's work, the narrative is sane, even if the events that it represents are not.

2 *Le dernier chameau* toured France for more than a year in 2004. *Le dernier chameau et autres histoires* [The Last Camel and other stories] was also published by JC Lattès in 2004. For more information on the show, see <http://www.theatreonline.com/guide/detail_piece.asp?i_Region=0&i_Programmation=10254&i_Genre=0&i_Origine=&i_Type=> (accessed 5 September 2007).

3 The French plays on the graphic resemblance between *concis* (concise) and *circoncis* (circumcised).

4 For a discussion of how the inheritance of the 'Gauls' vs. 'Franks' is the object of a constant cultural traffic, see Weber's first chapter ('Nos ancêtres les gaulois', Weber, 1991, 21–39).

5 See *Djurdjurassique Bled*, where he singles out a few words, asks the audience to 'repeat after him', then goes on to produce a complete sentence in Arabic before adding, to his bilingual audience's delight, that this material will be covered at the level of the 'doctorate' (Fellag, 1999, 51).

6 In *Ces Voix qui m'assiègent ... en marge de ma francophonie*, Djebar talks about 'Trois langues auxquelles s'accouple un quatrième langage: celui du corps avec ses danses ses transes, ses suffocations ...' (Djebar, 1999, 14).

7 See the end of the chapter entitled, 'Pour l'opacité', in *Poétique de la Relation*: 'Nous réclamons pour tous le droit à l'opacité' [We claim the right to opacity for all] (Glissant, 1990, 209).

8 In a portrait of the artist included in the published version of another of his shows, *Djurdjurassique Bled*, Pierre Lartigue writes that in Arabic, the name Fellag means 'bûcheron, coupeur de routes. Au figuré, bandit de grand chemin' [lumberjack, road cutter. Figuratively: highway man or highway robber] (Fellag, 1999, 95). We do not need to know this or even to believe that it is accurate to appreciate Fellag's work, and the meaning of the artist's proper name does not have to matter. But like 'French' and 'maghreb', Fellag is here presented as a linguistic unit whose translation into French raises potentially interesting questions. The explanation quoted above is part of a public portrait, printed at the beginning of one of the books that he signed. Fellag encourages us to imagine him as someone who stands in the middle of the road. Moreover, depending on whether we are in the literal or the figurative mood, the 'cutting' involved may be deemed legitimate or illegitimate.

9 For the 'oppositional' value of such practices, including the creation of a unique city map by pedestrians who cut across buildings, see Chambers, 1991, 6–7.

10 But here is another messy tunnel since 'bled', the derogatory reference to a backward village, is also 'bilad', the native land and the nation that the memory of the war of liberation glorifies.

11 Emily Apter notes (and deplores) that this tends to add canonical value to books that are 'translation-friendly (in a market sense)' and contributes to a widening of the gap between what is thought of as 'standard' and 'minor' languages (Apter, 2001, 65).

12 That a booby-trapped car was the cause of Abdiche's death now sounds like a horrifically ironic conclusion to his attempts at talking some sense into the typical Algerian driver.

13 To the extent that the representation of an insult already takes place in a book or on stage, Austin would eliminate this instance from the category of the performative, but I am arguing here that there is a doubly parasitical structure: within the diegesis, the insult cannot function as such. Austin warns his readers that '... a performative utterance will, for example, be *in peculiar way* hollow or void if said by an actor on the stage, or if introduced in a poem, or spoken in soliloquy ... Language in such circumstances is in special ways – intelligibly – used not seriously, but in ways *parasitic* upon its normal use ways which fall under the doctrine of the *etiolations* of language' (Austin, 1975, 22).

14 Dominique Caubet talks about 'contemporary creations' by popular artists and her interviewers included Algerian cartoonists such Gyps or Slim, raï singers, playwrights or stand-up comics.

15 *Mythologies* appeared during the Algerian war and more specifically at the end of what is now known as 'the Battle of Algiers'. Barthes criticizes the hypocrisy of a colonial regime that implicitly congratulates

itself through the representation of a proud soldier whose eagerness to serve is supposed to contradict those who worry that he is at the service of his oppressors (Barthes ironically refers to the 'zèle de ce noir à servir ses prétendus oppresseurs' [zeal shown by this Negro in serving his so-called oppressors] (Barthes, 1957, 223; 1972, 116).

16 As readers or spectators, we must therefore decide just how problematic this structure is for us: do 'we' belong to Fellag's 'we' or to his 'vous'?

17 Once again, 'quasi-national' would be more accurate since his definition of the 'nation' refers to the Maghreb of his ancestors. The whole region functions here as the equivalent of France.

18 On the issue of reading silence as 'an alternative form of political engagement', see Palladino and Moreira, 2006.

19 Introduced during the debate over the 'General Agreement on Tariffs and Trade' at the end of the 1980s, the principle of 'cultural exception' sought to exclude audiovisual services and productions from a purely commercial agreement. The concept has always been controversial and continues to be used in the larger debate that divides proponents and detractors of globalization.

20 The original expression is usually attributed to Jean-Yves Le Gallou, theoretician of the extreme right Front National party.

21 Preliminary versions of this chapter were presented at the Institute of European Studies at the University of California in March 2005 (See: 'Jay translation, ki ma qal Abdiche' <http://repositories.cdlib.org/ies/050324/>). A French version of the second part of the chapter was published as 'Fellag: plat national et demande d'amour subliminale', *Neue Romania* 33 (2005): 253–66. I thank Isaac Bazié (UQAM) and Peter Klaus (FU Berlin) for their invitation and the journal for permission to republish.

Chapter Two

1 For a list of René-Nicolas Ehni's publications, see the bibliography.

2 After the so-called 'journée des tomates' in February 1956, when Guy Mollet, then Prime Minister, was greeted by angry *pied-noir* demonstrators during his visit to Algeria, a decision was made to recall conscripts and to extend the period of military service from 18 to 27 months. The lives of half a million men and that of their families were directly affected and forever altered.

3 On Jean-Paul Sartre and Simone de Beauvoir's involvement, see Cohen, 2003; Cohen-Solal, 1998; Rioux and Sirinelli, 1991, 115–35. On the different networks that helped the NLF in France, see Hamon and Rotman, 1979.

4 See the volumes published by Autrement in 2000, especially Jean-Charles Jauffret's *Soldats en Algérie 1954–1962* (2000).

5 From that point of view, Ehni's work is closer to the texts written by Hélène Cixous (1997a; 1997b; 2000) or even Jacques Derrida (1996) about Algeria, although neither Derrida nor Cixous can be said to make a specific contribution to the memory of conscripts.

6 The most famous and controversial case in point is the book published by the late Paul Aussaresses (2001), a former general who continued to insist that torture had been justified during the war. But his position is the exception to the rule. Even Jacques Massu, the general who was in charge of the so-called Battle of Algiers and who died the year *Algérie roman* was published, had reacted to Aussaresses's statements and publicly declared that he regretted his role during the war. Even if his remorse comes too late for some commentators (Lamloum, 2002), the evolution of his position is well worth noticing, especially if we compare his last interviews to the book that he had published in 1971 (Massu, *La vraie bataille d'Alger*) and to which Vidal-Naquet had responded, one year later, with *La Torture dans la République* (Vidal-Naquet, 1972). See also Vidal-Naquet's *Les Crimes de l'armée française* (1975; 2001) and Labib's documentary (1987).

7 See Jean-Luc Godard's *Le Petit soldat* (1961), Alain Resnais's *Muriel ou le temps d'un retour* (1961), René Vautier's *Avoir vingt ans dans l'Aurès* (1971) or Yves Boisset's *R.A.S.* (1973).

8 See Laurent Herbiet's *Mon Colonel* (2006) or François Luciani's historical saga *L'Algérie des chimères* (2001).

9 For a comparative study of how films represent and construct wars and national memory in the United States and in France, see Stora, 1997b.

10 See *Le Monde*, 9 March 2002, 'La Torture en Algérie' <www.lemonde.fr> (accessed 16 October 2007).

11 At the time, Philippe Bernard began his article in *Le Monde* with a classic 'Ils ont fini par franchir le mur du silence. Pour la première fois depuis quarante ans, des militaires parlent à la télévision de l'indicible: la torture pendant la guerre d'Algérie.' [They finally broke the wall of silence. For the first time in forty years, soldiers talk about the unspeakable on television: torture during the Algerian war.] (Bernard, 2002). Such statements are less and less plausible after 2000.

12 'Si Manni se regarde vivre, il le fait exprès. Si ce vaurien se borne à faire des choses 'définitives' – à acheter des pulls, par exemple ce n'est que depuis la guerre en Algérie, depuis le moment où il a vu des meurtres inutiles, gratuits, sans rien faire pour protester contre le crime.' [If Manni observes his own life, he does so deliberately. This good-for-nothing only performs so-called 'definitive' actions – such as buying sweaters for example, but he only started after the Algerian war, a moment during which he witnessed useless, gratuitous murders, without doing anything to protest against the atrocity.] (Maples, 669–70).

13 The authors of the Internet site that introduces him to advertise

his play *Heïdi est partout* refers to the beginning of his career as his 'époque *"mode"*, glorifié par la compagnie de Jean-Paul Sartre, même si ou justement parce que, comme l'écrivit Simone de Beauvoir, il était *"irrécupérable par l'ordre théâtral"* et par quelque ordre que ce fût' [his fashionable period, glamorized by Jean-Paul Sartre's proximity, even if, or precisely because, as Simone de Beauvoir wrote, it was 'impossible for the theatrical order or any order at all, for that matter, to reappropriate him'] (<http://www.theatre-contemporain.net/spectacles/heidi_est_partout/> [accessed 10 October 2007]).

14 Even if the details of their position have not always reached the general public, one of the currently accepted stories is that Sartre's and Albert Camus's divergences marked the end of their friendship (Cohen-Solal, 1998).

15 Remarkably, *France-Observateur* confronted the issue of torture long before what is now considered to be the beginning of the war of independence in 1954 (Claude Bourdet, a former Resistant, asked 'Y-a-t-il une Gestapo en Algérie?' as early as 1951 before dissociating himself, in January 1955, from a 'we' that tortures in 'Votre Gestapo d'Algérie').

16 *Une embellie perdue*, which appeared in 1995, relates the details of the campaign that preceded Halimi's election to the National Assembly shortly after François Mitterrand became the French president in 1981 (Halimi, 1995, 204).

17 The name of the author's native village, Eschentzwiller (Sundgau), recurs in many of his texts, and in *Algérie roman* the narrator remembers that he wrote 'Alsagériens' on the first page of an anthology of German poetry that he was reading while on duty (Ehni, 2002, 98).

18 See Mouloud Feraoun's *Journal*. In December 1955 Feraoun pointed out that French anti-colonialists express a type of 'fraternity that comes too late': 'Nos amis français ou plus simplement nos camarades voudraient nous voir leur manifester une cordialité démonstrative qu'ils n'eussent jamais souhaitée naguère et ils étaient prêts à extérioriser pour nous des sentiments de fraternité qui, en d'autres temps, nous eussent profondément touchés et définitivement conquis. Nous ne sentions derrière ces tentatives aucune espèce d'hypocrisie.' [Our French friends or even our acquaintances would like to see us demonstrate a cordiality that they used to deem undesirable, and they were ready to express feelings of brotherhood that, previously, would have deeply touched us and definitively won us over. These attempts now smacked of hypocrisy.] (Feraoun, 1990, 23). Later, he talks of a 'brutal divorce' (47). See also Jules Roy's autobiographical narrative *Etranger pour mes frères* (1982). Assia Djebar's and Kateb Yacine's novels often allegorize the separation between France and Algeria as the end of a love story (see Djebar's *Les Nuits de Strasbourg* [1997a] or *Oran langue morte* [1997b] and Kateb's *Nedjma* [1956]).

19 Speech delivered on 16 July 1995 by Jacques Chirac, then President of the Republic, during the memorial to the victims of the round-up of the Vel d'Hiv in July 1942: 'La France, patrie des Lumières et des Droits de l'Homme, terre d'accueil et d'asile, la France, ce jour-là, accomplissait l'irréparable. Manquant à sa parole, elle livrait ses protégés à leurs bourreaux.' [France, the land of the Enlightenment and of human rights, the land of asylum and hospitality, that day, France committed the irreparable. Betraying its promise, it handed its children over to the executioners.] <http://www.elysee.fr/elysee/francais/interventions/discours_et_declarations/1995/juillet/allocution_de_m_jacques_chirac_president_de_la_republique_prononcee_lors_des_ceremonies_commemorant_la_grande_rafle_des_16_et_17_juillet_1942-paris.2503.html> (accessed 11 October 2007).

20 See Georges Didi-Huberman's analysis of the four photographs that the members of a Sonderkommando managed to take inside the camp of Auschwitz-Birkenau in 1944 (Didi-Huberman, 2003).

21 This narrative technique goes beyond an already difficult denunciation of the systematic occurrence of rape during the war of independence. The narrator writes as though it were obvious, as if we had always already known. On the frequency and banalization of rape during the war, see Michèle Bacholle-Boskovic's study of Beauvoir (1963) (Bacholle-Boskovic, 2003), Beauvoir and Halimi (1962), Delpard (2001), Sigg (1989) and Pouillot (2000).

22 'One could never, in the ordinary sense of the words, found a politics or law on forgiveness. In all the geopolitical scenes we have been talking about, the word most often abused is "forgive". Because it always has to do with negotiations more or less acknowledged, with calculated transactions, with conditions and, as Kant would say, with hypothetical imperatives. These *transactions* can certainly appear honourable. For example, in the name of "national reconcilation", the expression to which de Gaulle, Pompidou, and Mitterrand, all three, returned at the moment when they believed it necessary to take responsibility in order to efface the debts and crimes of the past, under the Occupation or during the Algerian war' (Derrida, 2001, 39–40).

23 See Odile Cazenave's 'Writing the Child, Youth, and Violence into the Francophone Novel from Sub-Saharan Africa: The Impact of Age and Gender' (Cazenave, 2005) and Valérie Loichot's *Orphaned Narratives* (2007).

24 See Fanon, 1963, 251. In other words, *Algérie roman* is inseparable from Fanon's *The Wretched of the Earth* (Fanon, 1963), but the paramyth is Ehni's response to Fanon's description of the encounter between the executioner and the victim. The son symbolizes the seemingly impossible union between both protagonists.

25 A first version of this text was published as 'A Literature Without

a Name: René-Nicolas Ehni's *Algérie roman*', in *Memory, Empire and Postcolonialism: Legacies of French Colonialism*, ed. Alec Hargreaves Lanham, MD: Lexington Books, 2005), 174–86. I thank the editor and the press for permission to reprint it here.

Chapter Three

1 In the chapter entitled '*Droit de cité* or apartheid', Balibar suggests that the colonial heritage is responsible for carving the space of strangers-insiders within Europe. They can only be integrated as fake citizens whose contractual relationship with the state they may never negotiate for themselves (Balibar, 2004, 40). This 'recolonization' process affects, would argue, not only immigrants but also all the subjects who are mythically treated as such.

2 Spectators who saw the film in a movie theatre may not have heard the interviews, but Haneke's conversation with Serge Toubiana can be said to be part of the film, or at least an important paratext, to the extent that it is sold as a 'supplement' to the DVD. The incorporation of their dialogue into the work of art proposes an interpretive grid, or rather a viewing position, to the spectator who either knows or does not know about October 1961 (Toubiana, 2005).

3 Philip Brooks' and Alan Hayling's Franco-British film (Channel Four, Point du Jour) was produced in 1992, at the beginning of the decade during which historians started bringing the war of independence to the French public's attention. It was shown again almost ten years later on the French-German Arte network on 17 October 2001.

4 A search through the archive of the Institut National de la Télévision INA) confirms that it was reprogrammed on Arte in 2001.

5 See Didier Daeninckx's *Meurtres pour mémoire*, Nacer Kettane's *Le Sourire de Brahim*, Leïla Sebbar's *La Seine était rouge*, Mehdi Lallaoui's *Une nuit d'octobre* or Nina Hayat's 'Le jardin du souvenir'. See also the films directed by Lallaoui and Agnès Denis (*Le Silence du fleuve*) as well as *Vivre au Paradis* (the adaptation that Bourlem Guerdjou made of Brahim Benaïcha's novel) and Alain Tasma and Patrick Rotman's *Nuit noire: 17 octobre 1961*. It was also in 2001 that Bertrand Delanoë, the Mayor of Paris, dedicated a plaque to the victims of October 1961. Jean-Luc Einaudi's 1991 *La Bataille de Paris, 17 octobre 1961* is often considered as the watershed that transformed the memorial landscape. Later, the publicity that surrounded Papon's condemnation for crimes against humanity consolidated the trend.

6 The association's website features a comprehensive 'biblio-filmography' that not only lists all the most recent books and films but also the testimonies published and censored immediately after October 1961.

<http://17octobre1961.free.fr/pages/association.htm> (accessed December 2007).

7 Although the charges had to do with Papon's role in the deportation of Jews during the Second World War, his trial was an opportunity to discuss the events of 1961 as well as the obstacles that continued to plague historians who wanted to analyse this period (See Amiri, 2004, 403–16; Golsan, 2000a; 2000b; and Le Cour Grandmaison, 2001).

8 Among the books republished at the beginning of the twenty-first century are two titles by Paulette Péju. *Les Harkis à Paris* and *Ratonnades à Paris* came out respectively just before and just after the demonstration. Both publications were seized by the police. The website of the '17 octobre 1961: contre l'oubli' association also mentions the special issue *Vérité-Liberté* edited by Paul Thibaud in 1961. See <http://17octobre1961.free.fr/pages/association.htm> (accessed December 2007).

9 The international visibility of Nora's work is such that his coinage 'lieu de mémoire' has passed into everyday speech. The volumes published between 1984 and 1992, but also the critiques that highlighted the limits of the historian's project in the Algerian context (Derderian, 2002; Apter, 1999, 2), have helped to forge a complex concept-tool that allows us to analyse the memorial mechanisms exhibited by any 'significant entity, whether material or non-material in nature' (Nora, 1996, xvii), archive as well as museum, commemorative plaques or more abstract forms of collective memory.

10 Neither Hargreaves nor Colin MacCabe is particularly impressed by the aesthetic qualities of the film. Hargreaves writes that '[w]hile well written and skillfully photographed and edited with strong acting performances, *Indigènes* breaks no new ground artistically' (2007, 205) and MacCabe states: 'The one French film that did touch both audience and jurors, Rachid Bouchareb's *Indigènes* [Days of Glory] was not an art film but an exercise in an all but historic American genre' (2006, 107). For both critics, the interest of the film does not lie in its artistic merit but in its ability to move its audience and to change history as it changes its public.

11 When we witness a christening, a wedding or a promise, we know what circumstances legitimize such speech acts. Here the speech act cannot be named outside of the event that coincides with it and there is no indication of which sort of enunciative conditions must be present for the performative act to be felicitous.

12 As some commentators have noticed, the disappearance of 'bougnoule' from the range of tolerated injurious terms is accompanied by the emergence of supposedly more neutral qualifiers. See the history of the contemporary word 'sauvageon' in Naba, 2003.

13 Since Haneke made the film knowledge has evolved. See, for example, Jim House and Neil MacMaster's proposal to stop trying to reach a

definitive body count and to consider instead that the demonstration was the culmination of a long series of brutal attacks (2006, 109–11). When George, who has no ideological interest in exaggerating the number of deaths, states that 200 Algerians died in October 1961, Haneke opts for one of the least conservative versions. He makes his character give a figure that he does not even think of contesting, instead of representing, as a fact, the continuing debate between historians who have or have not had access to the recently opened police archive (see Thibaud, 2001).

14 Austin writes that 'It is no surprise that the images that have generated the most discussion in accounts of the film have been the videotapes' (Austin, 2007, 532). He refers us to the 2007 issue of *Screen* that features a dossier on *Caché*. He singles out in particular the essays by Martine Beugnet, Elizabeth Ezra and Jane Sillars.

15 See especially Tarja Laine's reading of *Funny Games* (2004), Christopher Sharrett's study of *The Piano Teacher* (2004) and Frey (2006) on *Benny's Video* and *Caché*.

16 For a Rancierian analysis of the place of the child as 'director' and oppositional other in *Caché*, see Mecchia, 2007.

17 The much-commented on last scene of the film functions in the same manner. Some spectators will not spot Majid's son talking to Pierrot, George's son, among the crowd of students leaving their high school. And if we see them talking to each other, no clue enables us to decide whether they are friends (in spite of their parents' history), accomplices (maybe they sent the tapes together), enemies (Majid's son might want revenge) or casual acquaintances (are they unaware that they are symbolic cousins?).

18 *Two Brothers* is the story of two baby tigers separated by men. One is raised as a circus animal, the other one becomes a pet. When they meet again, they are expected to fight each other but some sort of recognition thwarts the violent script and enables both brothers to transcend the destiny that humans have imposed. They flee together, each helping the other by sharing what they have learned during their radically different upbringing. n their introduction to the issue of *Screen* that contains the dossier on *Caché*, the editors go even further and read all the posters advertising forthcoming films. They detect: '*Ma mère* (my mother – one of the adults responsible for sending Majid [Maurice Benijou] away), *Deux frères* (two brothers, or Georges and Majid), *La mauvaise éducation* (bad education – what Majid's son informs Georges that Majid suffered as a result of being ejected from George's family home) and *Mariages* (marriages – the family melodrama hinted at when Pierrot accuses his mother of having an affair with her colleague), which seem to spell out the various domestic and allegorical configurations in which Georges is implicated, as well as the various narrative and generic routes down which *Caché* as a film could have gone' (Ezra and Sillars, 2007, 217).

19 I am alluding to the impressive series of titles that begin with 'Pour en finir avec …' [To put an end to …] and urge readers to go beyond the moment of memory that they identify with the notion of 'repentance'. See Lefeuvre, 2006; Liauzu, 2003; and Bruckner, 2006.

Chapter Four

1 See Halimi's *Le Lait de l'oranger* for an account of the direct impact that the German occupation had on the family and the city in 1942 (1988, 71). See also Laskier (1991).

2 Beauvoir is one of the figures who regularly appear in the autobiographies, especially in *La Cause des femmes* and *Le Lait de l'oranger*. She had already co-signed and prefaced the story of the (unfinished) struggle to bring Djamila Boupacha's torturers to trial. Later, in *La Nouvelle Cause des femmes*, Halimi acknowledges the limits of their intellectual alliance, explaining how Beauvoir refused to involve directly herself in political action, a form of resistance that she feared to be a form of compromising with power (Halimi, 1997, 35).

3 For a discussion of the differences between how Halimi and Beauvoir dealt with the different phases of the Boupacha affair (and especially for an analysis of why Beauvoir was not in favour of helping Boupacha stay in France when the NLF insisted that she return to Algeria after the trial), see Stavro (2007) and Kruks (2005).

4 *Une affaire de femmes* is the title of Claude Chabrol's cinematographic interpretation of Marie-Louise Giraud's story. 'Une faiseuse d'anges' [an angel maker], as women who helped other women abort were then called, she is the last woman to have been executed in France. She was sentenced to death under the Vichy regime. The title of the film is an ironic comment on the fact that this is the story of men judging and condemning a woman.

5 During the last years of the war of independence, the 'Organisation de l'armée secrète' regularly targeted public figures such as Jean-Paul Sartre, the offices of hostile journals or papers (*Esprit*, *L'Express* or *Le Monde* [see Obuchowski, 1968, 93]) as well as Algerian civilians such as Mouloud Feraoun. See Le Sueur (2001), Shepard (2006), Schalk (2006), Kauffer (2004), as well as Anne-Marie Duranton-Crabol's *Le Temps de l'OAS* (1995). In *Avocate irrespectueuse*, Halimi also writes about being arrested by the paratroopers during the Algiers coup in May 1958 (2001, 15).

6 The cover states that the book is a series of 'propos recueillis par Marie Cardinal' [conversations with Marie Cardinal].

7 The book describes a period of hope quickly followed by disillusionment, and the delicate role that Halimi had to play as an elected representative who insisted that she was affiliated to, but not a member of,

the Socialist Party. The end of the story paints the picture of a woman who was close to François Mitterrand and had the impression of having been duped not only by the Left in general but by also by her friend, especially when stories about his dubious past (that she refused to believe) started to circulate.

8 From book to book, we regularly encounter a doctor from Grenoble, Anne Ferrey-Martin. Halimi discovers, when she first meets her, that she had given her daughter the name of 'Djamila' after reading *Djamila Boupacha*. Their paths cross several times, under different circumstances. n Grenoble she is in charge of a group of women who will eventually join Choisir, the association that could be imagined as a re-invented feminist political party. Later she will be accused of having illegally performed an abortion on one of her patients (1973b, 127–29). She reappears or perhaps disappears in *Une embellie perdue* since the book informs us that Annie has committed suicide: 'Annie ... nous tirait, de vie lasse, sa révérence' [Annie curtseyed out of her exhausting life] (1973b, 135). Annie symbolizes the impossibility of separating the issue of torture from later trials and the Bobigny trial from future political activities.

9 The epigraph set at the beginning of *La Cause des femmes* is Simone de Beauvoir's most famous formula: 'on ne naît pas femme, on le devient' [one is not born a woman, one becomes one] (Halimi's book came out when the French feminist movements of the 1970s were in full swing. They had not yet been reinterpreted or reinvented as 'French feminist theory'.)

10 Postcolonial novels have also made us reconsider the stereotypical association between eating disorders and whiteness, an assumption that used to Westernize the rejection of food and make it more difficult to interpret such behaviours in a context where women are also interpellated or disinterpellated as racialized subjects. Françoise Lionnet's study of Myriam Warner-Vieyra's *Juletane* emphasizes the link between food and an experience of increasing fragmentation and disintegration due to the character's inability to find her place in the compound that she shares with two other African women (Lionnet, 1995, 101–28).

11 It also implies that the little girl's chosen tactic belongs to the type of opposition that is usually not acknowledged as a legitimate political tool. As June Purvis points out, even the unsuccessful attempts at force-feeding were not read as evidence of the women's determination. Instead the failure to break their spirits was seen as a sign of their madness: 'This picture of irrational women, deliberately seeking their own torture was eagerly seized upon by male historians who sought to ridicule the WSPU [Women's Social and Political Union] and its politics' (Purvis, 1995, 104).

12 Even the allusion to the bowl adds a meaningful detail to the sentence as noted by Kébir Ammi whom I thank for his remark: in an Arabic family, the café-au-lait might have been served in a glass rather than in a bowl.

13 In *Fritna*, Halimi emphasizes the cultural hybridity of the nuclear family. And as a narrator, she takes her distance from the mother's insistance that her marrying a Berber was a misalliance: '... elle la descendante de la diaspora espagnole mariée à un "bédouin, berbère: ses ancêtres vivaient sous la tente ..."' [she, a descendant of the Spanish diaspora, had married a 'bedouin, a berber whose ancestors lived under a tent'] (Halimi, 1999a, 50).

14 Passages from *Fritna* retrospectively explain the context described in *Le Lait de l'oranger*. The narrator explains that, for Fortunée, 'we' could not simply refer to a unified Tunisian community. She remembers her mother's predilection for the 'poncifs racistes de la colonisation' [racist colonial clichés] (1999a, 70) and her 'haine des Arabes' [hatred for Arabs] (70). She quotes: '"Ces 'indigènes' (ma mère utilisait quelquefois le terme, pour faire plus chic et plus objectif à la fois), s'ils avaient le pouvoir, que feraient-ils de nous?" Ce "nous" englobait Français, Juifs, Italiens. Blancs, en un mot. La civilisation contre la barbarie.' ['If those "indigènes" had power (she sometimes used the word to sound more sophisticated and more objective at the same time), what would they do to us?' 'We' included the French, the Jews, the Italians. In a word, White people. Civilization against Barbarians.] (70).

15 The sterile and sick tree is also intertextually reminiscent of Boualem Sansal's novel, *L'Enfant fou de l'arbre creux* [The Mad Child from the Hollow Tree] (Sansal, 2000a). Sansal's and Halimi's trees are imprisoned in a courtyard. In Sansal's novel, the hollow tree is half alive, half dead, like the mad child who lives in its shadow, surrounded by the walls of a sinister jail that symbolizes Algeria as a whole. In Halimi's autobiography, the child is far from 'mad' but her relationship with the tree verges on the pathological, confusing love and parasitism.

16 Halimi's vision is closer to discourses that celebrate roots than to Deleuze and Guattari's famous developments on rhizomes. Her analysis of the orange tree is reminiscent of Césaire's vision of the Martinican people who must be urged to bear fruit freely: 'le sommer libre enfin/de produire de son intimité close/la succulence de ses fruits' (Césaire, 1983, 50).

17 Like Halimi, Césaire was elected to the National Assembly and had a clear preference for dis-affiliation as far as pre-existing political formations are concerned. They both remained extremely circumspect vis-à-vis parties and ideologies that prioritize one cause at the expense of another, suggesting, for example, that gender or race can only be addressed as part of a larger, more universal agenda. In the famous *Letter to Maurice Thorez* (Présence africaine, 1956), Césaire resigned from the Communist Party, denouncing a form of communism that treated black workers as unremarkable members of the proletariat. His position was similar to Halimi's critique of Marxist priorities. She was never convinced that 'Oppression de classe et oppression de sexe seraient combattues dans

la même démarche' [The struggle against class and gender oppression would go hand in hand] (Halimi, 1997, 32). In 1973 Césaire was one of the few representatives who supported Choisir's Bill of Law in favour of the legalizaion of abortion (1995, 85).

18 Although one of the crucial differences that distinguishes Halimi's autobiography from Williams' *The Alchemy of Race and Rights*, *The Rooster's Eggs* or *Open House* is that the latter describes her family (and especially her female relatives) as a strong source of support and inspiration whereas Halimi's career is prefigured by the little girl's constant struggle to free herself from her mother in particular and her milieu in general (Williams, 1992; 1997; 2004).

19 See, for example, the public debate between Elizabeth Badinter and Halimi, the former vehemently opposing 'parité' (the principle that makes it mandatory for political parties to present as many female as male candidates on their lists). For Halimi, the urgency of solving the blatant under-representation of French women in the Assembly and the Senate came first. See Badinter, 2003, and Halimi, 1999b.

20 French versions of various portions of this chapter were originally published as: '*Le lait de l'oranger* de Gisèle Halimi: l'élixir miraculeux des peuples colonisés', in *Migrances, diasporas et transculturalités franco-phones: littératures et cultures d'Afrique, des Caraïbes, d'Europe et du Québec*, ed. Hafid Gafaïti and Patricia Lorcin (Paris: L'Harmattan, 2005), 57–70, and 'Gisèle Halimi entre plainte et plaidoyer: "On naît avocate, on ne le devient pas"', in *Modern and Contemporary France* 12.3 (2004), 287–98. I thank the editors and the publishing houses for permission to republish.

Conclusion

1 'Erreurs de jeunesse', episode 5, series 12, directed by Claire de la Rochefoucauld, 18 January 2008 (France 2).

2 'Pieds-noirs' and 'pathos' were born respectively south or north of the Mediterranean, the second group of the binary pair (pathos, or Français de France) being today subsumed under Frenchness, as if only 'pied-noir' memories were marked, as if the specific history of participating in the war from within the Hexagon did not constitute one of the threads of popular memory (although it has been the object of experts' analysis; see Rioux, 1990).

3 This episode has nothing to do with the literary or cinematographic fictions of the 1980s, such as Azouz Begag's autobiographies (1986; 1989) or Yamina Benguigui's *Inch Allah dimanche* (2001) or her earlier documentary *Mémoires d'immigrés* (1997). Nor does it have the same logic as books such as Dalila Kerkouche's *Mon père ce harki* (2003).

4 *Guerre d'Algérie: la mémoire retrouvée?* is the title of a documentary made in 2003 by Jean-Paul Girbal. See also Benjamin Stora's 'La mémoire retrouvée de la guerre d'Algérie?', *Le Monde*, 19 March 2002, <www.lemonde.fr> (accessed 18 April 2008).

5 The series has been successively directed by Gérard Vergez, Christian François, Benoît d'Aubert, Christian Bonnet, Brigitte Coscas, Christophe Barbier, Claire de la Rochefoucauld and Thierry Petit. For full cast and credits, see <www.ina.fr>, <http://pj.france2.fr/pj_article.php3?id_article=329> or <http://www.imdb.com/title/tt1169586/fullcredits#writers> (accessed 18 April 2008).

6 Fanon interprets the colonizer's attempt at 'unveiling' the woman as a fantasy of rape. Assia Djebar's *La Femme sans sépulture* or Gisèle Halimi's *Djamila Boupacha* address rape in the context of the denunciation of torture.

7 *P.J. Saint Martin* was presented as an exception to the rule when a movement started to demand better representation of France's ethnic diversity in the media (see Rosello, 2005).

8 Unlike popular US series such *C.S.I.* (Jerry Bruckheimer Television and CBS Productions), and its spin-offs *C.S.I. NY* and *C.S.I. Miami*, *P.J. Saint Martin* does not rely on the power of special effects to produce a politics of truth and evidence that has to do with the immediate present. In *P.J. Saint Martin*, the camera must be able to negotiate close-ups to give us access to the page that constitutes the actors and actresses' facial expressions and the plot must maximize dialogues that allow characters to explain the influence of the past on their current situation.

9 Eight years earlier, Benjamin Stora and Bernard Favre's four-part documentary, *Les Années algériennes* can be said to mark the beginning of a new moment of memory during which the Algerian war ceases, gradually, to be taboo (Ina/France 2, broadcast September-October 1991).

10 Called La Malincha (the Captain's woman) due to her love affair with the Spanish conqueror (Hernan Cortéz), she becomes the emblematic figure of the translator, traitor and colonizer's mistress, as well as the mother of a new ethnos (she gives birth to a new type of ethnic Mexican).

11 This is precisely the topos that was at work in Halimi's reading of Djamila Boupacha's story. Prime-time television is now integrating such reconfigurations of silence and imagining the logical sequel to the Boupacha trial. Just as *Indigènes* brought our attention to the unglamorous present traces of otherwise heroicized pasts, the episode suggests that the grand theatre of history does not help us deal with the pathos of the quotidian.

12 *Journal officiel*, 2 August 1968, p. 0752. See <http://www.legifrance.gouv.fr/jopdf/common/jo_pdf.jsp?numJO=0&dateJO=19680802&numTexte=&pageDebut=07521&pageFin=> (accessed 18 April 2008). See also Gacon, 2002.

13 This is significantly different from what happens in Caribbean or African-American literature for example, where the child's overall skin colour functions as what denounces the rape of the black woman by the white man, but also constructs the child as 'in between' two categories that his or her so-called hybridity reinforces.

14 See *Béni ou le paradis privé* (Begag, 1989) or Thomas Gilou's *Michou d'Auber* in which a French woman turns her foster child into a blond 'Michou' to avoid confronting her husband's racism.

15 See the special issue of the journal *Mouvements* provocatively titled *Qui a peur du post colonial? Dénis et controverses*, which features texts by Pascal Blanchard, Christine Chivallon, Paul Gilroy, Achille Mbembe, Anibal Quijano, Françoise Vergès and Alec Hargreaves. See also Bancel and Blanchard, 2006.

16 During the war of independence, references to the Gestapo were used to denounce the methods used by the French military in Algeria. From that perspective, a simplified national narrative is mobilized to address contemporary events: the Gestapo stands for the enemy, the national other, and it is a scandal that the national 'we' should now turn into its worst nightmare. But just as the figures of the 'resistant' and the 'collaborator' import the self–other opposition within the national fabric and trouble the border between who is inside and who is out, who is the enemy and who is the ally, recent studies have brought to our attention the connections between memories of the Holocaust and of wars of decolonization. See Rothberg's study of Charlotte Delbo's first book, *Les Belles Lettres*. The author points out that this series of letters about the Algerian war predates by several years the first volume of Delbo's Holocaust trilogy (*Aucun de nous ne reviendra* [None of Us Will Return] originally appearing in 1965). He suggests that the early 1960s is a historic juncture where the memory of the Holocaust and the war of colonization come together in narratives: '... no one has yet attempted to consider this moment's status as a nodal point of intersecting histories or to speculate about how such intersections might inflect narratives of the era' (Rothberg, 2006, 160).

Bibliography

Abdiche, Boussad. 1984. *Reflets* (Chroniques). Algiers: Entreprise nationale du livre.

Abdiche, Boussad. 1986. *Circus'lation* (Billets). Algiers: Entreprise nationale du livre.

Abdiche, Boussad. 1988. *Mots pour maux* (Billets). Algiers: Entreprise nationale du livre.

Adorno, Theodor. 1998. 'The Meaning of Working Through the Past'. In *Critical Models: Intervention and Catchwords*. Trans. Henry W. Pickford. New York: Columbia University Press, 89–103.

Agamben, Giorgio. 1998. *Homo Sacer: Sovereign Power and Bare Life*. Trans. Daniel Heller-Roazen. Stanford, CA: Stanford University Press.

Agamben, Giorgio. 1999. *Remnants of Auschwitz: The Witness and the Archive*. Trans. Daniel Hezzel-Roazen. London: Zone Books.

Alloula, Malek. 1981. *Harem Colonial: images d'un sous-érotisme*. Paris: Garance. Revised edition: Séguier, 2001.

Amiri, Linda. 2004. 'La Répression policière en France vue par les archives'. In *La Guerre d'Algérie 1954–1962, la fin de l'amnésie*. Ed. Mohammed Harbi and Benjamin Stora. Paris: Laffont, 403–16.

Amrouche, Jean. 1989. *Chants berbères de Kabylie*. Preface by Mouloud Mammeri. Texts presented by Tassadit Yacine. Paris: l'Harmattan.

Appadurai, Arjun. 2006. *Fear of Small Numbers*. Durham, NC: Duke University Press.

Apter, Emily. 1999. *Continental Drift: From National Character to Virtual Subjects*. Chicago: Chicago University Press.

Apter, Emily. 2001. 'Balkan Babel: Translation Zones, Military Zones'. *Public Culture* 13.1: 65–80.

Aussaresses, Paul. 2001. *Services spéciaux, Algérie 1955–1957*. Paris: Perrin.

Austin, Guy. 2007. 'Drawing Trauma: Visual Testimony in *Caché* and *J'ai 8 ans*'. *Screen* 48.4: 529–53.

Austin, John L. 1975. *How to Do Things with Words*. 2nd ed. Cambridge, MA: Harvard University Press,.

Bacholle-Boskovic, Michèle. 2003. '*La Femme sans sépulture* d'Assia Djebar ou une Histoire pas enterrée'. *Expressions Maghrébines* 2.1: 79–90.

Badinter, Elizabeth. 2003. *Fausse Route*. Paris: Odile Jacob.

Balibar, Etienne. 2004. *We, the People of Europe? Reflections on Transnational Citizenship*. Trans. James Swenson. Oxford and Princeton: Princeton University Press.

Bancel, Nicolas and Pascal Blanchard. 2005. 'Comment en finir avec la fracture coloniale'. *Le Monde*, 17 March. <www.lemonde.fr> (accessed 20 April 2008).

Bancel, Nicolas and Pascal Blanchard. 2006. *Culture postcoloniale. 1961–2006: Traces et mémoires coloniales en France*. Paris: Autrement.

Bancel, Nicolas and Pascal Blanchard. 2007. 'La Fracture coloniale: retour sur une reaction'. *Mouvements* 51.3: 40–51. <http://www.cairn. info/article.php?ID_REVUE=MOUV&ID_NUMPUBLIE=MOUV_ 051&ID_ARTICLE=MOUV_051_0040> (accessed 25 May 2008).

Bancel, Nicolas, Pascal Blanchard and Sandrine Lemaire (eds). 2005. *La Fracture coloniale. La société française au prisme de l'héritage Colonial*. Paris: La Découverte.

Barthes, Roland. 1972. *Mythologies*. Trans. Annette Lavers. New York: Hill and Wang. Originally published as *Mythologies*. Paris: Seuil, 1957.

Barthes, Roland. 1980. *La Chambre claire*. Paris: Gallimard.

Baudrillard, Jean. 1991. *La Guerre du Golfe n'a pas eu lieu*. Paris: Galilée.

Beauvoir, Simone de. 1963. *La Force des choses*. Paris: Gallimard.

Beauvoir, Simone de and Gisèle Halimi. 1962. *Djamila Boupacha*. Paris: Gallimard.

Begag, Azouz. 1986. *Le Gone du Châaba*. Paris: Seuil.

Begag, Azouz. 1989. *Béni ou le Paradis privé*. Paris: Éditions du Seuil.

Belghoul, Farida. 1986. *Georgette!* Paris: Barrault.

Benaïcha, Brahim. 1992. *Vivre au paradis: d'un oasis à un bidonville*. Paris: Desclée De Brouwer.

Benguigui, Yamina (direction and screenplay). 1997. *Mémoires d'immigrés: l'héritage maghrébin*. France: Bandit productions and Canal +.

Benguigui, Yamina (direction and screenplay). 2001. *Inch'Allah dimanche*. Algeria/France: APR selection, Bandits long.

Bergner, Gwen. 1995. 'Who Is That Masked Woman? Or, the Role of Gender in Fanon's Black Skin, White Masks'. *PMLA* 110.1 *Special Topic: Colonialism and the Postcolonial Condition*: 75–88.

Bergot, Erwan. 1991. *Algérie, les appelés au combat*. Paris: Presses de la Cité.

Bergot, Erwan. 1992. *Les Appelés en Algérie: la bataille des frontières*. Paris: France Loisir.

Bernard, Philippe. 2002. 'Soldats de la torture ordinaire'. *Le Monde* 2 March. <www.lemonde.fr> (accessed 10 October 2007).

Beugnet, Martine. 2007. 'Blind spot'. *Screen* 48.2: 227–31.

Blume, Mary. 2005. 'For comic, despair is cloaked in humor'. *International Herald Tribune*, 17 February. <http://www.iht.com/articles/2005/02/17/features/blume.php?page=1> (accessed September 2007).

Bonnaud, Robert. 2002. 'La Paix de Nementchas'. In *Esprit. Ecrire contre la guerre d'Algérie 1947–1962*. Paris: Hachette, 186–206.

Bordo, Susan. 1993. *Unbearable Weight: Feminism, Western Culture and the Body*. Berkeley. CA: University of California Press.

Boudjedra, Rachid. 1997. *La Vie à l'endroit*. Paris: Grasset.

Bracher, Nathan. 2007. 'Bruckner and the Politics of Memory: Repentance and Resistance in Contemporary France'. *South Central Review* 24.2: 54–70.

Brooks, Roy. 2004. *Atonement and Forgiveness: A New Model for Black Reparations*. Berkeley, CA: University of California Press.

Brooks, Roy (ed.). 1999. *When Sorry isn't Enough: The Controversy over Apologies and Reparations for Human Injustice*. New York: New York University Press.

Bruckner, Pascal. 2006. *La Tyrannie de la pénitence: essai sur le masochisme occidental*. Paris: Grasset and Fasquelle.

Butler, Judith. 1993. *Bodies that Matter*. London and New York: Routledge.

Butler, Judith. 1997. *Excitable Speech: A Politics of the Performative*. Routledge: New York and London.

Butler, Judith. 2004a. *Precarious Life: The Powers of Mourning and Violence*. London: Verso.

Butler, Judith. 2004b. *Undoing Gender*. New York and London: Routledge.

Butler, Judith. 2005. *Giving an Account of Oneself*. New York: Fordham University Press.

Caubet, Dominique. 2004. *Les Mots du bled*. Paris: l'Harmattan.

Cazenave, Odile. 2005. 'Writing the Child, Youth, and Violence into the Francophone Novel from Sub-Saharan Africa: The Impact of Age and Gender'. *Research in African Literatures* 36.2: 59–71.

Cédelle, Luc. 2008. 'Mme Veil condamne les propositions de M. Sarkozy'. *Le Monde*, 17 February <www.lemonde.fr> (accessed 31 May 2008).

Certeau, Michel de. 1984. *The Practice of Everyday Life*. Trans. Steven Randall. Berkeley, CA: University of California Press.

Césaire, Aimé. 1946. *Les Armes miraculeuses*. Paris: Gallimard.

Césaire, Aimé. 1983. *Cahier d'un retour au pays natal*. Paris: Présence africaine.

Chambers, Ross. 1991. *Room for Maneuver*. Chicago: Chicago University Press.

Cheng, Anne Anlin. 2000. *The Melancholy of Race: Psychoanalysis, Assimilation, and Hidden Grief*. New York: Oxford University Press.

Cixous, Hélène. 1997a. 'Pieds nus'. In *Une enfance algérienne*. Sous la direction de Leïla Sebbar. Paris: Gallimard, 53–63.

Cixous, Hélène. 1997b. *OR – Les Lettres de mon père*. Paris: Editions des femmes.

Cixous, Hélène. 2000. *Les Rêveries de la femme sauvage*. Paris: Galilée.

Cliff, Michelle. 1980. *Claiming an Identity They Taught me to Despise*. Pittsburgh, PA: Persephone Press.

Cohen, Jim, Elsa Dorlin, Dimitri Nicolaïdis, Malika Rahal and Patrick Simon. 2007. 'Le tournant postcolonial à la française'. *Qui a peur de postcolonial? Dénis et controverses*. Special issue of *Mouvements* 51.3: 7–12. <http://www.cairn.info/article.php?ID_REVUE=MOUV&ID_NUMPUBLIE=MOUV_051&ID_ARTICLE=MOUV_051_0007> (accessed 25 May 2008).

Cohen, Jim, Elsa Dorlin, Dimitri Nicolaïdis, Malika Rahal, Patrick Simon (eds). 2007. *Qui a peur du postcolonial? Dénis et controverses*. Special issue of *Mouvements* 51.3.

Cohen, William. 2003. 'The Algerian War and the Revision of France's Overseas Mission'. *French Colonial History* 4: 227–39.

Cohen-Solal, Anne. 1998. 'Camus, Sartre and the Algerian War'. *Journal of European Studies* 28: 43–50.

Cole, Joshua. 2003. 'Remembering the Battle of Paris: 17 Octobre 1961 in French and Algerian Memory'. *French Politics, Culture and Society* 21.3: 21–50.

Conan, Éric and Henry Rousso. 1998. Trans. Nathan Bracher. *Vichy: an Ever-present Past*. Hanover, NH: University Press of New England. Originally published as *Vichy, un passé qui ne passe pas*. Paris: Fayard, 1994.

Coquery-Vidrovitch, Catherine. 2007. Review of Daniel Leveuvre's *Pour en finir avec la repentance*. *Etudes Coloniales*, 27 April <http://etudescoloniales.canalblog.com/archives/2007/04/index.html> (accessed 28 May 2008).

Daeninckx, Didier. 1984. *Meurtres pour mémoire*. Paris: Gallimard.

Delpard, Raphaël. 2001. *20 ans pendant la guerre d'Algérie: Générations sacrifiées*. Paris: Michel Lafon.

Déotte, Jean-Louis. 2004. 'The Differences Between Rancière's *Mésentente* (Political Disagreement) and Lyotard's *Différend*'. *SubStance* 33.1: 77–90.

Derderian, Richard. 2002. 'Algeria as a lieu de mémoire: Ethnic Minority

Memory and National Identity in Contemporary France'. *Radical History Review* 83 (spring): 28–4.

Derrida, Jacques. 1998. *Monolingualism of the Other, or, The Prosthesis of Origin*. Trans. Patrick Mensah. Stanford, CA: Stanford University Press. Originally published as *Le Monolinguisme de l'autre*. Paris: Galilée, 1996.

Derrida, Jacques. 2001. *On Cosmopolitanism and Forgiveness*. New York and London: Routledge.

Didi-Huberman, Georges. 2003. *Images maglré tout*. Paris: Minuit.

Djaout, Tahar. 1987. *L'Invention du désert*. Paris: Seuil.

Djebar, Assia. 1980. *Femmes d'Alger dans leur appartement*. Paris: Editions des femmes. New edition: Albin Michel, 2002.

Djebar, Assia. 1997a. *Les Nuits de Strasbourg*. Arles: Actes Sud.

Djebar, Assia. 1997b. *Oran, langue morte*. Arles: Actes Sud.

Djebar, Assia. 1999. *Ces Voix qui m'assiègent ... en marge de ma francophonie*. Paris: Albin Michel.

Djebar, Assia. 2002. *La Femme sans sépulture*. Paris: Albin Michel.

Duranton-Crabol, Anne-Marie. 1995. *Le Temps de l'OAS*. Paris: Complexe.

Dussert, Eric. 2000. Review of *Pintades* de René Nicolas Ehni. *Le Matricule des Anges* 30 (March–May) <http://www.oike.com/lmda/din/tit_lmda.php?Id=7115> (accessed 16 October 2007).

Ehni, Nicolas-René. 1964. *La Gloire du vaurien*. Paris: Julliard; Christian Bourgois, 1964; UGE, 1974; Christian Bourgois, 2000.

Ehni, Nicolas-René. 1968a. *Ensuite nous fûmes à Palmyre*. Paris: Gallimard.

Ehni, Nicolas-René. 1968b. *Que ferez-vous en Novembre?* Paris: Christian Bourgois.

Ehni, Nicolas-René. 1971. *Babylone, vous y étiez, nue parmi les bananiers*. Paris: Christian Bourgois. New editions: UGE, 1973; Christian Bourgois, 2000.

Ehni, Nicolas-René. 1974. *Pintades*. Paris: Christian Bourgois, repr. 2000.

Ehni, Nicolas-René. 1978. *La Raison lunatique: roman du pays* (avec Louis Schittly). Paris: Presse d'aujourd'hui.

Ehni, Nicolas-René. 1981. *Côme, confession générale: La Gloire du vaurien II*. Paris: Christian Bourgois.

Ehni, Nicolas-René. 1988a. *Rahab et les héritiers de la gloire*. Paris: BF Editions.

Ehni, Nicolas-René. 1988b. *Le Voyage en Belgique*. Paris: Christian Bourgois.

Ehni, Nicolas-René. 1994. *Vert-de-Gris*. Paris: La Nuée Bleue.

Ehni, Nicolas-René. 2000. *Quand nous dansions sur la table, suivi de Lettre à Dominique*. Paris: Christian Bourgeois.

Ehni, Nicolas-René. 2002. *Algérie roman*. Paris: Denoël,.

Einaudi, Jean-Luc. 1991. *La Bataille de Paris, 17 octobre 1961*. Paris: Seuil.

Elgey, Georgette. 2007. 'L'Année où l'opinion a basculé'. *Historia* 730: 58–59.

Evans, Martin. 1997. *The Memory of Resistance: French Opposition to the Algerian War (1954–1962)*. Oxford and New York: Berg.

Ezra, Elizabeth and Jane Sillars. 2007. 'Hidden in Plain Sight: Bringing Terror Home'. *Screen* 48.2: 215–21.

Fanon, Frantz. 1963. *The Wretched of the Earth*. Trans. Constance Farrington. New York: Grove. Originally published as *Les Damnés de la terre*. Paris: Maspero, 1962.

Fanon, Frantz. 1968. 'L'Algérie se dévoile'. In *Sociologie d'une révolution. L'an V de la révolution algérienne*. Paris: Maspéro, 16–50.

Fanon, Frantz. 1991. *Black Skin, White Masks*. Trans. Charles Lam Markmann. New York: Grove. Originally published as *Peau noire, masques blancs*. Paris: Seuil, 1952.

Fellag. 1999. *Djurdjurassique Bled (texte du spectacle)*. Paris: JC Lattès.

Fellag. 2001. *Rue des petites daurades*. Paris: JC Lattès.

Fellag. 2003a. *Comment réussir un bon petit couscous. Suivi de Manuel bref et circoncis des relations franco-algériennes*. Paris: JC Lattès.

Fellag. 2003b. *Le dernier chameau et autres histoires*. Paris: JC Lattès.

Fellag. 2007. *L'Allumeur des rêves berbères*. Paris: JC Lattès.

Felman, Shoshana and Dori Laub. 1992. *Testimony: Crises of Witnessing in Literature, Psychoanalysis, and History*. New York: Routledge.

Feraoun, Mouloud. 1990. *Journal*. Alger: Bouchêne.

Ferro, Marc (ed). 2003. *Le Livre noir du colonialisme. 16eme–21ème siècle: de l'extermination à la repentance*. Paris: Laffont.

Forster, E.M. 1956. *Aspects of the Novel*. London: Harvest Books [1927].

Frey, Mattias. 2006. '*Benny's Video*, *Caché*, and the Desubstantiated Image'. *Framework: The Journal of Cinema and Media* 47.2: 30–36.

Froidure, Michel. 2006. *Où était Dieu? Lettres de révolte et d'indignation d'un appelé en Algérie (1956–1958)*; preceded by 'Cette colère qui m'habite', interview with Tassadit Yacine (texts compiled, presented and edited by Tassadit Yacine). Metz: Mettis.

Gacon, Stéphane. 2002. *L'Amnistie: De la Commune à la guerre d'Algérie*. Paris: Éditions du Seuil.

Gallo, Max. 2006. *Fier d'être français*. Paris: Fayard.

Gallo, Max. 2007. *L'Ame de la France. Une histoire de la Nation*. Paris: Fayard.

Garapon, Antoine. 2008. *Peut-on réparer l'Histoire? Colonisation, esclavage, Shoah*. Paris: Odile Jacob.

Gilroy, Paul. 2004. *After Empire. Melancholia or Convivial Culture?* London and New York: Routledge.

Gilroy, Paul. 2007. 'Shooting crabs in a barrel'. *Screen* 48.2: 233–35.

Girbal, Jean-Paul. 2003. *La Mémoire retrouvée*. France: Cinégénération Editions.

Glissant, Edouard. 1990. *Poétique de la Relation*. Paris: Gallimard.

Glissant, Edouard. 1995. *Introduction à une poétique du divers*. Paris: Gallimard.

Golsan, Richard. 1996. *Memory, the Holocaust and French Justice: the Bousquet and Touvier Affairs*. Hanover, NH: University Press of New England.

Golsan, Richard. 2000a. 'Papon: The Good, the Bad, and the Ugly'. *SubStance* 29.1: 139–52.

Golsan, Richard (ed). 2000b. *The Papon Affair: Memory and Justice on Trial*. New York and London: Routledge.

Gomez, Carlos. 2007. 'Nouveau voyage au bout de l'enfer'. *Le Journal du dimanche*, Sunday, 30 September <http://www.lejdd.fr/cmc/culture/200739/nouveau-voyage-au-bout-de-l-enfer_59921.html> (accessed 3 October 2007).

Guyotat, Pierre. 1967. *Tombeau pour cinq cent mille soldats*. Paris: Gallimard [coll. 'Imaginaire', 1980].

Guyotat, Pierre. 1970. *Eden, Eden, Eden*. Preface by Michel Leiris, Roland Barthes and Phillippe Sollers. Paris: Gallimard.

Guyotat, Pierre. 1972. *Littérature interdite*. Paris: Gallimard.

Halimi, Gisèle. 1973a. *Avortement, une loi en procès: l'affaire de Bobigny*. Choisir; préface de Simone de Beauvoir. Paris: Gallimard. New edition: *Le Procès de Bobigny. Choisir la cause des femmes*. Gallimard, 2006.

Halimi, Gisèle. 1973b. *La Cause des femmes. Propos recueillis par Marie Cardinal*. Paris: Grasset. Subsequent editions: Paris: Livre de Poche, 1974; Paris: Gallimard-Folio, 1992.

Halimi, Gisèle. 1988. *Le Lait de l'oranger*. Paris: Gallimard.

Halimi, Gisèle. 1994. 'Plaidoyer pour une démocratie paritaire'. In *CHOISIR – La Cause des femmes, Femmes: Moitié de la terre, moitié du pouvoir*. Paris: Gallimard.

Halimi, Gisèle. 1995. *Une embellie perdue*. Paris: Gallimard.

Halimi, Gisèle. 1997. *La Nouvelle Cause des femmes*. Paris: Gallimard.

Halimi, Gisèle. 1999a. *Fritna*. Paris: Seuil.

Halimi, Gisèle. 1999b. *La Parité dans la vie politique. Rapport de la commission pour la parité entre les femmes et les hommes dans la vie politique*. Preface by Lionel Jospin. Ed. Virginie Barre. Paris: La Documentation Française.

Halimi, Gisèle. 2001. *Avocate irrespectueuse*. Paris: Plon.

Hamon, Hervé and Patrick Rotman. 1979. *Les Porteurs de valises: La Résistance française à la guerre d'Algérie*. Paris: Albin Michel.

Harbi, Mohammed and Benjamin Stora (eds). 2004. *La Guerre d'Algérie: 1954–2004, la fin de l'amnésie*. Paris: Robert Laffont.

Hargreaves, Alec. 2007. 'Indigènes: A Sign of the Times'. *Research in African Literatures* 38.4: 204–16.

Hayat, Nina. 2003. 'Le jardin du souvenir'. *L'Algérie des deux rives: 1954–1962*. Raymond Bozier (ed.). Paris: Mille et une nuits, 109–18.

Hirsch, Marianne. 2008. 'The Generation of Postmemory'. *Poetics Today* 29:1: 103–28.

Hirsch, Marianne. 1997. *Family Frames: Photography, Narrative, and Postmemory*. Cambridge, MA: Harvard University Press.

Holly, Michael Ann. 2003. 'Mourning and Method'. In *Compelling Visuality. The Work of Art in and out of History*. Ed. Claire Farago and Robert Zwijnenberg. Minneapolis, MN: University of Minnesota Press, 156–78.

House, Jim and Neil MacMaster. 2006. *Paris 1961: Algerians, State Terror and Memory*. Oxford: Oxford University Press.

Huyssen, Andreas. 2000. 'Present Pasts: Media, Politics, Amnesia'. *Public Culture* 12.1: 21–38.

annucci, Ugo. 2001. *Soldat dans les gorges de Palestro*. Lyon: Aléas.

Jauffret, Jean-Charles. 2000. *Soldats en Algérie 1954–1962. Expériences contrastées des hommes du contingent*. Paris: Autrement, collection Mémoires.

Jay, Paul. 2005. *Des années sans cerise*. Lyon: Aléas.

Jordi, Jean-Jacques. 2002. 'Les Pieds-noirs: constructions identitaires et reinvention des origines'. *Hommes and Migrations* 1236: 14–25.

Kateb, Yacine. 1956. *Nedjma*. Paris: Seuil.

Kauffer, Rémi. 2004. 'OAS: la guerre franco-française'. In *La Guerre d'Algérie 1954–2004: la fin de l'amnésie*. Ed. Mohammed Harbi and Benjamin Stora. Paris: Robert Laffont, 451–76

Kerkouche, Dalila. 2003. *Mon père ce harki*. Paris: Seuil.

Kettane, Nacer. 1985. *Le Sourire de Brahim*. Paris: Denoël.

Krapp, Peter. 2005. 'Amnesty: Between an Ethics of Forgiveness and the Politics of Forgetting'. *German Law Journal* 6.1: 185–95. <http://www.germanlawjournal.com/article.php?id=548> (accessed 10 October 2007).

Kristeva, Julia. 1984. *Powers of Horror: An Essay on Abjection*. Trans. Léon Roudié. Columbia: Columbia University Press. Originally published as *Pouvoirs de l'horreur*. Paris: Seuil, 1983.

Kristeva, Julia. 1988. *Etrangers à nous-mêmes*. Paris: Fayard.

Kritzman, Lawrence. 1995. *Auschwitz and After: Race, Culture, and 'the Jewish Question' in France*. New York: Routledge.

Kruks, Sonia. 2005. 'Simone de Beauvoir and the Politics of Privilege'. *Hypatia: A Journal of Feminist Philosophy* 20.1: 178–205.

Labib, Jean. 1987. *Déchirures algériennes* (documentary). Paris: INA.

LaCapra, Dominick. 1998. *History and Memory After Auschwitz*. Ithaca, NY: Cornell University Press.

Laine, Tarja. 2004. '"What are you looking at and why?" Michael Haneke's *Funny Games* (1997) with his audience'. *Kinoeye* 4.8 <http://www.kinoeye.org/index_04_01.php> (accessed December 2007).

Lallaoui, Mehdi. 2001. *Une nuit d'octobre*. Paris: Editions Alternatives.

Lamloum, Olfa. 2002. 'La mort de Massu vue par la presse algérienne'. *Le Monde*, 13 October <www.lemonde.fr> (accessed April 2004).

Lanser, Susan. 2004. 'Sexing Narratology: Toward a Gendered Poetics of Narrative Voice'. In *Narrative Theory: Political Narratology*. Ed. Mieke Bal. London: Routledge.

Laskier, Michael. 1991. 'Between Vichy Antisemitism and German Harassment: The Jews of North Africa during the Early 1940s'. *Modern Judaism* 11.3: 343–70.

Laurini, Robert. 1995. *Ceux du contingent*. Gueret: Fédération nationale des anciens combattants.

Le Cornec, Michel. 2000. *Appelés en Algérie* (photographs by Marc Flament). Monaco: Editions du patrimoine.

Le Cour Grandmaison, Olivier. 2001. *Le 17 octobre 1961: Un crime d'Etat à Paris*. Paris: La Dispute.

Le Sueur, James. 2001. *Uncivil War: Intellectuals and Identity Politics during the Decolonization of Algeria*. Philadelphia: University of Pennsylvania Press.

Lefeuvre, Daniel. 2006. *Pour en finir avec la repentance coloniale*. Paris: Flammarion.

Lemalet, Martine. 1992. *Lettres d'Algérie, 1954–1962: la guerre des appelés*. Paris: JC Lattès.

Lentz, Jean-Marie. 2005. *Algérie 1959–1961: un appelé raconte*. Paris: L'Officine.

LeSueur, James. 2001. *Uncivil War: Intellectuals and Identity Politics During the Decolonization*. Philadelphia: University of Pennsylvania Press.

Liauzu, Claude (ed.). 2003. *Violence et colonisation: Pour en finir avec les guerres des mémoires*. Paris: Editions Syllepse.

Lionnet, Françoise. 1995. *Postcolonial Representations: Women, Literature, Identity*. Ithaca, NY: Cornell University Press.

Loichot, Valérie. 2007. *Orphan Narratives: The Postplantation Literature of Faulkner, Glissant, Morrison, and Saint-John Perse*. Charlottesville, VA: University of Virginia Press.

Lyotard, Jacques. 1988. *The Differend: Phrases in Dispute*. Trans. Georges van den Abbeele. Minneapolis, MN: University of Minnesota Press. Originally published as *Le Différend*. Paris: Minuit, 1982.

MacCabe, Colin. 2006. 'Film: Cannes 2006'. *Critical Quarterly* 48.3: 105–09.

Mammeri, Mouloud. 1989. *Cheikh Mohand a dit*. Paris: CERAM.

Maples, Robert. 1966. Review of *La Gloire du vaurien*. *The French Review* 39.4: 669–70.

Massu, Jacques. 1971. *La vraie bataille d'Alger*. Paris: Plon. New edition: Rocher, 1997.

Matéos-Ruiz, Maurice. 1998. *L'Algérie des appelés*. Biarritz: Atlantica.

Mauss-Copeaux, Claire. 2002. *Les Appelés en Algérie: La Parole confisquée*. Paris: Hachette.

McCusker, Maeve. 2007. *Patrick Chamoiseau: Recovering Memory*. Liverpool: Liverpool University Press.

Mecchia, Giuseppina. 2007. 'The Children Are Still Watching Us, *Caché/Hidden* in the folds of time'. *Studies in French Cinema* 7.2: 131–41.

Mekhaled, Boucif. 1995. *Chronique d'un massacre: 8 mai 1945, Sétif-Guelma-Kherrata*. Paris: Syros.

Merchet, Jean-Dominique. 2006. '"*Indigènes*" fait craquer Chirac'. *Libération*, 25 September <http://www.liberation.fr> (accessed December 2007).

Naba, René. 2003. *Du Bougnoule au Sauvageon: Voyage dans l'imaginaire Français*. Paris: Harmattan.

Naficy, Hamid. 2001. *An Accented Cinema: Exilic and Diasporic Filmmaking*. Princeton, NJ: Princeton University Press.

Nallet, Albert. 2004. *On n'efface pas la vérité. Comment j'ai vécu la guerre d'Algérie: témoignages*. Lyon: Aléas.

Nora, Pierre. 1996. *Realms of Memory: Rethinking the French Past*. Vol. 1: *Conflicts and Divisions*. Trans. by Arthur Goldhammer. New York and Chichester: Columbia University Press.

Obuchowski, Chester. 1968. 'Algeria, the Tortured Conscience'. *The French Review* 42.1: 90–103.

Olaïzola, Pierre. 2002. *Algérie! Nous aurions dû tant nous aimer*. Anglet: Sauve Terre.

Orbach, Susie. 2001. *Hunger Strike: Starving Amidst Plenty*. New York: Other Press.

Palladino, Paolo and Tiago Moreira. 2006. 'On Silence and the Constitution of the Political Community'. *Theory & Event* 9.2. <http://muse.jhu.edu/journals/theory_and_event/v009/9.2palladino_moreira.html> (accessed 1 June 2008).

Paoli, Paul-François. 2006. *Nous ne sommes pas coupables. Assez de repentances!* Paris: La Table Ronde.

Péju, Paulette. 2000. *Ratonnades à Paris précédé de Les Harkis à Paris*. Paris: La Découverte. 1ˢᵗ edition: Paris: François Maspero, 1961.

Perkins, Kenneth. 2004. *A History of Modern Tunisia*. Cambridge: Cambridge University Press.

Planche, Jean-Louis. 2006. *Sétif 1945: Histoire d'un massacre annoncé*. Paris: Perrin.

Porton, Richard. 2005. 'Collective Guilt and Individual Responsibility: An Interview with Michael Haneke'. *Cinéaste* 31.1: 50–51.

Pouillot, Henri. 2000. *La Villa Susini: tortures en Algérie, un appelé parle, juin 1961–mars 1962*. Paris: Térésias.

Purvis, Jane. 1995. 'The Prison Experiences of the Suffragettes in Edwardian Britain'. *Women's History Review* 4: 103–33.

Rancière, Jacques. 1999. *Dis-agreement. Politics and Philosophy*. Trans. Julie Rose. Minneapolis, MN: University of Minnesota Press. Originally published as *La Mésentente: politique et philosophie*. Paris: Galilée, 1995.

Rancière, Jacques. 2007. *The Future of the Image*. Trans. Gregory Elliott. London: Verso.

Rancière, Jacques. 2004. *The Politics of Aesthetics: The Distribution of the Sensible*. Afterword by Slavoj Žižek. Trans. Gabriel Rockhill. London: Continuum.

Ricoeur, Paul. 2004. *Memory, History, Forgetting*. Trans. Kathleen Blamey and David Pellauer. Chicago: University of Chicago Press. Originally published as *La Mémoire, l'histoire, l'oubli*. Paris: Seuil, 2000.

Ricoeur, Paul and Sorin Antohi. 2005. 'Memory, History, Forgiveness: A Dialogue Between Paul Ricoeur and Sorin Antohi', *Janus Head* 8.1: 14–25.

Rigney, Ann. 2005. 'Plenitude, Scarcity and the Circulation of Cultural Memory'. *Journal of European Studies* 35.1: 11–28.

Rioux, Jean-Pierre. 1990. *La Guerre d'Algérie et les Français*. Paris: Fayard.

Rioux, Jean-Pierre and Jean-François Sirinelli. 1991. *La Guerre d'Algérie et les intellectuels français*. Paris: Editions complexe.

Roman, Joël. 2002. Introduction. *Esprit: Ecrire contre la guerre d'Algérie*. Paris: Hachette, 5–20.

Rosello, Mireille. 2005. 'Good Cops, Black Cops: Ethnicity and Solidarity on French TV'. *Journal of Romance Studies* 5.3: 79–89.

Rothberg, Michael. 2006. 'Between Auschwitz and Algeria: Multidirectional Memory and the Counterpublic Witness'. *Critical Inquiry* 33 (autumn): 158–84.

Rotman, Patrick. 2002. *L'Ennemi intime*. Paris: Seuil.

Rousso, Henry. 2002. *The Haunting Past: History, Memory, and Justice in Contemporary France*. Trans. Ralph Schoolcraft. Preface by Philippe

Petit. Foreword by Ora Avni. Philadelphia. University of Pennsylvania Press. Originally published as *La Hantise du passé: entretien avec Philippe Petit*. Paris: Les Editions Textuel, 1998.

Roy, Jules. 1982. *Etranger pour mes frères*. Paris: Stock.

Said, Edward. 1983. *The World, the Text, and the Critic*. Cambridge, MA: Harvard University Press.

Sansal, Boualem. 2000a. *L'Enfant fou de l'arbre creux*. Paris: Gallimard.

Sansal Boualem. 2000b. 'Interview with Daniel Bermond'. *Lire* (September).

Sarkozy, Nicolas. 2007. Speech delivered in Caen, 9 March <http://www.u-m-p.org/site/index.php/s_informer/discours/nicolas_sarkozy_a_caen> (accessed 31 May 2008).

Sartre, Jean-Paul. 1976. *Critique of Dialectical Reason: Theory of Practical Ensembles*. Trans. Alan Sheridan-Smith. Ed. Jonathan Rée. London: NLB.

Scarry, Elaine. 1985. *The Body in Pain: The Making and Unmaking of the World*. New York: Oxford University Press.

Schalk, David. 2006. *War and the Ivory Tower: Algeria and Vietnam*. With a preface by Benjamin Stora and George Herring. 2nd edition. Nebraska, University of Nebraska Press. Originally published New York: Oxford University Press, 1991.

Sebbar, Leïla. 2003. *La Seine était rouge, Paris, octobre 1961*. Paris: Editions Thierry Magnier [1999].

Sebbar, Leïla, Christelle Taraud and Jean-Michel Belorgey. 2006. *Femmes d'Afrique du Nord, Cartes postales (1885–1930)*. Paris: Bleu autour.

Sedgwick, Eve. 2003. *Touching Feeling: Affect, Pedagogy, Performativity*. Durham, NC: Duke University Press.

Shakespeare. 1906. *The Tempest* in *The Complete Works of William Shakespeare Reprinted From the First Folio*. Ed. Charlotte Porter and H.A.Clarke. Introduction by John Churton Collins. London: Harrap.

Sharrett, Christopher. 2004. 'The Horror of the Middle Class in Michael Haneke's *La Pianiste (The Piano Teacher*, 2001)'. *Kinoeye* 4.8. <http://www.kinoeye.org/index_04_01.php> (accessed December 2007)

Shepard, Todd. 2006. *The Invention of Decolonization: The Algerian War and the Remaking of France*. Ithaca, NY: Cornell University Press.

Sigg, Bernard. 1989. *Le Silence et la honte: névroses de la guerre d'Algérie*. Preface by Daniel Zimmermann. Paris: Messidor.

Silverman, Max. 2007. 'The Empire Looks Back'. *Screen* 48.2: 245–49.

Silvestre, Charles. 2002. 'Pour Ben M'hidi et Audin'. *L'Humanité*, 19 March. <http://www.humanite.fr/2002–03–19_International_Pour-Ben-M-hidi-et-Audin> (accessed 10 October 2007)

Smaïl. 1997. *Vivre me tue*. Paris: Balland.

Spivak, Gayatri. 1993. 'The Politics of Translation'. In *Outside in the Teaching Machine*. New York and London: Routledge, 179–200.

Stavro, Elaine. 2007. 'Rethinking Identity and Coalitional Politics, Insights from Simone de Beauvoir'. *Canadian Journal of Political Science/ Revue canadienne de science politique* 40.2: 439–63.

Stora, Benjamin. 1992. *La Gangrène et l'oubli*. Paris: Editions La Découverte.

Stora, Benjamin. 1997a. *Appelés en guerre d'Algérie*. Paris: Gallimard.

Stora, Benjamin. 1997b. *Imaginaires de guerre: Algérie-Vietnam en France et aux Etats Unis*. Paris: La Découverte.

Stora, Benjamin. 2001. 'Décloisonner les mémoires autour de la guerre d'Algérie'. Interview granted to Eugénie Barbez. Colloquium INA: *Regards croisés sur la guerre d'Algérie*, 17 November. <http://www. ina.fr/voir_revoir/algerie/itv_stora.fr.html> (accessed 1 October 2005).

Stora, Benjamin. 2002. 'La mémoire retrouvée de la guerre d'Algérie?' *Le Monde*, 19 March <www.lemonde.fr> (accessed 18 April 2008).

Stora, Benjamin. 2003. 'Guerre d'Algérie: 1999–2003, les accélérations de la mémoire'. *Hommes et migrations* 1244 (July–August): <http:// www.hommes-et-migrations.fr/articles/1244/1244.pdf>   (accessed June 2007).

Stora, Benjamin. 2005. 'Quand une mémoire (de guerre) peut en cacher une autre (coloniale)'. In Bancel *et al.*, 2005, 59–67.

Stora, Benjamin and Thierry Leclere. 2007. *La Guerre des mémoires: La France face à son passé colonial*. La Tour d'Aigues: L'Aube.

Terdiman, Richard. 1985. *Discourse/Counter-Discourse: The Theory and Practice of Symbolic Resistance in Nineteenth-Century France*. Ithaca, NY: Cornell University Press.

Thibaud, Paul. 2001. 'Le 17 octobre 1961: Un moment de notre histoire'. *Esprit* 279 (November): 6–19.

Tillion, Germaine. 1960. *Les Ennemis complémentaires*. Paris: Minuit.

Toubiana, Serge. 2005. Interview with Michael Haneke. DVD 2 of *Caché*. Directed by Michael Haneke, France, Austria, Germany, Italy production.

Venuti, Lawrence. 1998. *The Scandals of Translation. Towards an Ethics of Difference*. London and New York: Routledge.

Verdier, Michel. 2002. *Bandes de brêles: les appelés en Algérie. Quand violence et torture deviennent banalité*. Louge-sur-Maire: Humusaire.

Vidal-Naquet, Pierre. 1972. *La Torture dans la République*. Paris: Minuit. New edition 1998.

Vidal-Naquet, Pierre. 1989. *Ce jour qui n'ébranla pas Paris*. Paris: La Découverte.

Vidal-Naquet, Pierre. 2005. Interview with Hervé Nathan. 'L'Etat n'a pas à dire comment enseigner l'histoire'. *Libération*, 14 April <http://www.liberation.fr> (accessed December 2007).

Vidal-Naquet, Pierre (ed.). 1975. *Les Crimes de l'armée française*. Paris: Maspero.

Vidal-Naquet, Pierre (ed.). 2001. *Les Crimes de l'armée française: Algérie 1954–1962*. With a new preface by Pierre Vidal-Naquet. Paris: La Découverte.

Vittori, Jean-Pierre. 1997. *Nous, les appelés d'Algérie*. Paris: Stock.

Weber, Eugen. 1991. *My France: Politics, Culture, Myth*. Cambridge, MA: Harvard University Press.

Weiner, Ruth. 1999. 'Performance Review: Djurdjurassique Bled'. *Theatre Journal* 51.4: 470–72.

Williams, Patricia. 1992. *The Alchemy of Race and Rights*. Cambridge, MA: Harvard University Press.

Williams, Patricia. 1997. *The Rooster's Egg*. Cambridge, MA: Harvard University Press.

Williams, Patricia. 2004. *Open House: Of Family, Friends, Food, Piano Lessons, and the Search for a Room of My Own*. New York: Farrar, Straus and Giroux.

Wilson, Emma. 2007. 'Days of Glory/Flanders: Emma Wilson on Two Prize-winning, Politically Ambitious French War Films'. *Film Quarterly* 61.1: 16–22.

Winter, Jay. 2000. 'The Generation of Memory: Reflections on the "Memory Boom" in Contemporary Historical Studies'. *Bulletin of the German Historical Institute Washington* 27: 69–92.

Wood, Nancy. 1999. *Vectors of Memory: Legacies of Trauma in Postwar Europe*. Oxford and New York: Berg.

Young, Robert. 2001. *Postcolonialism: An Historical Introduction*. London: Blackwell.

Index

Printed and bound by CPI Group (UK) Ltd, Croydon, CR0 4YY

13/04/2025

14656573-0006